The Power That Worketh in Us

THE POWER THAT WORKETH IN US

F. HENRY EDWARDS

Reorganized Church of Jesus Christ of Latter Day Saints
Herald Publishing House
Independence, Missouri

Library of Congress Cataloging-in-Publication Data

Edwards, F. Henry (Francis Henry), 1897–
   The Power That Worketh in Us.

   Bibliography: p.
   1. Spiritual life—Reorganized Church of Jesus Christ of Latter Day Saints authors. I. Title.
BX8656.E415   1987   248.4'89333   87-8402
ISBN 0-8309-0481-6

93 92 91 90 89 88 87   1 2 3 4 5 6 7

SCRIPTURE REFERENCES

All biblical references are to the Holy Scriptures (Inspired Version) unless otherwise indicated. The designation "IV" following a Bible reference indicates a difference in versification between the Inspired Version and other translations and versions.

The 1966 edition of the Book of Mormon is used for all references to that book of scripture.

CONTENTS

Introduction

If we start out to tell a story, or to write a book, we need a clearly understood point of departure and an awareness of where we wish to arrive. Either or both may be modified to a degree; but, if we are to succeed, the modifications must point toward greater clarity. I hope that this book will justify its existence more and more clearly as it moves toward completion.

What I have in mind, and on my heart, is of the utmost importance. I want to write about God. But, even more specifically, I want to write about the God who is worshiped by believers in the Father and the Son and the Holy Ghost. I cannot write adequately about any of them apart from the others, but although this is so, my emphasis will be on the Holy Ghost.

Some readers may be surprised at my omission of the scientific doctrine of evolution. I do not know enough about it and, anyway, that is not what the book is about. Certainly this doctrine is not the stumbling block today that it was when I was young. So, let me say that I have come to accept without undue difficulty the oft repeated affirmations of the scriptures concerning the creation and maintenance of our world:

Before the mountains were brought forth, or ever thou hadst

formed the earth and the world, even from everlasting to everlasting, thou art God.—Psalm 90:2. See also Isaiah 44:6; Jeremiah 32:17; Colossians 1:16, 17; Hebrews 1:2, 10-12.

God spake unto Moses, saying, Behold, I am the Lord God Almighty, and Endless is my name, for I am without beginning of days or end of years.—Doctrine and Covenants 22:2. See also Mosiah 1:102; III Nephi 4:45-48.

None of us have full understanding of words having to do with eternity such as *endless* or *everlasting*, although they point the way toward understanding which in God's own time will be complete. Our use of them is conditioned by our mortality. Isaiah sensed our lack, and in the name of God wrote

my thoughts are not your thoughts, neither are your ways my ways.... For as the heavens are higher than the earth, so are my ways higher than your ways, and my thoughts than your thoughts.—Isaiah 55:8-9

My health has been such that I have found myself dependent on many friends: more than I can name here. Among them are members of the staff of Resthaven, notably Mrs. Patsy Boos who located many rare books for me. Among the residents who were especially helpful was Mrs. Roscoe Davey, who found for me needed references marked in her late husband's books.

The editorial copy editor for this book was Imogene Goodyear. She became ill about the time the manuscript was ready for her to work on it. Nevertheless, she edited it as her strength permitted, doing so at no little inconvenience. My best thanks are extended to her, both for her editorial contribution and for making it at such personal cost.

I must also acknowledge in a separate category the invaluable help given me by my sons, Lyman and Paul. When I was not sure that my health would permit me to complete the manuscript I was heartened to think that they could check it for me. But for them, the book would never have been finished.

The atmosphere at Resthaven has been conducive to thought and prayer. As signs near the entrances indicate, "Gentleness is spoken here."

F. Henry Edwards
Resthaven, Independence, Missouri
November 4, 1986

The world is charged with the grandeur of God.

—Gerald Manly Hopkins

Chapter 1

Our World from God

We live in a world which is not of our making. At any point in our lives we find ourselves already launched. We and our neighbors are active in the business of living: eating and drinking, thinking and feeling, planning and achieving, venturing and arriving. And all this is going on by the exercise of powers which we may have polished, but which we did not create, and amid resources whose nature we must discover and obey before we can use them.

The challenge and the glory of life derives from what we do with what we have been given. We rejoice in the achievements of the heroes and heroines of our race, and should feel grateful for what they have done to clear and brighten the way before us. But we need to remember that they, like us, and we like them, all live by what has been given us.

The "given" encompasses all of life and the universe in which we live—both our inner and our outer selves—the world as we have come to know it, and the unknown world which invites us to discover it. We have much to contribute, but the talents which enable us to contribute and the structure of the universe with which we must deal, are all part of the "given" which is basic to our existence. God has determined the "bounds of [our] habitation."[1] In him "we live, and move, and have our being."[2]

Although our world is much too vast and too complex for any person or any group of persons to fully understand it, we cannot avoid thinking about it. By building on the thoughts and conclusions of those who have gone before, and by using the world's resources more effectively, we have come to know more about it than did any of our forebears. For example, for the first time in history people can look down from space and see the earth and, returning, can show us revealing pictures of what they have seen. But no matter how clear and accurate the pictures, nor from what vantage point they are taken, no camera can reveal all we want to know about our world. Nor can any other machine or combination of machines do so, whatever their field.

Every day researchers find more about our world—its composition, its nature, its resources, its threats. Always, the more we discover about the earth or the wider universe of which it is part, the more we find there is to find. We are enveloped in both mystery and challenge.

We tend to think of our world as external to us. But this is not so. It becomes obvious, once we apply ourselves, that plants and animals and other living things are part of our world. The sun and moon and stars have life appropriate to their nature and place. Something of this has been known down the generations, but only in the past few score years have our eyes been opened to the fact that we live in a vast universe.

The infinitely varied possibilities in our world beckon in every direction. The vision and the hope and the courage and the sheer hard work of count-

14

less men and women are vital elements in our advance. But this advance is rarely solitary. What persons of genius have perceived those of lesser stature have soon corroborated and given body. "No man is an island."[3]

Our world is not just skyscrapers and planes and X rays. It includes the people who build and occupy the skyscrapers, who fly and ride the planes, who create and see by the X rays. It includes us and the spirit and purpose which motivate us; it is persons who live in vital but unstable relationships with each other.

We cannot know our world until we become informed about the people who are an integral part of it. Indeed, inquiry into its resources, its beauty, its threats, is never complete until we consider these in relation to its people. And the most important thing about people is what they are like in their innermost selves and—most of all—in their relationships to God and others.

Our world is a world of persons, but not of individuals. We grow in the qualities of personhood in families and communities, not as hermits. Here knowledge and skill, mental and physical health, geography and climate, and a host of other factors, are all significant. But the direction in which they point, the ends they serve or obstruct, the victories they serve or the defeats they suffer, are determined by the spirit of the men or women who use the gains from their endeavors.

To say that our world is a world of persons is to say that some aspects of life lie beyond the range of science. To recognize this is not to disparage the role of science, which is of great importance, but to take note of its built-in limitations. Science deals with that which can be repeated under like conditions. It has little concern for that which is individual and unpredictable. Science can be of great service in ministering to what people share in common, and which can therefore be observed and measured in the mass. But beyond their necessary sharing, people are most distinctive when they are most individual and particular. They then tend to resent being known by numbers, or being considered as mere cogs in wheels. Although they overlap, there is fundamental difference between the world of science and that of personality, and between scientific methods and the insights of intuition and inspiration.

We live in a world created for us as the arena for our maturing: not for existence only, but for life after the order of the Son of God.

I took time from writing this to watch the landing of the spaceship *Columbia* and so of a new advance into the space age. As I watched I felt myself enveloped in a deep and penetrating sense of wonder. This wonder had its beginning, of course, in a quickened awareness of the genius behind the whole space conception, the contributing insights which provided solutions to the many challenges which arose, the coordination which made a whole out of its parts, the courage with which this work of many thousands of men and women was put to the test before the whole world. But it was not long until the wonder turned to awe. This took nothing from my gratitude to and for the space pioneers. But, going still further, I found myself stirred to the depths of my soul as I rejoiced that God has made his creatures capable of such achievements. And in that spirit I went on to know with assurance that other insights and achievements, far beyond our present understanding, beckon us over our present horizons.

Those who worked on the *Columbia* were not selected for their religious faith. They were chosen rather for their technical skills and competence. But their success demands by its very excellence that such stupendous material advances shall be controlled, so far as we can possibly contrive to do so, by persons of goodwill.

We have become more aware that it is impossible to understand the universe except as we consider at the same time the mind which observes it. We now know that we cannot separate our knowledge of the universe from the mind which studies it. Our mental equipment needs the assistance of other faculties. To leave them out is to omit factors which may disturb the whole enterprise of understanding. But to leave out consideration of the emotional and spiritual factors in any assessment of the meaning and functioning of the universe can be similarly disastrous. If we should move into some other planet and find it inhabited, the spirit in which we arrive or that in which we would be received would be determinative.

Our world is not ours forever. We are tenants, not owners. We seek to prepare for the tomorrows, but all our preparation can be brought to naught by unanticipated convulsions of nature, by unforeseen accidents, by illness or by death, or by our own folly. As we seek further understanding or security we must do so with instruments and insights which are both faulty. We can share the cultivated insights furnished by our universities. But we cannot command genius.

As moderns we have little sense of creaturehood. We are aware of our mortality but, ignoring the limitations which this fact puts on all our activities, we tend to act as though we are, rightfully, our own law-givers. Not infrequently we abandon this in favor of servitude to some interest or assumed responsibility, transforming mere activities into life-determining pursuits. We are creatures endowed with a passion for things eternal. When we deny this part of our nature this gives rise to disturbing inner conflicts, and these give rise to external conflicts. Most of our social maladjustments are better treated from within than from without.

This has not happened all at once, but has become more and more apparent as modern devices have augmented human powers (i.e., the power to see has been multiplied by the use of telescopes, X rays, television, etc.). It is not suggested that these devices be abandoned, but that our enslavement to them be controlled, as our bodies are insisting we do when we become the victims of excessive use of our automobiles. War as an instrument of aggression has always been a sickening thing. Now we can see what it means in terms of outrage, homelessness, death, mutilation, hunger. And yet, perhaps even worse, we still regard it as an essential instrument of such sovereignty as we will not yield.

As moderns we allow the most important of our moral assets to lie idle, ignoring the insights which are granted in worship. Before long we become slaves of our own inventions.

Paul noted that many of our transgressions result from copying the fashions of our times, and wrote to the saints in Corinth of those who "measuring themselves by themselves...are not wise."[4] The antidote for such foolishness, he wrote, is to respond to God's grace and forgiveness whereby he calls us to become members of his family by adoption. His invitation says: "Here is the security and love—the belonging—to which you have no right of yourselves but to which you are called, and into which you are freely accepted." By entering into covenant with God we move from no place to some place, from no roots to cosmic roots. By the acts of members of the Lord's family all live as though we belong to each other, and those newly adopted enter with assurance.

The practice of adoption was known among the Hebrews. (Moses was an adopted son of the daughter of Pharaoh, and Esther was the adopted daughter of Mordecai).[5] It was more common, however, among the Romans among whom adopted children were legally entitled to all the rights and privileges of natural-born children. Against this background the apostle Paul wrote to the saints in Rome:

Ye have received the Spirit of adoption; whereby we cry Abba Father. The Spirit itself beareth witness with our spirit, that we are the children of God; heirs of God, and joint heirs with Christ; if so be that we suffer with him, that we may be also glorified together.

My wife and I adopted our daughter Ruth when she was a month old. While she was a little girl friends occasionally mentioned adoption, but if Ruth heard any such mention she ignored it, not having any idea that she was in any way involved. While she was yet young, however, she went to my wife crying because some other youngster had said that she was "adopted." "Of course you were adopted," said Alice. "We picked you out to be our daughter. Lyman was there and helped to select you, and you are the only sister Paul ever had. All of us love you very much." Ruth dried her eyes and went off to play. Alice stayed to watch further developments, but left when she heard Ruth declaring somewhat aggressively that she had been especially selected to be our little girl.

Our world is from God, a gift given in the hope that in it we shall share with gratitude the further gifts which God gives so freely to the end that we shall here prepare for a fullness of eternal life. To this end the spirit in which we respond is of fundamental importance.

REFERENCES

1. Acts 17:26.
2. Acts 17:28.
3. John Donne, *Devotions Upon Emergent Occasions* XVII.
4. II Corinthians 10:12.
5. Exodus 2:10; Ether 2:7.
6. Romans 8:15-17. See also Romans 8:23, 9:4; Galatians 4:5; Ephesians 4:2.

Create in me a clean heart, O God: and renew a right spirit within me. Cast me not away from thy presence; and take not thy Holy Spirit from me. Restore unto me the joy of thy salvation; and uphold me with thy free Spirit. Then will I teach transgressors thy ways; and sinners shall be converted unto thee. . . . O Lord, open thou my lips; and my mouth shall show forth thy praise.

—Psalm 51:10-13, 15

Chapter 2

Spirit Is Basic

A human being *has* a body, but *is* a spirit. In a very significant sense, the spirit is life. By virtue of the spirit which animates, humans can communicate with other spirits and may receive communications from them. Although not a Spirit in the ultimate sense, as is God, by the nature of creation a human being is a spirit—a person.

The word *spirit* is often used to denote that which is non-material. Properly used, this is permissible. But there is a basic difference between matter and spirit. To achieve their full value they depend on each other. Ideally, matter is the vehicle through which spirit is expressed. Spirit is needed to give matter function and meaning, to enable matter to minister to fullness of life.

Fundamentally, our use of the word *spirit* has to do with persons and personality. We speak of the spirit of a person, meaning that he or she is kind or self-serving, generous or avaricious, outgoing or recessive. In related fashion we think of spirit as a common mind, shared by a group of persons, and talk of the spirit of a team (football) or of a nation (Scotland) or of an age (Elizabethan).

As reason influences and conditions our whole animal nature by its presence, so that we are never merely animals, so, also, our spirit permeates and modifies all of our lesser inclinations. Our personality may thus be spiritually directed.

Among thoughtful persons spirit is often experienced as an inner impulse calling and enabling them to rise above the self-regarding temptations of the moment. "The spirit of man...goeth upward."[1] When the *Titanic* sank in 1912, I remember being impressed by the fact that when it was realized the lifeboats were insufficient to carry all the passengers the officers announced: "Women and children first." The men stepped back with little or no demur. Soon the loaded boats pulled away, and the men left behind sank with the ship. These men were not a carefully selected group. At first it appeared as though the only thing they had in common was their place aboard. But there was more. They shared (probably without ever talking about it) what the French have long known as *noblesse oblige,* which means, in general terms, that *privilege entails obligations.* The men of the *Titanic* sensed this, and accepted its guidance.

Spirit is creative. Spirit perceives beauty and truth and goodness within the limits of its gifts and—again within the limits of its gifts—may find satisfaction in imitating or reproducing them. The spirit of persons enables them to extend their powers by the construction of tools. Forms are changed to more perfectly express human will, as persons find within an inner fount of energy by which to use things material for spiritual ends, or, according to the spirit which empowers, to promote more immediate ends.

The forms of energy we are most familiar with in modern life do not explain the deeper penetrations with which we become familiar in worship and in loving service. Things mental and things physical, each in its place, are of great importance in our personal and corporate lives. But they lack ultimate significance until and unless they are influenced by forces spiritual. The former are more readily perceived, and their values weighed. But the latter demand that growth shall precede understanding. They become means of revelation to those who are already familiar with the energies of grace.

Until the fairly recent past reputable historians made strenuous efforts to secure and coordinate all the facts which they thought had a bearing on the periods they were reviewing. Their major difficulty with this procedure, as became apparent from time to time, was that some of the most important facts were beyond their reach—for the passions which often determined a course of action might be surmised, but were rarely truly known. This is illustrated in the comments of Emil Ludwig in explaining his purpose in writing his widely approved biography of Napoleon:

In the episodes of his life I have tried to grasp the innermost moods (of which his rise was a natural and logical outcome), and to trace his movement towards the climax at St. Helena. To examine this man's inner life; to explain his resolves and his refrainings, his deeds and his sufferings, his fancies and his calculations, as issuing from the moods of his heart—the disclosure of this great chain of effects, was at once the means and the end of the portrayal.

Dr. Ludwig's very able reconstruction of the activating forces on the life of Napoleon has carried conviction to many readers. Actually, however, it is but a projection of his own experience and judgment against the known and verifiable facts. It was probably quite accurate. But what is beyond reasonable doubt is that Napoleon's spirit—his ambition, his courage, his ruthlessness—determined his actions and in so doing influenced the entire future of Europe.

A person's basic problems and achievements are in the realm of spirit. They have to do with the innermost self: "He that is slow to anger is better than the mighty; and he that ruleth his spirit than he that taketh a city."[2] One's spirit guides one's thoughts and actions. We are strongly influenced from without, but at the core of our being is the spirit which marks our essential selfhood. Perceiving this, the Psalmist wrote long ago: "Thou desirest truth in the inward parts; and in the hidden part thou shalt make me to know wisdom."[3]

It is because of the nature of the human spirit that the best of all human achievements have come to pass. A great cathedral or a great painting, a great poem or a great symphony, the rise and fall of a great nation or the scanty records of an ancient civilization are all expressions of the human spirit.

It has been said that human beings are "thinking animals" or "tool-making animals." Such designations have elements of truth, but are not fully descriptive. At their best persons are those with whom God wishes to converse, for they are made in the image of God, and God communicates with those most responsive to his revelation of himself and his purpose. God's powers have been entrusted to those who are set in place among others in order that they may choose, if they will, to cooperate in the salvation of all. People and their ways cannot be fully understood except in terms of their relationship to their Maker and to other human beings.

This relationship is required by our human situation. If we are to exist at all we must be created to some pattern, and that pattern is the best that we can imagine, determined in love by our heavenly Father. John wrote, "As many as received him, to them gave he power to become the sons of God."[4] The Psalmist wrote, "Thou wilt show me the path of life; in thy presence is the fulness of joy; at thy right hand are pleasures for evermore."[5] Jesus himself said, "It is the Spirit that quickeneth: the flesh profiteth nothing; the words that I speak unto you, they are spirit, and they are life."[6]

The refinement and extension of education is a major responsibility of successive generations. Without this there is no progress, for there is no salvation in ignorance. Nor is there any salvation in education of itself. In the long run the value of education depends on the spiritual qualities of those educated. The horrors of recent wars have told us this for the nations most wicked were the nations best educated. There is sound wisdom in the Harvard inscription:

When God had carried us safe to our New England
When we had built our houses; made secure
The needs of life; established civil law;
And raised convenient places for God's worship;
The next thing that we longed for was to advance
Knowledge, and hand it on from sire to son,
Dreading to leave our cause to the forgetful
When we shall lie in dust.

A danger in the pressures of modern times is that we will forget the importance of the partnership which our forebears saw so clearly. This was noted with concern in another Harvard connection by President Nathan Pusey in a major address:

When we look at the troubled state of the present world...one thing becomes manifest. This is the failure of recent educational practice to prepare men in terms of heart and will to prevent the strife, misunderstanding, and willfulness which now arise, or constructively and resolutely to cope with them once arisen....Indifference to religion in the world of education would therefore seem—whatever the situation may have been a generation ago—at least now to be a luxury we can no longer afford.

The foundations of permanent international peace are not political; they are spiritual. What is most needed in the pursuit of peace is the wide diffusion of that spirit which will impel both those in authority and their supporters to "seek peace and pursue it" in every way within their power with wisdom and work, persistence, and at sacrifice. When we have built up a tremendous aggregate of small trends toward selfishness, it is too late to expect the statesmen of the time to withstand the pressures which we have combined to create. As I write, the newspapers are reporting that Americans and Russians are co-operating to get needed food to people in Ethiopia. In such selfless action lies the possible foundation of hope. But it must be augmented. There are times when justice is more important than charity.

It takes at least two to make war. War comes, as James reminded his compeers, "of your lusts that war in your members."[7] They come of greed and oppression and injustice, of covetousness and fear and resentment. This is as true today as it was when James wrote nearly two thousand years ago. They come of pride of possessions and of resentment of opportunities unequally distributed, and of laws enacted by the strong to safeguard these inequities. They come of memories better allowed to die, but which are cherished—Mafia like—as though to abandon them would be disloyal to hate-engendered group standards. All these and many more ministers of conflict have their roots in spiritual lacks, and must be combated on that level if the will to peace is to have enduring success. Here, as elsewhere, spirit is basic.

We need sound convictions about matters of fundamental importance if our knowledge is to work for the common good. Without this, knowledge can be a hazard, for to know more is not necessarily to be better. There is no marked deficiency of knowledge in the world. In fact the increase of knowledge over the years preceding the outbreak of the world wars was not enough to prevent them or to limit their bestiality. What the world needs more than anything else is an increase in the number of actively good men and women. This may appear to be trite, but its lack of glamor is no evidence against its truth. The human spirit, not just the understanding of things material, is the determining factor in human progress and survival. Spirit is basic.

In November 1920, I went with President Frederick M. Smith from our church headquarters in Amhurst Park, London, England, to show him where to catch a train for Scotland. We allowed ourselves plenty of time. Soon I noticed that the "underground" was unusually full for the time of day. Later, on the surface, the crowd was larger, and everyone seemed to be going in the same direction. Then I remembered that this was Armistice Day, and that King George was to lay a wreath at the Cenotaph in tribute to the Unknown Soldier. So we joined the others and soon heard one of the great military bands playing patriotic airs. By the time we got to Whitehall the crowd was what Jim Daugherty would have called "densely thickulated." We came to an involuntary halt, and just looked and listened and felt emotional. There was little talking. We could not see very well, but we were aware of what was happening. When the king placed the wreath at the foot of the Cenotaph the band struck up the great hymn of Isaac Watts:

> O God, our help in ages past;
>   Our hope for years to come,
> Our shelter from the stormy blast,
>   And our eternal home.[8]

Before the first line was completed just about everyone there had joined in with compelling fervor: the king and the royal family and the heads of government and the poorest and most ill-clad person there. After President Smith had left and I was returning home, it dawned on me that the character of the assembly had changed when the crowd began to sing. Until then the onlookers were just that. But when I heard President Smith booming along beside me I knew he had not changed his status as an American citizen, but that this was swallowed up in something larger than any earthly loyalty. He, with the rest of us, was singing his faith. Spirit is basic.

We need the guidance of a Spirit and a power not our own. The spirit manifest among us has not proved adequate to the tasks committed to us. The opening of our eyes to others' needs and the diminution of reasons for conflict which presumably will follow, have been made possible by social and political endeavors of recent decades. There is a renewed emphasis on the worldwide importance of ministering to basic human needs regardless of ability to meet the costs involved. In response to this need Christian people have taken a significant part. But many who make no profession of Christianity show compassion which matches that of Christians. If the righteousness of the Saints is to exceed this, it seems axiomatic that we must heed and become the servants of a Spirit which unchristian people do not know, but which is vital to success: the Spirit of God.

REFERENCES

1. Ecclesiastes 3:21.
2. Proverbs 16:32.
3. Psalm 51:6.
4. John 1:12.
5. Psalm 16:11.
6. John 6:63.
7. James 4:1-3.
8. *Hymns of the Saints*, 200.

O God, Whose Voice Is in the Wind

Tune: All Saints, New. C.M.D.

O God, whose voice is in the wind,
Whose law is carved in stone,
We praise thee for the varied ways
We make thy kingdom known;
For skills of science and of art
And every new design
We use to sow the gospel seed,
To make all kingdoms thine.

Let music fill the starry skies
Like angel-songs of old;
May all mankind, through these new gifts,
The face of God behold;
May we be worthy of the saints
Who pioneered of yore,
And preached the Word in many climes
To earth's remotest shore.

May airwaves be thy lengthened arm,
To show abroad thy love
So we may learn to live on earth
As the redeemed above;
To spread the vision glorious,
By sermon, stage, and song;
Till all shall own the Christ as Lord,
And all to him belong!

—Ernest K. Emurian

This hymn was written, by request, for the dedication of the million dollar Protestant Radio and Television Center, on the campus of Emory University, at Emory University, Ga., Jan. 19, 1955.   Taken from *The Pulpit*, April 1955.

Chapter 3

Creation

In the beginning God created the heaven and the earth. And the earth was without form, and void; and darkness *was* upon the face of the deep. And the Spirit of God moved upon the face of the waters. And God said, Let there be light: and there was light. And God saw the light, that *it* was good: and God divided the light from the darkness. And God called the light Day, and the darkness he called Night.[1]

The creation was a love enterprise. But the love of God did not originate there. Nor did it begin when persons of spiritual insight first recognized it. Creation is of the very nature of divinity and—with divine holiness—it is central to all the works of God.

That creation was by the power of God is recognized throughout the scriptures. The Psalmist wrote, and the people sang: "O Lord, how manifold are thy works! in wisdom hast thou made them all: the earth is full of thy riches."[2] And in the Hebrew letter it is stated that "through faith we understand that the worlds were framed by the word of God."[3]

Jesus was associated with his Father in the work of creation.* The Psalmist wrote, "By the word of the

---

*In my earlier book, *The Joy in Creation and Judgment*, were chapters on creation with major emphasis on the Father and the Son, and some overlapping was inevitable. Here I have done my best to avoid duplication. Since my concern here is with the Holy Spirit, this will tend to occupy the center of attention.   F.H.E.

Lord were the heavens made."[4] This was echoed in both the New Testament and the Book of Mormon.

The Holy Spirit was also actively concerned in the creation of the world: "The earth was without form and void.... The Spirit of God moved upon the face of the waters,"[5] bringing order out of chaos.

It is apparent that the Father, the Son, and the Holy Spirit were all concerned in the creation, and that from the beginning creation was love-centered and intended to be a spiritual enterprise.

The scriptures reveal further that "I, the Lord God, formed man from the dust of the ground, and breathed into his nostrils the breath of life; and man became a living soul."[6]

This in-breathing is not reported of any other creature. Human beings were quite evidently of a different order, and were given dominion over all the lesser creation.[7] Although related to the animals, people are not merely animals, for they were created in the image of God. According to the Joseph Smith version of the Holy Scriptures "I, God, created man in mine own image, in the image of mine Only Begotten created I him, male and female created I them."[8]

Even though we are made in God's image we are still creatures. We are not God. We were created for a God-like purpose, and endowed with something of his Spirit to that end. This assurance, which underlies much of the scriptures, does not rest ultimately on human reason. It grows, rather, in worship and service and the indwelling of the Spirit of God. It gives us a point of reference for orienting our lives meaningfully and, if heeded, makes us humble and grateful and cooperative. Apparently it was against such a background that Moses composed the great prayer which later became part of the Book of Psalms:

Lord, thou hast been our dwelling-place in all generations. Before the mountains were brought forth, or ever thou hadst formed the earth and the world, even from everlasting to everlasting, thou art God.[9]

We are created in the image of God, but this likeness is conditioned by our finiteness. God is of infinitely greater moral grandeur than we are. His goodness is so far higher than our best as to be of a different order. As God said to Isaiah:

My thoughts are not your thoughts, neither are your ways my ways, saith the Lord. For as the heavens are higher than the earth, so are my ways higher than your ways, and my thoughts than your thoughts.[10]

God's love is far above ours; it reaches beyond eternity and eludes our full understanding until eternity opens our eyes. Our only possibility of true holiness does not rest in our up-reaching goodness, but in his Spirit's ministries. We need redemption, not merely education.

Yet we are in the image of God. Contemplation of the greatness of God as he looked on the majesty of creation moved David to write the following:

O Lord our Lord, how excellent is thy name in all the earth! who hast set thy glory above the heavens....When I consider thy heavens, the work of thy fingers, the moon and the stars, which thou hast ordained; What is man that thou art mindful of him? and the son of man, that thou visitest him? For thou hast made him a little lower than the angels, and hast crowned him with glory and honor. Thou madest him to have dominion over the works of thy hands; thou hast put all things under his feet; All sheep and oxen, yea, and the beasts of the field; the fowl of the air, and the fish of sea, and whatsoever passeth through the paths of the seas. O Lord our Lord, how excellent is thy name in all the earth![11]

God is a person in the fullest sense. We are persons, too, within the limits of our finitude, and have capacity to understand and distinguish between values, and must live according to our choices. But though we are relatively free and responsible, we have not been left alone. Another of the great Psalms expresses this conviction:

Whither shall I go from thy Spirit? or whither shall I flee from thy presence?...If I take the wings of the morning, and dwell in the uttermost parts of the sea; even there shall thy hand lead me, and thy right hand shall hold me. If I say, surely the darkness shall cover me; even the night shall be light about me. Yea, the darkness hideth not from thee; but the night shineth as the day; the darkness and the light are both alike unto thee.[12]

Creation was and is a love enterprise. And love at its best calls for communication and a degree of understanding between the lovers. Parents know this. Long before their children are born, parents prepare for their coming. Although children appear to be totally without understanding they are environed in love from the beginning. By the grace of God they have built-in capacities for recognition and response. Their first faltering words are welcomed joyously, and by this they are encouraged to continue. And all the time they are learning to talk they are assimilating family affection. They enter into play patterns without realizing that they are entering into an approved social order. And so, after a time, love opens doors through which they enter into personhood in their own right.

In much richer fashion than human beings can attain, the love of God is his way of basic communication with us. It is wiser, more devoted, more sustained than anything we can achieve. And God introduces it to us with a steadily growing capacity for understanding. He uses families and friends, and

35

special messengers like the prophets, so that in time—if we are alert to what is happening below the surface of things—we find ourselves parts of diverse circles of affection.

Our creation and the endowment reserved for us above all other created beings confirms that the creation is for a purpose consistent with the grandeur of our Creator. Acording to a revelation given to Joseph Smith in June 1830 Moses asked what was this purpose, and was answered:

For mine own purpose have I made these things. Here is wisdom and it remaineth in me.... And worlds without number have I created, and I also created them for mine own purpose.[13]

Although the fullness of God's purpose will always exceed our understanding we can learn "here a little and there a little."[14] Our understanding will grow with our knowledge of God and our obedience to his commands. In this growth Jesus and the Holy Spirit, the testimonies of the New Testament witnesses, and the prophets and psalmists lead the way.

The affirmation that "God created the heaven and the earth" invites further questions, for the record also reveals that at each stage in creation God pronounced his work "Good."[15] Almost instinctively we ask Good for what? and Good for whom? If our answer is to satisfy it must not be trivial. It must correspond to the grandeur of God. Men of prophetic caliber among the Hebrews said that creation was a good beginning to the establishment of the covenant. The late, widely esteemed theologian, Karl Barth, agreed: "The covenant is the goal of creation; creation is the way to the covenant." It was the covenant which gave creation its exalted meaning.

Our world was intended as the starting point of an expanding social fellowship after the Son of God's own heart. To this end the race was launched and told to be fruitful and multiply and replenish the earth, to subdue it and to have dominion over it. But the fullness of the divine intention was not only in the perfecting of human skills, but in the growth of humankind in God's likeness. In the name of God Isaiah said, "God himself that formed the earth and made it; he hath established it; he created it not in vain, he formed it to be inhabited."[16]

In accord with his plan for further creation,

The Lord God took the man [Adam] and put him into the garden of Eden, to dress it, and to keep it. And...the Lord commanded the man, saying, Of every tree of the garden thou mayest freely eat; but of the tree of the knowledge of good and evil, thou shalt not eat of it....For in the day thou eatest thereof thou shalt surely die.[17]

Both Adam and Eve ate the forbidden fruit. The full meaning of the prohibition we do not know, but some results were immediately apparent. They saw their own nakedness with new eyes, and were ashamed and sought to hide from God.[18] Moreover, they could not have been unaware of the bounty of God and of the ingratitude they had shown. Although death did not come within the short day between sunrise and sunset, it loomed over the horizon. And in the meantime they had to learn to live beyond Eden.

Life beyond Eden was not life apart from the love of God, for it soon became apparent that their skills and ingenuity could not of themselves satisfy all their needs and the needs of their descendants. Their hard work must be augmented by rain and seasonal warmth, the coming of which were beyond their command. However, both these and other needs were filled, and the generosity of the Creator begat

37

gratitude. Among the many gifts of God granted in creation and growth is appreciation. I have felt that it was probably in appreciation of these sustaining gifts that Adam and Eve turned to gratitude and worship and like-mindedness.

It is not likely that they spent all their time in the fields. Beauty and order were all around them. And there were animals which had been placed in their care, and which were endowed according to their distinctive natures. So, almost imperceptibly, appreciation merged into something far deeper. Their situation caused them to sense grandeur in all they saw and felt. It merged into awe, the finest of the emotions, and to love, its counterpart. According to the scripture record:

Adam called upon the name of the Lord, and Eve also, his wife; and they heard the voice of the Lord, from the way towards the garden of Eden, speaking unto them, and they saw him not; for they were shut out from his presence. And he gave unto them commandments, that they should worship the Lord their God; and should offer the firstlings of their flocks for an offering unto the Lord. And Adam was obedient unto the commandments of the Lord. And after many days, an angel of the Lord appeared unto Adam, saying, Why dost thou offer sacrifices unto the Lord? And Adam said unto him, I know not save the Lord commanded me. And then the angel spake, saying, This thing is a similitude of the sacrifice of the Only Begotten of the Father, which is full of grace and truth.[19]

Apparently Adam and his wife had learned something of the primary authority of their Creator, for they were obedient even before the meaning of the commands was explained to them. Having come this far, there was seemingly no reason why the Lord could not lead them further, and they were instructed as follows:

Thou shalt do all that thou doest, in the name of the Son. And thou shalt repent, and call upon God, in the name of the Son for evermore. And in that day, the Holy Ghost fell upon Adam, which beareth record of the Father and the Son, saying, I am the Only Begotten of the Father from the beginning, henceforth and for ever; that as thou hast fallen, thou mayest be redeemed, and all mankind, even as many as will.[20]

Thereafter Adam, blessed of God, prophesied of the goodness of God, and Eve testified of their joy in the promise of redemption "and the eternal life which God giveth unto all the obedient."[21]

Devout consideration of the reasons for our creation and placement in such a world as ours invariably leads to awareness of the majesty of divinity to awe, and to worship. The great leaders of ancient Israel thought of creation as a preparation for the Covenant, and considered it in their major assemblies. Joshua, when he was about to die, gathered all the tribes to Shechem and there recalled to them the faith-promoting incidents of their history and then continued:

Choose you this day whom ye will serve; whether the gods which your fathers served that were on the other side of the flood, or the gods of the Amorites, in whose land ye dwell; but as for me and my house, we will serve the Lord.[22]

Glory in the gracious sovereignty of God inspired many of the psalms. This note is sounded many times, but I have always found help in the Psalms.

The earth is the Lord's, and the fulness thereof; the world and they that dwell therein. . . . Who shall ascend unto the hill of the Lord? or who shall stand in his holy place? He that hath clean hands, and a pure heart; who hath not lifted up his soul unto vanity, nor sworn deceitfully. He shall receive the blessing from the Lord, and righteousness from the God of his salvation.[23]

Awareness of our creation in love begets recognition that we have been offered a significant part in a great adventure. The preparation for our participation was undertaken by our Creator before we were born, and has been shared by him ever since that time, as the cost of the birth and life of a child is borne by the parents. To ignore the debt we owe to parents or Creator, living by their love without appreciation, receiving their gifts without gratitude, stunts the soul. But to respond to the love which sustains us, sharing it with gratitude, lights up the whole adventure of being. Who can put a price tag on family affection, or—even more—on the love of our heavenly Father. Its reward is in its sharing. And we rob ourselves as well as those who love us when we fail to share the riches which love offers.

The sense of awe envelops us totally as we experience it. It has been described as the greatest of the emotions, and this is probably sound, but it goes much further. It is a revelation for which we must be in an elevated state of heart and mind. We can understand this better if we think in the mood of worship of Isaiah's awe-inspiring experience in the temple:

In the year that King Uzziah died I saw also the Lord sitting upon a throne, high and lifted up, and his train filled the temple. Above it stood the seraphim; and each one had six wings; with twain he covered his face, and with twain he covered his feet, and with twain he did fly. And one cried unto another, and said, Holy, holy, holy is the Lord of hosts; the whole earth is full of his glory. And the posts of the door moved at the voice of him that cried, and the whole house was filled with smoke. Then said I, Woe is me! For...I am a man of unclean lips, and I dwell in the midst of a people of unclean lips; for mine eyes have seen the King, the Lord of hosts. Then flew one of the seraphim unto me, having a live coal in his hand, which he had taken with the tongs from off the altar; and he laid it upon my mouth, and said, Lo, this hath touched thy lips; and thine iniquity is taken away, and thy sin purged.

Also I heard the voice of the Lord, saying, Whom shall I send, and who will go for us? Then said I, Here am I; send me.[24]

Note these aspects of the revelation:

- The splendor of the vision of God: His glory and exaltation. He was "high and lifted up."
- The unmatched holiness of God, filling the whole earth.
- The reaction of Isaiah: "Woe is me! For I am a man of unclean lips, and I dwell in the midst of a people of unclean lips."
- The forgiveness of the repentant prophet.
- Isaiah's commissioning: "Who will go for us?"
- His acceptance: "Here am I, send me."

There was a tremendously impressive purpose underlying the whole revelation. It was both sublime and commanding. It is dimly approximated when we are arrested by a view of the majesty of the ocean or the unmatched magnificence of a mountain range, or the sheer loveliness of a small flower. These, however, give only hints of the awe engendered by the vision of God.

Creation is not finished—belonging to the past and never to be repeated. Rather, it is continuous, preserving what is still needed by a prolongation of the creative process. To this maintenance of creation the psalmists give testimony: "Thou sendest forth thy Spirit, they are created; and thou renewest the face of the earth."[25]

In the Apocrypha we read: "How can anything endure, if thou wouldst not? Or be preserved if not called by thee?"

God has shared his creative power with those he has created, giving us the capacity to appreciate the examples of his creative genius all around us. Some have been especially blessed with outstanding creative gifts in the arts and sciences. Many were given such "extras" as music and painting, and the ability

41

to create fine literature and drama. These gifts belong to the fullness of life. Persons who create things and thoughts of beauty and truth have done more to make life glorious than all the wealthy distributors of "goods." These artistic "extras" are particularly important in the field of social relationships. They make for the enrichment of personality. Parents express their love for their children through their efforts to provide these riches for them—often at considerable sacrifice. They are an important element in the language of love.

REFERENCES

1. Genesis 1:1-5 K.J.
2. Psalm 104:24.
3. Hebrews 11:3.
4. Psalm 33:6.
5. Genesis 1:2 KJ.
6. Genesis 2:8.
7. Genesis 1:30 IV.
8. Genesis 1:29 IV.
9. Psalm 90:1.
10. Isaiah 55:8-9.
11. Psalm 8:1, 3-9.
12. Psalm 139:7-12.
13. Doctrine and Covenants 22:21.
14. Isaiah 28:10.
15. Genesis 1:10, 18, 21, etc.
16. Isaiah 45:18.
17. Genesis 2:18-22 IV.
18. Genesis 3:7 KJ.
19. Genesis 4:4-7 IV.
20. Genesis 4:8-9 IV.
21. Genesis 4:11 IV.
22. Joshua 24:14-15.
23. Psalm 24:1, 3-5.
24. Isaiah 6:1-8.
25. Psalm 104:30.

Oh Lord, grant me such love that humility may be my sanctuary, and Thy service the joy of my soul, and death itself the entrance of an eternal life, when I may live with Thee, my Strength, and my Refuge, my God and everlasting Hope.

—Jeremy Taylor (1613-1667)

Chapter 4

The God of the Covenants

One of the great words of the Bible is *berith*, which is translated *covenant*. The Covenant proposed by God and renewed on his initiative from time to time was not an arrangement between equals. It arose out of the very nature of God, and reflected his unfailing loving-kindness. The covenant was the gift of God for the guidance of those he had created. It was set to overcome the effect of the fall, which had come about through disobedience. By its nature it required a considerable amount of freedom on the part of those consenting to it. But the expanse of such freedom must be limited since human beings are finite, while infinite forces and powers are involved in achieving godliness.

For many years students of the Old Testament thought the covenant relation between God and human beings began with Moses, or even with Abraham. More recently, however, it has been thought that God did not wait that long before calling persons to faithfulness and service. Dr. Arnold B. Come suggests "a covenant of works" to explain this relationship after the fall. It is of interest to Latter Day Saints to note in this connection that according to the Joseph Smith New Translation of the Holy Scriptures the covenant principle was operative shortly after Adam and Eve were expelled from Eden.[1]

The covenant which was made with Abraham some generations after the flood is set forth in such detail that it is widely accepted as a good starting point for the study of the nature of the covenants in general:

The Lord said unto Abram [Abraham], Get thee out of thy country, and from thy kindred, and from thy father's house, unto a land that I will show thee. And I will make of thee a great nation, and I will bless thee, and make thy name great; and thou shalt be a blessing; and I will bless them that bless thee, and curse them that curse thee; and in thee shall the families of the earth be blessed.[2]

The King James version of the Bible mentions this call of Abram [Abraham] quite abruptly and until the patriarch's call is discussed in Paul's Galatian letter we are left wondering what prompted Abraham's response in faith. The older version does mention that Abraham paid tithes to Melchisedek, the king of Salem[3] but again gives few details. Some of these are added in the Inspired Version where we are told that Melchisedek was a high priest after the order of the covenant which God made with Enoch.[4] Modern revelation adds that "Abraham received the priesthood from Melchisedek who received it through the lineage of his fathers, even till Noah.[5]

When we consider the covenant with Abraham in light of his connection with Melchisedek and his environment in Haran—where idolatry was deeply rooted—these conclusions appear reasonable:

From Melchisedek, and from his family knowledge of the covenant with Enoch and Noah, Abraham was probably prepared in some degree for the extension of the covenant to himself.

When, later, the covenant was renewed and his seed promised it became clear that fulfillment of the promises was possible if God so determined, but only if this was so.

The birth of Isaac and his subsequent preservation when Abraham was about to sacrifice him provided the necessary link to the future.

His sense of family obligation, understandable since it had been sustained through several generations, fitted Abraham for the transmission of the covenant responsibility.

Abraham was regarded as a prophet.[6] This was probably in recognition of his attitude and way of life, and especially because of his freedom from idolatrous activities.

Abraham and his son, Isaac, and Isaac's son, Jacob, were all faithful to the covenant, as was Joseph. Before the death of Jacob the covenant was confirmed to Ephraim, the younger son of Joseph.[7]

In an arrangement made by Joseph, his family went to Egypt as guests of the Pharoah. They remained there for four hundred years, their status deteriorating until they were virtually slaves. When their situation was desperate, the Lord raised up from among them Moses, who became one of the great leaders of all time, and through him wrought their deliverance. After it was clear what the Lord had done for them, Moses proposed a covenant in the name of God:

Ye have seen what I did unto the Egyptians, and how I bare you on eagle's wings, and brought you unto myself. Now therefore, if ye will obey my voice indeed, and keep my covenant, then ye shall be a peculiar treasure unto me above all people; for all the earth is mine; and ye shall be unto me a kingdom of priests, and a holy nation.[8]

And, in light of the deliverance which God had brought to pass "All the people answered together, and said All that the Lord hath spoken we will do."[9]

This deliverance, Moses said, was wrought because of the love of God for Israel, and to fulfill his purpose in them:

The Lord did not set his love upon you, nor choose you, because ye were more in number than any people; for ye were the fewest of all people. But because the Lord loved you, and because he would keep his oath which he had sworn unto your fathers.[10]

The covenant was given to Moses on Mount Sinai. Here he was also given instructions for the building of a tabernacle and an ark and a table and other furnishings which it should enclose. This the people also agreed to. The men who were "of a willing heart" brought precious goods from their treasures, and the women "that were wise-hearted" fashioned the drapes and the garments which Moses called for.[11] These were then entrusted to Bezaleel of the tribe of Judah and to Aholiab of the tribe of Dan whom the Lord said he had filled "with the Spirit of God in wisdom, and in understanding, and in knowledge, and in all manner of workmanship."[12]

Despite the repeated demonstrations of God's love the Children of Israel, because of their regard for their immediate and temporal concerns and the influence of their pagan neighbors, frequently fell away from the covenant.[13] Moses pleaded for their forgiveness and renewal[14] and on their promise of repentance a "lesser covenant" which was "after the law of a carnal commandment" was given. The people as a whole had limited insight and understanding; they needed guidance to make their way of life consistent with their covenant commitments. This was spelled out in the law as Moses now set it forth. Both the covenants and the law reflected the loving purpose of God. They were given in love, and it was intended that they should be obeyed in love. It was hoped that as this was done the people would grow in understanding the holiness of God.

Understanding of the principles revealed in God's covenants with us is important for sound insight into the nature and purpose of God. The covenants are a vital part of the divine plan for our redemption. This is seen more clearly if we consider some of the principles embodied in the covenant as it was agreed to and renewed from time to time.

The sound, unvarying basis for the covenants is the previously demonstrated power and love of God. It is by the grace of God that we "live, and move, and have our being,"[15] and his love underlies all our relationships with him. Not all are alert to this, so it is necessary that those who would enter into the covenant first consider the love of God which has already been demonstrated. Thus, when the covenant was proposed for Israel Moses narrated God's mighty acts.[16]

Our heavenly Father is deeply involved in all that he requires of us. By his Spirit he quickens our understanding and steels our wills. The Lord Jesus is our constant example. And when our task seems impossible he may provide the offering as he did for Abraham.[17] It was out of his own costly experience that the Apostle Paul wrote to the saints in Rome: "I beseech you therefore, brethren, by the mercies of God, that you present your bodies a living sacrifice, holy, acceptable unto God, which is your reasonable service."[18]

Sacrifice in the service of God is not a sorrowful experience except as we dwell on it rather than on its purpose and glory. In the scriptures, sacrifice and thanksgiving are frequently joined together. The Psalmist invited the Children of Israel to sing of this:

O that men would praise the Lord for his goodness, and for his wonderful works to the children of men! And let them sacrifice the sacrifice of thanksgiving, and declare his works with rejoicing.[19]

The sacrifices of God are a broken spirit; a broken and a contrite heart, O God, thou wilt not despise. Do good in thy good pleasure unto Zion; build thou the walls of Jerusalem. Then shalt thou be pleased with the sacrifices of righteousness.[20]

The covenants call for sacrifice. Every covenant calls for the abandonment of non-covenant ways, and the adoption of ways pertinent to the life of the new covenant. This cannot always be achieved immediately. Indeed, those who practice the arts of repentance, and do so earnestly, find themselves in constant need of the Spirit of God to keep them in God's way.

The covenants are grounded in the inscrutable wisdom of God. In the final analysis, we have no explanation of why God chose the Children of Israel (or why he chooses us) other than to say that it is done out of his own wisdom and grace. This is the verdict of believers in view of the total revelation given us in the Lord Jesus as it has been confirmed by the Holy Spirit.

A major problem we encounter as we study the choices underlying our creation is that God cannot direct us by merely telling us. Words do not convey enough. And, also, since we are called to be members of his family we need to learn together. Even before this, God must demonstrate his great love for us so that the covenant is offered in love. This he did in the morning of creation and again on Sinai, and—most fully—on Calvary.

It is not good for persons to be alone.[21] This truth was witnessed between Adam and Eve. It is also true between us and God. We need God. As the presence of the human spirit is vital to our continuing earthly life, so the ministry of the Holy Spirit is vital to our spiritual maturing. There is no satisfactory substitute. In recognition of this, the Mosaic covenant began, "Hear, O, Israel; The Lord our God is one Lord; and thou shalt love the Lord thy God with all thine heart, and with all thy soul, and with all thy might."[22]

We do not determine the basis on which we will be accepted of God. Being finite, we lack the understanding required to do so. So God has written the terms of this partnership into the structure of the universe. The prophets announce the offer of the covenant, and people accept or reject it: "Obey my voice, and I will be your God, and ye shall be my people; and walk ye in all the ways that I have commanded you, that it may be well unto you."[23]

The scriptures do not teach that the divine requirement of righteousness is in any way relaxed for any chosen people. Nor do individuals, whatever their service, stand in any preferential relation to God. Those who fulfill their calling grow like their Lord. Their reward is in further stewardship.[24]

The covenants are based on free choice. While this choice is secondary to those already made for us in our creation and placement in time and geography, it is nevertheless real, and is needed to consummate the covenant relation. To give solid foundation for this free choice the prophets always called attention to the mighty acts of God on people's behalf before inviting them to enter into the covenant.[25] Without

such a foundation persons would have to choose
blindly—yet must choose if they are to be responsible.

But, the choice of an individual invariably had in
sight the choice of a people:

God made a covenant with Noah, and said, This shall be the
token of the covenant I make between me and you, and for every
living creature with you, for perpetual generations.[26]

Unity under the covenant was well understood
among the Hebrews. Indeed, our modern emphasis
on individualism would have seemed strange to
them. Hebrews who understood their religion did
not set their personal religious life apart from that of
others. This corporate view of religion was not felt to
be inconsistent with deep, personal religious life, but
it was the corporate religion which came first in both
time and importance. They thought of their relation
to God as normally inseparable from their relation to
the people of God.

God is faithful to his covenant commitments. Since
the covenant has been inaugurated and renewed by
the grace of God, and not because of the demonstrated worthiness of people, its fulfillment may be
deterred by human unfaithfulness but will not be
abandoned:

God is not a man, that he should lie; neither the son of man,
that he should repent; hath he said, and shall he not do it? or hath
he spoken and shall he not make it good?[27]

The gifts and calling of God are without repentance.[28]

They did evil again before thee; therefore leftest thou them in the
hand of their enemies, so that they had the dominion over them;
yet when they returned, and cried unto thee, thou heardest them
from heaven; and many times didst thou deliver them according
to thy mercies.[29]

Let the wicked forsake his way, and the unrighteous man his
thoughts; and let him return unto the Lord, and he will have

mercy upon him; and to our God, for he will abundantly pardon.[30]

Revelation received in the early days of the Restoration spoke of the "new and everlasting covenant; even that which was from the beginning."[31]

In the preface to the Doctrine and Covenants the essence of apostasy is said to be that people

have strayed from mine ordinances, and have broken mine everlasting covenant; they seek not the Lord to establish his righteousness, but every man walketh in his own way, and after the image of his own god.[32]

The same revelation says that the purpose of the Restoration is that "faith also might increase in the earth: that mine everlasting covenant might be established."[33]

Later prophecy anticipated the song of the redeemed:

The Lord hath brought again Zion;
The Lord hath redeemed his people, Israel,
According to the election of grace,
Which was brought to pass by the faith
and covenant of their fathers.[34]

The covenants we have noted briefly have an important place in the history of redemption. The principle was never abandoned, but was reinterpreted and carried forward by the Lord Jesus into the new age which he inaugurated. The covenant with Israel had provided "a shadow of heavenly things"[35] but had not been faultless.[36] Now, however, it was superseded by what James called "the perfect law of liberty."[37]

REFERENCES

1. Genesis 5:1-2.
2. Genesis 12:1-3.
3. Genesis 14:18-20 KJ.
4. Genesis 9:17-19; 14:17 IV.
5. Genesis 13:13, 14:27 IV.
6. Genesis 20:7 KJ.
7. Genesis 48:17-20.
8. Exodus 19:4-6.
9. Exodus 19:8.
10. Deuteronomy 7:7-8.
11. Exodus 25:2; 28:3.
12. Exodus 31:3, 35:31.
13. Deuteronomy 11:28.
14. Deuteronomy 30:19.
15. Acts 17:28.
16. Deuteronomy 4:31-39.
17. Genesis 22:13.
18. Romans 12:1.
19. Psalm 107:21-22.
20. Psalm 51:17-19.
21. Genesis 2:23.
22. Deuteronomy 6:4-5.
23. Jeremiah 7:23.
24. Matthew 25:21, 23 ff.
25. Exodus 19:4.
26. Genesis 9:18.
27. Numbers 23:19.
28. Romans 11:29.
29. Nehemiah 9:28.
30. Isaiah 55:7.
31. Doctrine and Covenants 20:1a.
32. Doctrine and Covenants 1:3d.
33. Doctrine and Covenants 1:4d.
34. Doctrine and Covenants 83:17a.
35. Hebrews 8:5.
36. Hebrews 8:7.
37. James 1:25.

Oh come, let us sing unto the Lord; let us make a joyful noise to the Rock of our salvation. Let us come before his presence with thanksgiving, and make a joyful noise unto him with psalms. For the Lord is a great God, and a great King above all gods.

—Psalm 95:1-3

Chapter 5

The Book of Psalms

Of the thirty-nine books of the Old Testament probably none other has exercised such a profound and far-reaching influence as the Book of Psalms. It has been a major source of spiritual insight and uplift in both Judaism and Christianity, and it is difficult to think of any of the great arts not indebted to it. Its value for private devotions has been recognized by many publishers whose joint editions of the New Testament and the Book of Psalms appear year after year.

The Book of Psalms is a compilation of poems which were intended to be sung in Hebrew worship. Some of these poems were probably written by David about a thousand years before the birth of Jesus. David was not, however, the sole author; Korah and Aseph are known to have written some. But the majority of the psalms carry no evidence of their authors, and the dates of composition are known for only a few.

Many of the psalms reveal a high degree of spiritual and prophetic insight. They are unique in that while other scriptures contain God's word addressed to people, many of the psalms express persons' adoration of God and appreciation of his handiwork.

It is difficult to trace the beginnings of psalmody. It

is interesting, however, that after Saul became king Samuel the prophet retired to his home in Ramah, and there sought to fulfill an ambition which he had been too busy to pursue. He founded a school specializing in the study and production of music, musical instruments, and poetry. He soon gathered around him men and women of all ages, spiritually motivated, who devoted their lives to this calling. Their enterprise was called "The School of the Prophets"—a designation used by the early Reorganization for a school which had a different emphasis.

Samuel located his school at Naioth. Later, when Saul became subject to fits of melancholy, it was suggested that he might be helped by the music of one of whom an attendant said, "I have seen a son of Jesse the Beth-lehemite, that is cunning in playing, and a mighty valiant man, a man of war, and prudent in matters, and a comely person, and the Lord is with him."[1] So David joined the school, and with his coming the great age of Israel's music was ushered in.

David became widely known and Saul was insanely jealous. Fearing for his life, David sought the protection of Samuel and was sent to Naioth. Here David increased his musical skills and, between times, talked with Samuel about the arts of statesmanship. It was well that he did so, for shortly thereafter both Saul and his son, Jonathan, were killed in battle with the Philistines, and David—prepared and popular—became king. One of his first problems was the promotion of unity among the tribes of Israel. To this task he brought many skills. His music was one of the most useful. An associated factor was the capture of Jerusalem. This David accomplished, making Jerusalem the capital of the united nation. As soon as he could do so he augmented the sense of unity and strength of his people by taking the Ark of the Covenant to the capital. Its transportation and installation were occasions of great joy and celebration in which both the Levites and singers trained in the School of the Prophets had prominent parts. The Hebrews were becoming known as a musical people. Down the years, while David's son, Solomon, was building the temple, the psalms were sung in the homes and in the fields and at seasonal festivals and in all manner of public gatherings.

When the temple was completed the Levites were ready also. The ordering of worship was their hereditary responsibility and privilege.[2] At appropriate times in the services the story of Israel's deliverance from Egypt was chanted. Psalms were sung, too, many of them with the people responding or sharing the text antiphonally, so that all had a part in the worship of God and in expressing their gratitude for his mighty acts on their behalf.

The Hebrew word from which the Book of Psalms is named means *praises*. Thanksgiving and praise are dominant notes of the book. We praise God to give wholehearted expression to our delight in him. Doing so, we find that it is as we rejoice in God that he makes himself known to us in a spiritually uplifting personal sharing. The urge to praise God is evidence of our spiritual health. As the late C. S. Lewis wrote, "Praise is spiritual health made visible."[3]

The phrasing of the psalms is rarely abstruse, making the counsels and testimonies easily remembered. Following are some quotations which illustrate this. The recall of them and others like them are pertinent and helpful in many diverse situations:

Bless the Lord, O my soul; and all that is within me, bless his holy name.[4]

O Lord, our Lord, how excellent is thy name in all the earth.[5]

Let the words of my mouth, and the meditations of my heart, be acceptable in thy sight, O Lord, my strength, and my redeemer.[6]

Wait on the Lord, be of good courage, and he shall strengthen thy heart, wait, I say, on the Lord.[7]

God is our refuge and strength, a present help in trouble. Therefore we will not fear, though the earth...be removed.[8]

Ease in remembering is augmented by the Hebrew poetic device called *parallelism* according to which a thought expressed in the fore part of a sentence is slightly modified to present what is essentially the same idea as the latter part of the sentence. Psalm 104:33 has a forthright illustration of parallelism:

I will sing unto the Lord as long as I live:
I will sing praise to my God while I have my being.

There are many other parallelisms. Noting these makes remembrance easier as does the poetic form.

The Book of Psalms is not to be skimmed through any more than is a modern hymnal. It is a treasury of praise designed for use in the spirit of worship and should be kept handy in the mind, rather than on the shelf. When the book is needed the need is usually urgent; then there is little time to search for it—no more than there is time for a performer on the stage to study his or her lines.

Study of the psalms shows that they were wrought out of deep spiritual experience and insight. Some may be the fruit of clear and enlightening inspiration. While they often sound an attractive note of spontaneity, there is evidence of prolonged seeking and finding. Consider the message of the writer of Psalm 103, whose testimony has enriched thirty centuries of worshipers:

Bless the Lord, O my soul; and all that is within me, bless his holy name. Bless the Lord, O my soul, and forget not all his benefits; who forgiveth all thine iniquities; who healeth all thy diseases; who redeemeth thy life from destruction; who crowneth thee with loving-kindness and tender mercies; who satisfieth thy mouth with good things; so that thy youth is renewed like the eagle's.[9]

In seeking for the noblest expression of the Holy Spirit in the Old Testament many turn to the psalms rather than to the prophets. Sections of Psalm 139 have been discussed in this connection:

O Lord thou hast searched me and known me. . . . Thou hast beset me behind and before, and laid thine hand upon me. . . . Whither shall I go from thy Spirit? or whither shall I flee from thy presence?

Search me, O God, and know my heart, try me, and know my thoughts and see if there be any wicked way in me, and lead me in the way everlasting.[10]

Many values accrue to the devotional life of Christians from the frequent use of the Book of Psalms. The testimonies of the writers of three thousand years ago still quicken our spiritual responses. In Victorian England it was a widely observed custom for everyone in the house to be present to share in "morning prayers." The style of these gatherings varied, but they were likely to have one thing in common: the reading of the scriptures, generally from the psalms. More recently the practice has yielded to the encroachment of industry, the spread of secularism, and other factors. In many Christian homes throughout the world, however, the practice is continued. For such occasions the psalms are an unfailing resource. Relatively brief psalms or sections of the longer psalms are especially fitted for such occasions.[11]

The people of God trust him for his loving-kindness.

This so impressed the compiler of the psalms that he chose Psalm 150 as a fitting end to the book:

Praise ye the Lord. Praise God in his sanctuary; praise him in the firmament of his power. Praise him for his mighty acts; praise him according to his excellent greatness....Let everything that hath breath praise the Lord. Praise ye the Lord.[12]

This makes an excellent introduction to a service of worship.

By their constitution, some groups are more familiar with the psalms than others. This is true, for instance, in public assemblies where denominational lines are ignored. Here there are often many who have sung anthems from the psalms. Others, with no specific memories of the psalms, find that they fit their mood of solemnity, grandeur, and commemoration. One historic situation illustrates this: The majestic Psalm 90 is usually attributed to Moses (although the first clear mention of it was in the third section of the Psalms of David which appeared after Moses died). It was read by the actor Edward Everett Hale at midnight from the steps of the Boston State House as the nineteenth century slipped away and gave place to the twentieth.

Lord, thou hast been our dwelling-place in all generations. Before the mountains were brought forth, or ever thou hadst formed the earth and the world, even from everlasting to everlasting, thou art God. Thou turnest man to destruction; and sayest, Return, ye children of men. For a thousand years in thy sight are but as yesterday when it is past, and as a watch in the night. Thou carriest them away as with a flood; they are as a sleep; in the morning they are like the grass which groweth up; in the evening it is cut down, and withereth.[13]

The psalms bear testimony of the Spirit of God as known among the faithful. They were written, however, before the Lord's earthly ministry. We read them, therefore, from a vantage point which the children of Israel did not fully share. We should read the psalms (and the whole of the Old Testament) in the light of the New. When we read the truly inspiring psalm which says that "the law of the Lord is perfect, converting the soul" we do not spend much time reflecting that the composer of Psalm 19:7 had the Mosaic Law in mind. Instead, our thoughts leap ahead to the teaching of the apostle James about the "perfect law of liberty."[14]

Nevertheless, we need to remember with gratitude that the psalms provided the initial thrust which transformed John Bunyan from an unlettered tinker into a Christian poet of genius. It was from the psalms, too, that John Milton wrote a hymn which is still loved and widely used:

Let us with a gladsome mind
Praise the Lord for he is kind,
For his mercies aye endure
Ever faithful, ever sure.

And it was in Psalm 90 that Isaac Watts found the inspiration from which he wrote "O God Our Help in Ages Past" which Roland Prothero described as "perhaps the finest hymn in the English language."

Many of the best loved hymns familiar to Christians are paraphrases of the psalms or are patterned on them. Among those which come readily to mind are the following:

"Praise the Lord, ye heavens adore him"[15]
"All creatures of our God and king"[16]
"The Lord is my shepherd," "My Shepherd will supply my need"[17]
"Joy to the world"[18]
"Lead on, O king eternal"[19]
"Let the words of my mouth"[20]
"Oh, for a closer walk with God"[21]

The joyous Hebrew exclamation, Hallelujah! (Praise the Lord), was adopted from the Jewish ritual and has remained a treasured Christian response down the centuries.

Most of the psalms were written long before they were brought together to form our Book of Psalms. Some may have been parts of earlier collections. It is altogether likely that some revisions occured in the editorial process, as in the compilation of innumerable hymnbooks, including *Hymns of the Saints* and its precursors. Since the moral and spiritual tone of the life of the Jews was greatly enriched by the influence of the prophets of the golden age of prophecy, and the Book of Psalms as we know it was compiled after that time, this may explain the elevated prophetic message of many of the psalms.

Some of the psalms, however, are of a distinctly sub-Christian quality.[22] That they are there has troubled many sincere Christians. They are evidence of the troubled ground through which the spiritual pilgrimage of the Israelites led. They are not without parallels from among the war-time prayers of professing Christians of our own day. "One way to treat them," said C. S. Lewis, "is simply to leave them alone." But Dr. Lewis could not be satisfied with this. Nor can we. He went on to say that the ones subject to criticism were framed under conditions of great provocation. Whatever explanation we develop, two things are clear: These psalms were composed in pre-Christian times; the bitterness expressed was not inspired by the Spirit of God. The appearance of these psalms should never be used to justify similar expressions or actions on the part of disciples.

Deep calleth unto deep. . . .
The Lord will command loving-kindness in the daytime,

And in the night his song shall be with me,
And my prayer unto the God of my life.[23]

REFERENCES

1. I Samuel 16:18.
2. I Chronicles 15:16-34.
3. *Reflections on the Psalms*, 94.
4. Psalm 103:1.
5. Psalm 8:1.
6. Psalm 19:14-15.
7. Psalm 27:14.
8. Psalm 46:1-2.
9. Psalm 103:1-5.
10. Psalm 139:1, 5, 7, 23, 24.
11. Psalms 23, 46, 103:119-120, 127:1, 139:7-11, and others.
12. Psalm 150:1, 2, 6.
13. Psalm 90:1-6.
14. James 1:25.
15. Psalm 140; *HS* 66.
16. Psalm 148; *HS* 72.
17. Psalm 23; *HS* 124, 125.
18. Psalm 98:4-9; *HS* 258.
19. Psalm 31:1-3, 5; *HS* 374.
20. Psalm 19:14; *HS* 461.
21. Psalm 89:30-33; *HS* 117.
22. Psalms 69:23; 109:8; 139:19-22.
23. Psalm 42:7-8.

*Follow peace with all men, and
holiness, without which no man shall
see the Lord. Looking diligently lest any
man fail of the grace of God; lest any
root of bitterness springing up trouble
you, and thereby many be defiled.*

—Hebrews 12:14-15

Chapter 6

The Divine Holiness

The King James and similar versions of the Old Testament do not give many details of the religious life of the ancients. What we have been accustomed to calling the "Inspired Version" gives more, but there are still gaps of information about the rapidly growing population of the earth. Abraham was one of the stalwarts of the early years, but not until the time of Moses did we learn of the calling of Abraham to lead his people in the worship of the true and living God.

The Hebrews were monotheists. They knew that the pagan deities worshiped by the peoples of the surrounding nations were the fruit of the imagination and fears of their worshipers. Elijah derided Baal and his priests.[1] And one of the psalmists wrote: "God standeth in the congregation of the mighty; he judgeth among the gods."[2] Another prayed that the enemies of the God of Israel should be "confounded and troubled for ever, yea, let them be put to shame, and perish; that men may know that thou whose name alone is JEHOVAH, art the Most High over all the earth."[3]

The pagan gods reflected the limitations of their human creators. They were known to be demanding, quarrelsome, and unclean. In contrast to them

Jehovah had declared himself to be holy, and called on his worshipers to be holy also: "The Lord spake unto Moses, saying, Speak unto all the congregations of the children of Israel, and say unto them, Ye shall be holy; for I the Lord your God am holy."[4]

The term *holy* was originally applied to God only, but after a time it was used to describe people and instruments of worship:

Thou art a holy people unto the Lord thy God; the Lord thy God hath chosen thee to be a special people unto himself, above all people that are upon the face of the earth.[5]

As might be expected, the term was applied to the priests who were separated from others in order to serve God and the people: "The Lord said unto Moses, Speak thou unto the priests the sons of Aaron. . . . They shall be holy unto their God."[6]

It was also applied to the people as a whole:

Behold, the Lord hath proclaimed unto the end of the world, Say ye to the daughter of Zion, Behold thy salvation cometh; behold, his reward is with him, and his work before him. And they shall call them, The holy people, The redeemed of the Lord; and thou shalt be called, Sought out, A city not forsaken.[7]

God is separated from us by his unmatched holiness. The call to be holy as God is holy is therefore a call to live with openness to a greatness which we cannot discover ourselves; we can know it only as it is revealed. The prophets and psalmists were the advance guards in this revelation, being specially endowed to understand and declare the righteousness of God. Amos said, "Let judgment run down as waters, and righteousness as a mighty stream."[8]

Since holiness is of the nature of God, and so partakes of his glory and eternity, we cannot define it with precision; we can only experience its meaning in the presence of the Holy. But definitions can be helpful when associated with experience. Rudolph Otto's comment is enlightening. He described holiness as the response of the body and soul to lofty mysteries, deeply felt and only partially understood. It involves elements of wonder, reverence and awe and is best understood, but not exhausted, in sacraments and symbols.[9]

Holiness was the hallmark of the living God worshiped by the Children of Israel and it distinguished their worship from that of the pagans by whom they were surrounded. It was extolled by Moses, who sang "Who is like unto thee, O Lord, among the gods? who is like thee,"[10] and who said in the name of the Lord

I am the Lord your God; ye shall therefore sanctify yourselves, and ye shall be holy. . . . I am the Lord that bringeth you out of the land of Egypt, to be your God; ye shall therefore be holy, for I am holy.[11]

and caused to be engraved on a plate of pure gold to be hung in the tabernacle: "HOLINESS TO THE LORD."[12]

God's holiness is his unique moral character. The earlier meaning of "separateness" had an element of "beyondness." The core idea was that God is greater in every sense than any of his creation. Isaiah said, "I saw . . . the Lord . . . high and lifted up."[13]

And again, in his name: "My ways are higher than your ways, and my thoughts are higher than your thoughts."[14]

Holiness is as characteristic of God as is love. Indeed, each of these fundamental qualities of divinity fulfills the other: love which is not good is devastating and holiness without love is self-defeating.

The prophets of Israel rejoiced in the spiritual integrity of the Lord. Malachi declared under inspiration: "I am the Lord: I change not."[15] Many years later the apostle James wrote that in God there is "no variableness, neither shadow of turning."[16] And modern revelation reveals that "His course is one eternal round."[17]

The Hebrews were especially impressed by God's faithfulness manifest in his unfailing devotion to the covenant he had made with them: "Thy mercy, O Lord, is in the heavens, and thy faithfulness reacheth unto the clouds."[18] "Thy faithfulness is unto all generations."[19]

They thought of God as the rock on whom salvation is built:

> He only is my rock and my salvation; he is my defense; I shall not be moved.[20]

> Be thou my strong habitation, whereunto I may continually resort; thou hast given commandment to save me; for thou art my rock and my fortress.[21]

The holiness of God was made manifest among them in demonstration of his mercy and justice. Isaiah wrote, "In mercy shall the throne be established; and he shall sit upon it in truth in the tabernacle of David, judging, and seeking judgment and hasting righteousness" [22]

Hosea related righteousness to the covenant: "I will betroth thee unto me for ever; yea, I will betroth thee unto me in righteousness, and in judgment, and in loving-kindness, and in mercies."[23]

Moses' affirmation of the holiness of God set the pattern for Hebrew prophecy. Although the roots of understanding came to be an important part of the heritage of succeeding generations, this needed to come to fruition in their constantly changing circumstances. This called for further inspired leadership and for participation in worship in which the people—singly and in groups—learned to look beyond the immediately visible but transient to the invisible but eternal. In this endeavor the law was intended as a major aid, translating the divine purpose into the relationships of daily life.

The holiness of God was one of the great themes of the psalmists:

O give thanks unto the Lord, for he is good; for his mercy endureth for ever. Let the redeemed of the Lord say so, whom he hath redeemed from the hand of the enemy; And gathered them out of the lands, from the east, and from the west, from the north, and from the south. They wandered in the wilderness in a solitary way; they found no city to dwell in. Hungry and thirsty, their soul fainted in them. Then they cried unto the Lord in their trouble, and he delivered them out of their distresses. And he led them forth by the right way, that they might go to a city of habitation. O that men would praise the Lord for his goodness, and for his wonderful works to the children of men![24]

The holiness which the early leaders sought to develop in the lives of their compeers was an attitude and a process. The attitude was one of grateful adoration. The process was one of growth in understanding and response. At its best it required the practice of obedience to the highest and best they knew under the guidance of the covenant and the worship which centered in it. It was registered in more and more meaningful freedom from the power of sin.

The spiritual qualities which constitute holiness are not the outgrowth of moral striving, for there is more to righteousness than morality. Righteousness is related to ultimates about which human beings are not fully informed. While all the best gifts of faithful believers are involved, so also is the guidance and empowering of the Holy Spirit.

The richer and more complex any reality is, the

more difficult it is to enter into the fullness of its meaning, and the longer it is likely to take to do so. This is especially true in the realm of the Spirit. Righteousness, or holiness, is of the very nature of God, and to become righteous as he is righteous requires that we seek earnestly to learn of him in order that we may obey him with joyous understanding. We do not need to approach him in a servile manner, but yet with something of the awe which greatness evokes in the spiritually perceptive. Our heavenly Father welcomes all who come to him humbly and in faith. Ezekiel was divinely commanded: "Son of man, stand upon thy feet, and I will speak unto thee."[25]

David was more concerned with being at-one with God than he was with any self-justification when he wrote: "Search me, O God, and know my heart; try me, and know my thoughts; and see if there be any wicked way in me, and lead me in the way everlasting."[26]

The holiness of God is most penetratingly perceived in heartfelt worship. We should not be surprised, therefore, to find that the call to worship is, first of all, a call to rejoice in the goodness of God, who seeks to bless us, knowing our need. Holiness in the faithful is life permeated by love and made venturous by the power of God. The meaning of holiness emerges in the process of guided endeavor to respond to the best we know. Because, as human beings, we have been pursuing our own course for so long, its newly disclosed way has to be made known, and its ramifications explained.

Since the time of the prophets and psalmists the people of God have known that the only thing which counts with God, in the long run, is holiness:

Judge me, O Lord, according to my righteousness, and according to mine integrity that is in me.[27]

Zion shall be redeemed with judgment and her converts with righteousness.[28]

Judgment also will I lay to the line, and righteousness to the plummet.[29]

REFERENCES

1. I Kings 18:27.
2. Psalm 82:1.
3. Psalm 83:2, 17-18.
4. Leviticus 19:1-2. See also Leviticus 21:8.
5. Deuteronomy 7:6. See also Deuteronomy 14:2, 26.
6. Leviticus 21:1, 6.
7. Isaiah 62:11-12.
8. Amos 5:24.
9. *The Interpreter's Bible,* 872-3.
10. Exodus 15:11.
11. Leviticus 11:44-45.
12. Exodus 28:36.
13. Isaiah 6:1.
14. Isaiah 55:9.
15. Malachi 3:6.
16. James 1:17.
17. Doctrine and Covenants 2:1c; 34:1a.
18. Psalm 36:5 KJ.
19. Psalm 119:90.
20. Psalm 62:6.
21. Psalm 71:3.
22. Isaiah 16:5.
23. Hosea 2:19.
24. Psalm 107:1-8.
25. Ezekiel 2:1.
26. Psalm 139:23-24.
27. Psalm 7:8.
28. Isaiah 1:27.
29. Isaiah 28:17.

I have learned
To look on Nature, not as in the hour
Of thoughtless youth, but hearing
    oftentimes
The still sad music of humanity,
Nor harsh, nor grating, though of ample
    power
To chasten and subdue. And I have felt
A presence that disturbs me with joy
Of elevated thoughts; a sense sublime
Of something far more deeply interfused,
Whose dwelling is the light of setting
    suns,
And the round ocean and the living air,
And the blue sky, and in the mind of man;
A motion and a spirit, that impels
All thinking things, all objects of all
    thought,
And rolls through all things.

—W. Wordsworth:
"Lines Composed Near Tintern Abbey"

Chapter 7

The Prophets of the Old Testament

It is an important part of the strategy of redemption for the Lord to make himself known at appropriate times and places through people of his own choosing and appointment. Amos put it this way: "Surely the Lord God will do nothing, until he revealeth the secret unto his servants the prophets."[1]

The process of revelation began with Adam and continued through Adam's faithful descendants prior to the flood. Afterward the tradition of prophecy was continued in Noah and Abraham and others. It was related to the perpetuation of the covenant.

The prophets of the Old Testament were unique among all the spiritual leaders of antiquity. They were the glory of their race. There were persons of prophetic stature elsewhere (e.g., Zoroaster) but their ministries did not compare with those of the prophets of the Old Testament and they had no successors. There was in Israel a succession of prophetic voices for which there is no parallel in the ancient world.

The prophets served at critical times in the history of their people but their prophetic ministry was not the product of that history. They were men of God before they were men of their times. At times their personal characteristics shine through their proclamations (e.g., the loving-kindness of Hosea and the aristocracy of Isaiah 11). But, despite their personal differences, between them, under God, they laid the moral foundations on which the Lord Jesus and his apostles were to build the church.

The prophets were of exceptional spiritual caliber. They were especially called and endowed by God to minister to their contemporaries and to later generations by declaring the will and purpose of God and so the demands of righteousness to which all are called. They were finite, but of unusual spiritual power. They were hated by many whose wickedness they denounced, and were heard seemingly with apathy by others who suffered because of that wickedness. But the soundness of their preaching was such that they could not be ignored, especially when their ministries were vindicated by subsequent events. They are now recognized as the spiritual leaders of their times.

The writer of the Hebrew letter evidently regarded the prophets as forerunners of the Lord Jesus. He wrote, "God, who at sundry times and in diverse manners spake in times past unto the fathers by the prophets, hath in these last days spoken to us by his Son."[2]

Disclosure of the future was not the primary function of the prophets. But, because they saw more deeply into the divine nature and purpose than did others, they were messengers of hope. In the political and spiritual confusion of their times they proclaimed with power that the God of the covenant would not permit his purposes to be frustrated. Isaiah said, in the name of God,

So shall my word be that goeth forth out of my mouth; it shall not return unto me void, but it shall accomplish that which I please, and it shall prosper in the thing whereto I sent it.[3]

74

A major factor in the work of the prophets was their conviction that they were called of God. This conviction was shared by the sensitive among their followers, who noted the coherence of their messages with the words of earlier prophets. The prophetic word carried assurance, moreover, because of the prophetic confidence that it would be attested by the Spirit which had already borne witness to the prophet. Amos said of his own call, "The Lord took me as I followed the flock, and the Lord said unto me, Go, prophesy unto my people Israel."[4] In his conviction of the divinity of his commission Amos went without fear. Isaiah had a similar experience. After telling of his remarkable vision of God in the temple at Jerusalem he continued: "I heard the voice of the Lord, saying, Whom shall I send, and who will go for us? Then said I, Here am I; send me. And he said, Go."[5] And it was in the assurance of this call that Isaiah went forth in his ministry.

The constant repetition by the prophets of "thus saith the Lord," was an important part of every prophetic affirmation. It was not used without deep intent for each message had a two-fold character: it conveyed an important message, and it revealed something of the nature of God. In the use of this phrase the prophet was saying, in essence, "Listen carefully, and with all your hearts. Does not this sound like what Moses and the other prophets have said? Is it not what you would expect the God of the covenant to say at a time like this? This is not a report of a momentary experience. God has burned it into my heart!"

The prophets were sent by God, and their authority and the burden of their message came from God—not from them. They were involved in what they said, for they retained their freedom under guidance. But their involvement was in seeing and learning and reporting, in apprehending what was to be conveyed, and in expressing it with all their powers. Their situation was like that of concerned persons chosen for their capacity to understand and placed in the doorway of the hall of knowledge and truth, which they saw illumined by light from within. Since they declared the word of God, whose vision is not limited by time, the essence of their messages—the principles they set forth—were of permanent worth. Their prophetic word was sound and challenging. It invited further examination so that those in ages to come might attest its wealth.

Each of the prophets fitted his time and place. Any comparison to determine which was the greatest is hazardous. Nevertheless, there is considerable evidence supporting the Hebrew tradition ascribing this honor to Moses out of whose personal experience the promises given to the fathers had been brought into focus in the founding of their nation. Moses affirmed the uniqueness of God and made it a cardinal tenet of the national faith. In this the later prophets concurred.

As God's representatives, the prophets condemned with fierce passion the evils they saw about them—oppression, violence, debauchery, greed, theft, lust for power, callous inhumanity, faithlessness to trust. Jeremiah wrote:

Will ye steal, murder, and commit adultery, and swear falsely, and burn incense unto Baal, and walk after other gods whom ye know not; And come and stand before me in this house, which is called by my name, and say, We are delivered to do all these abominations? Is this house, which is called by my name, become a den of robbers in your eyes? Behold, even I have seen it, saith the Lord.[6]

What had crept up on them, and so had come to be more or less taken for granted, was now seen as much more than the rapacity of strong men. It was clearly portrayed as flagrant treason against God; the guarantor of their national life and calling.

Knowing how carefully they had considered the word given them, so as to be sure not to be carried away by their own passionate concerns, the prophets applied to others the same kind of scrutiny as they had to their own messages. When the word for which others claimed inspiration did not pass their tests, they did not hesitate to denounce them. Jeremiah felt sure of the Lord's approval when he wrote the following:

The Lord said unto me, The prophets prophesy lies in my name; I sent them not, neither have I commanded them, neither spake unto them; they prophesy unto you a false vision and divination, and a thing of naught, and the deceit of their heart.[7]

Recognizing the soundness of the prophetic word does not necessarily come in a moment. It may take time to overcome our ill-founded presuppositions. This was true of the Jews of the apostolic era, and is true today among those who find it difficult to welcome the deeper meaning of stewardship. But the Lord is patient with those of us who find the way difficult, so long as we persist. He commissioned Peter and the other apostles to go into all the world and preach the gospel, but it took Peter several years to realize that "all the world" included the Gentiles.[8]

The prophets of the Old Testament were deeply religious. They loved God and sought to live by the covenant they and their fellows had made with him. They took their prophetic messages with the utmost seriousness such as justified the taking of the risks which their prophecy entailed. They addressed specific persons, possibly without thought of anyone standing in the shadows of the days to come. But they do not seem to have been aware of any time element. And, in truth, what they had to say is as pertinent today, in principle, as it was then. It was, and is, the word of God.

Despite the changing emphases which the changing times sounded forth, the prophets had one central theme: they told of God who is holy and eternal, whose love never fails. They did this by telling of the divine purpose in creation, in the choice and nurture of the Children of Israel, in the means of grace, and, as later became apparent, of the relation between suffering and salvation. Love was a constant note in their testimony, even when they spoke of the perils which disobedience invited.

The prophets saw life on earth as the sphere in which the chosen people were called to work out the day-by-day meaning of the covenant. As they saw it, understanding was to be won in both worship and obedience. Against this background they regarded the frantic search of generation after generation of the Israelites for allies with whom to advance their national ambitions as both wicked and foolish. Isaiah wrote,

Woe to the rebellious children, saith the Lord, that take counsel but not of me; and that cover with a covering, but not of my Spirit, that they may add sin to sin; that walk to go down into Egypt, and have not asked at my mouth; to strengthen themselves in the strength of Pharaoh, and trust in the shadow of Egypt! Therefore shall the strength of Pharaoh be your shame, and the trust in the shadow of Egypt your confusion.[9]

The prophets were not popular during their lifetimes, for few want authoritative guidance which will require basic changes in their way of living.

Obviously those whose way of life was challenged were not readily receptive, and the poor tended to be apathetic. The sanctity of the prophetic message was often clouded because the Spirit on which awareness of sanctity depends had been lost. Jeremiah wrote:

I spake not unto your fathers, nor commanded them in the day that I brought them out of the land of Egypt, concerning burnt offerings as sacrifices. But this thing commanded I them, saying, Obey my voice, and I will be your God, and ye shall be my people; and walk ye in all the ways that I have commanded you, that it may be well unto you. But they hearkened not, nor inclined their ear, and walked in the counsels, and in the imagination of their evil heart, and went backward, and not forward.[10]

The prophets brought the word of God *to* people; they also pleaded with God *for* people. They were messengers of God after God's own heart. Their greatness as prophets depended, in large measure, on the quality of their love for those whose wickedness they denounced. Said Amos to the Lord concerning Judah: "O Lord God, cease, I beseech thee; by whom shall Jacob arise? for he is small."[11] The principle of loving the sinner whose sin is denounced is a common biblical theme (e.g., Genesis 18:2-32), but it is set forth most clearly by Jesus. To the Pharisees he said, "I am not come to call the righteous, but sinners to repentance."[12] And it was undoubtedly from his Lord and in light of his own experience that Paul made this the central theme of his ministry, writing to the saints in Rome: "God commendeth his love toward us, in that, while we were yet sinners, Christ died for us,"[13] and,

When sin abounded, grace did much more abound; that as sin hath reigned unto death, even so might grace reign through righteousness unto eternal life by Jesus Christ our Lord.[14]

REFERENCES

1. Amos 3:7.
2. Hebrews 1:1-2.
3. Isaiah 55:11.
4. Amos 7:15.
5. Isaiah 6:8-9.
6. Jeremiah 7:9-11. See also Micah 3:11.
7. Jeremiah 14:14. See also Jeremiah 17:16.
8. Acts 10:11-16.
9. Isaiah 30:1-3. See also Isaiah 10:20.
10. Jeremiah 7:22-24.
11. Amos 7:5.
12. Matthew 9:14.
13. Romans 5:8.
14. Romans 20-21.

Justice and judgment are the habitation of thy throne; mercy and truth shall go before thy face. Blessed is the people that know the joyful sound; they shall walk, O Lord, in the light of thy countenance. In thy name shall they rejoice all the day; and in thy righteousness shall they be exalted.

—Psalm 89:14-16

Chapter 8

The Prophets of the Exile

The golden age of prophecy is usually dated between the eighth and sixth centuries before Christ, although Samuel and Elijah (who made it clear that God will not tolerate rivals) had important influence in preparing the way for those who were to come after them and build on their foundations.

We have already given some attention to these early prophets and to Amos, Hosea, Isaiah I, and Micah and their denunciation of formal worship tainted by greed and injustice, we now turn to the prophets who ministered during the difficult period of the exile from their homeland: Isaiah II, Jeremiah, and Ezekiel. Perhaps we should identify Isaiah II more clearly. We know very little about him, but it appears that he contributed chapters forty to sixty-six of the Book of Isaiah, since the literary characteristics of these chapters are markedly different from the earlier ones. This major prophet is now referred to quite generally as Isaiah II or, possibly more frequently, as Deutero-Isaiah.

Jerusalem was sacked by Nebuchadnezzar the Assyrian in 597 B.C. Many of the well-to-do, prominent, and talented were taken into captivity in and around Babylon. An uprising in Jerusalem a few years later brought Nebuchadnezzar back with a large army, and the seige which followed lasted for two years and led to more deportations. But Nebuchadnezzar died in 562 B.C., and shortly thereafter the Assyrians were defeated by Cyrus, who permitted the return of the Hebrews to their homeland. Our primary concern, however, is less with these historical events than with their bearing on the maturing of the Hebrew understanding of the nature and purpose of God, and the purpose of the covenant. For the moment this seemed to be shattered.

The Jews, like many of their contemporaries, regarded God as uniquely related to their land, particularly to its sacred places. The exiles in Babylon were troubled as to how they could worship God in a strange land, away from his temple. Some thought that God had abandoned them, rather than that they had failed him. This was not true, and Isaiah reminded them of their faithlessness and called on them to repent. Even those who did repent were nevertheless still cut off from their homeland and from its sacred places. They needed guidance or they would lose their sense of mission and with it their national unity. Their only hope was in recognizing and repudiating their self-centered way of life.

Under God, Isaiah II lifted the thoughts of the exiles from their own despair and reminded them of the goodness and greatness of God, who is Lord of all the earth:

Woe unto him that striveth with his Maker!...Shall the clay say to him that fashioneth it, What makest thou?...Woe unto him that saith to his father, What begettest thou? or to the woman, What hast thou brought forth?[1]

Who hath directed the Spirit of the Lord, or being his counsellor hath taught him? With whom took he counsel, and who instructed him, and taught him in the path of judgment, and taught him knowledge, and showed unto him the way of understanding?[2]

The task of the prophets was to convince the exiles that God reigned in Babylon as well as in Jerusalem. This seemed like a denial of all they had believed. But gradually the wisest of them saw that their trust must be in God, and that he could make even their exile serve his covenant purpose:

Why sayest thou, O Jacob, and speakest O Israel, my way is hid from the Lord, and my judgment is passed over from my God? Hast thou not known? Hast thou not heard, that the everlasting God, the Lord, the Creator of the ends of the earth, fainteth not, neither is weary? There is no searching of his understanding. He giveth power to the faint, and to them that have no might he increaseth strength. Even the youths shall faint and be weary, and the young men shall utterly fail; but they that wait upon the Lord shall renew their strength; they shall mount up with wings as eagles; they shall run and not be weary; and they shall walk and not faint.[3]

A second major prophet who ministered against a background of seeming national disaster was Jeremiah, a member of a prominent priestly family whose home for generations had been at Anathoth, a nearby suburb of Jerusalem. Jeremiah was born about 645 B.C. and was called to be a prophet while still very young—probably about 626 B.C. He wrote of his call:

The word of the Lord came unto me, saying, Before I formed thee in the belly I knew thee; and before thou camest forth out of the womb I sanctified thee, and I ordained thee a prophet unto the nations. . . . Then the Lord put forth his hand, and touched my mouth. And the Lord said unto me, Behold I have put my words in thy mouth.[4]

Jeremiah regarded the siege of Jerusalem and the suffering it entailed as fulfillment of the warnings which his prophetic predecessers had sounded, and he said so forthrightly.[5] He said, further, that the captivity of those taken to Babylon would be "for their good."[6] But when the situation seemed most hopeless the vision of Jeremiah was lifted away from the present to the assurances of the future:

Behold, the days come, saith the Lord, that I will raise unto David a righteous Branch, and a King shall reign and prosper, and shall execute judgment and justice in the earth. In his days Judah shall be saved, and Israel shall dwell safely; and this is his name whereby he shall be called, THE LORD OUR RIGHTEOUSNESS.[7]

Jeremiah attested his faith in eventual triumph by causing a piece of land near his home in Anathoth to be purchased and the purchase to be publicized. It appeared to be an empty gesture, but Jeremiah said, "Thus saith the Lord of hosts, the God of Israel; Houses and fields and vineyards shall be possessed again in this land."[8]

Jeremiah continued the socio-spiritual declarations of the earlier prophets of the period (Amos, Hosea, Isaiah I, Micah), but in view of his own intensely personal experiences, akin to those of Hosea and Ezekiel, he also sounded an important note of personal responsibility:

Behold, the days come, saith the Lord, that I will make a new covenant with the house of Israel, and with the house of Judah; not according to the covenant that I made with their fathers, in the day that I took them by the hand to bring them out of the land of Egypt; which my covenant they brake, although I was a husband unto them, saith the Lord; but this shall be the covenant that I will make with the house of Israel; After these days, saith the Lord, I will put my law in their inward parts, and write it in their hearts; and will be their God, and they shall be my people.[9]

A similar emphasis was sounded in the early ministry of Ezekiel, a young priest who was among the first of the exiles. The "word of the Lord" came to him[10] and he saw "the appearance of the likeness of the glory of the Lord"[11] and a voice said to him: "Son of man, stand upon thy feet, and I will speak unto thee." And, wrote Ezekiel, "The spirit entered into me when he spake unto me, and set me upon my feet, . . . and he said unto me, Son of man I send thee to the children of Israel."[12] Thereafter, like Jeremiah, he delivered to his people the word of judgment rather than the word of deliverance which they awaited. And when the captives sought to blame their fathers for their plight he affirmed the responsibility which each one has before God:

Behold, all souls are mine; the soul of the father, so also the soul of the son is mine; the soul that sinneth, it shall die. . . . When the son hath done that which is lawful and right, and hath kept all my statutes, and hath done them, he surely shall live.[13]

When the destruction of Jerusalem was complete, however, and the Israelites needed guidance to help them retain and enlarge their vision of God's purpose in their selection and preservation, Ezekiel prophesied of the judgments to come on the surrounding nations, which were cruel, filthy, and greedy.[14] He augmented this by his narration of a vision of dry bones which had been given him[15] and to which the Lord had given the meaning:

These bones are the whole house of Israel. . . . Thus saith the Lord God; Behold, O my people, I will open your graves, and . . . bring you into the land of Israel. And ye shall know that I am the Lord. . . . And shall put my Spirit in you, and ye shall live, and I shall place you in your own land; then shall ye know that I the Lord have spoken it, and performed it, saith the Lord.[16]

He called them "God's sheep":

Thus saith the Lord God; Behold I, even I, will both search my sheep, and seek them out. As a shepherd seeketh out his flock in the day that he is among the sheep that are scattered; so will I seek out my sheep, and will deliver them out of all the places where they have been scattered in the cloudy and dark day. . . . Ye my flock, the flock of my pasture, are men, and I am your God, saith the Lord.[17]

He promised them deliverance for his name's sake:

Thus saith the Lord God: I do not this for your sakes, O house of Israel, but for mine holy name's sake, which ye have profaned among the heathen, whither ye went....And the heathen shall know that I am the Lord; saith the Lord God, when I shall be sanctified in you before their eyes.[18]

When Jerusalem was destroyed and the elite were taken to Babylon, the captives lost their power of political self-determination. They were not badly treated. A few leaders with political experience were taken to Babylon; the remainder were settled in small groups and allowed to pursue their own way of life. This, of course, required some adjustments. Of these probably the most difficult, and also the most important, was the organization of their religious life apart from the temple and the sacrificial system to which they had been accustomed. But they did what they could and were surprised to find how satisfactory the results were.

Their music was an unexpected treasure. Their conquerors had insisted that the ransom they exacted should include the children of the royal family, youths from the Levitical aristocracy, and craftsmen, scholars, and musicians, who could enrich the culture of the capital. The adjustments made within the limits prescribed would have been intolerable under different circumstances for they gave rise to questions about God and the nature of worship. But the music of the captives was too closely knit to the fabric of their lives for them to reserve it for the entertainment of their conquerors. Soon their singing became a safety valve and a solace; it went far to perpetuate their unity as a people.

Down the years many of the children of Israel had

come under condemnation because of their backsliding. But now, alien and enslaved, a thousand miles from their homeland, they became stable and steadfast in their love for the covenant. So long as the temple existed, the music of the well-trained Levitical choirs had served to embellish the sacrifices. But now the temple had been destroyed and the sacrifices discontinued. They could have said, "How shall we sing the Lord's song in a strange land?" Indeed there were some who did so,[19] as though the place of worship was of primary importance. But although it was a hundred years since Isaiah had written

To what purpose is the multitude of your sacrifices unto me? saith the Lord; I am full of the burnt offerings of rams, and the fat of fed beasts; and I delight not in the blood of bullocks, or of lambs, or of he goats.[20]

Now, at last, they were beginning to understand.

The policy of their captors toward the defeated changed with the victory of Cyrus. But the Jews had been in Chaldea for seventy years, and the farmers who had come from Judea had become accustomed to the centralized military and commercial affairs of their present neighbors. Among the Jews were now competent artisans and businessmen who were being encouraged to settle in such new cities as Alexandria and Antioch. Many did so, and of these a high proportion melted into the general population and were lost to sight. Others found satisfaction in the study and worship available in the synagogues. A few of their descendants became Christians.

A second group of the exiles rejoiced in the opportunity to return to the land of their fathers, and here they hoped to recapture their ancient glories. They rebuilt the temple and looked to Ezekiel as their prophet-leader. It is not unlikely that the point of view underlying the books of Ezra, Nehemiah, and the two books of Chronicles was determined by them.

The remainder of the exiles probably had no formal organization, and may have intermingled with the second group already named. But they were distinguished by their concern for the more enlightened fulfillment of their basic calling. They were attracted to the words of Isaiah II:

It is a light thing that thou shouldest be my [the Lord's] servant to raise up the tribes of Jacob, and to restore the preserved of Israel; I will also give thee for a light to the Gentiles that thou mayest be my salvation unto the end of the earth.[21]

Within a few years the Jewish population in many cities of the Roman Empire were sufficiently numerous to command consideration. They were being influenced by their neighbors, just as they also had their spheres of influence. The moral standards and practices of the Jews were far more elevated than those of most of their neighbors, and many Gentiles who had no intention of becoming Jews nevertheless attended Jewish worship in the synagogues. Those who did this were apparently welcomed although they had no standing under the Jewish law.

Many of the diaspora (the Jews dispersed among the Gentiles after the exile) were kindly disposed toward their distant relatives who had returned to their homeland. They observed the festivals, but were inclined to be less insular in their religious outlook than were those in Jerusalem and its environs. Those who could afford to do so were likely to attend such festivals in Palestine as the Passover. But the trips were costly and yielded little historic satisfaction when the temple was no longer there.

Another cause of division came when the pressures of business and social contacts led them to use the Greek rather than the Aramaic or Hebrew languages. In time the Hebrew scriptures were translated into Greek (the Septuagint). Thereafter, since Greek and Latin were the two major languages of the world, there were many Jews by descent who were unfamiliar with the language of their fathers. This was not a complete loss, for the Septuagint became a major aid in spreading the gospel among the Greek-speaking peoples of the world.

The defeat and exile of the Jews marked the destruction of the Hebrew state. There was to be a brief period of limited independence under the Hasmoneans (the Maccabees) but the political stature of the earlier years was never regained. From the external evidence available it seemed that the national hopes of the Hebrews had been quenched forever. But this was far from true. The late Dr. Georgia Harkness wrote: "The exile is a watershed in Hebrew history." And Burton H. Streeter, an outstanding British theological historian, wrote that "the exile is an event as central for the comprehension of the Old Testament as the crucifixion is for that of the New Testament."[22] Neither of them even hinted that Hebrew history is over.

It is not possible to discuss here the spiritual gains made by the Hebrew people because of the exile and the accompanying ministry of the prophets of that age. We should note, however, that it was in the midst of major tragedy that the Jews and the Christians who shared their history began to enter fully into an inspired understanding of the greatness of God: his love, his wisdom, his holiness, his power, and his unfailing purpose for good. Those who sincerely trust in God need not think of themselves as captives in an alien land: they are sons and daughters of God protected by his love and and invincible power. Isaiah II wrote:

Thus saith the Lord the King of Israel, and his Redeemer the Lord of hosts; I am the first, and I am the last; and besides me there is no God. And who, as I, shall call, and shall declare it, and set it in order for me, since I appointed the ancient people? and the things that are coming, and shall come, let them show unto them. Fear ye not, neither be afraid; have I not told thee . . . and have declared it? ye are even my witnesses. Is there a God beside me? yea, there is no God; I know not any.[23]

REFERENCES

1. Isaiah 45:9, 10 ff.
2. Isaiah 40:13-14.
3. Isaiah 40:27-31.
4. Jeremiah 1:4-5, 9.
5. Jeremiah 21:8-20.
6. Jeremiah 24:5.
7. Jeremiah 23:5-6.
8. Jeremiah 32:15.
9. Jeremiah 31:31-33.
10. Ezekiel 1:3.
11. Ezekiel 1:28.
12. Ezekiel 2:2-3.
13. Ezekiel 18:4, 19.
14. Ezekiel 25 to 32.
15. Ezekiel 37:1-14.
16. Ezekiel 37:11, 12, 13, 14.
17. Ezekiel 34:11, 12, 31.
18. Ezekiel 36:22-23.
19. Psalm 137:4.
20. Isaiah 1:11.
21. Isaiah 49:6.
22. *The God Who Speaks*, The MacMillan Co., 1937, 77.
23. Isaiah 44:6-8.

THE MYSTERY OF LIFE
Albert Einstein

The most beautiful thing we can experience is the mysterious. It is the source of all true art and science. He to whom this emotion is a stranger, who can no longer pause to wonder and stand rapt in awe, is as good as dead: his eyes are closed. This insight into the mystery of life, coupled though it be with fear, has also given rise to religion. To know that what is impenetrable to us really exists, manifesting itself as the highest wisdom and the most radiant beauty which our dull faculties can comprehend only in their most primitive forms—this knowledge, this feeling, is at the center of true religiousness.

—In *Living Philosophies*
Simon and Schuster

Chapter 9

Themes of the Old Testament Prophets

The Living God

The prophets of Israel assessed the importance of events in terms of their effect on the people involved. In doing this they affirmed the primary importance of spiritual perception. It was axiomatic with them that the dedication of life to what is approved of God is the only sound way to express religious commitment. Isaiah, one of the greatest of them, began his prophetic ministry with denunciation of evildoing and then continued as follows

Wash ye, make you clean; put away the evil of your doings from before mine eyes; cease to do evil; learn to do well; seek judgment; relieve the oppressed, judge the fatherless, plead for the widow.[1]

Basic to their faith was their devotion to the living God.

When the Hebrews conquered Canaan many of the early settlers, who were worshipers of Baal, remained where they had lived before the wars. After a time marriages were contracted between them and their conquerors who found no inconsistency in adding the worship of this pagan god to their Hebrew worship. The religious situation degenerated until a climax was reached during the reign of Ahab, king of the northern tribes, whose wife was a worshiper of

Baal. During Ahab's reign Samaria was stricken by a "sore famine" and since Baal was the god of fertility his worship grew apace.

One of the leaders of the faithful Hebrews was Obadiah, who had sufficient influence with Ahab to arrange a meeting between the king and Elijah, the prophet. Here it was agreed that the 450 priests of Baal should meet with Elijah and the people of the vicinity. The meeting was at Mount Carmel, and apparently Elijah took charge. He set forth the issues, saying, "How long halt ye between two opinions? If the Lord be God, follow him; but if Baal, then follow him."[2]

The demonstration went forward as Elijah had planned. The priests called frantically for Baal to send fire to consume the offering they had prepared, but with no success. Toward evening Elijah had the people draw near so they could see exactly what was done, and he could be secured against any future charges of trickery. He prepared an offering and deluged it with water before calling on the Lord to demonstrate his power by accepting the offering. Fire from heaven consumed the offering and the altar and the water which had been poured on them.[3] The people accepted the demonstration, agreeing that they would no longer worship gods of their own devising. The priests of Baal were killed. But the entrenchment of paganism in their homes and the persistence of Queen Jezebel kept pagan worship alive, though the worshipers of the true God were strengthened.

The testimony of the living God continued throughout the prophetic age. Jeremiah wrote, "The Lord is the true God, he is the living God, and an everlasting king."[4]

Hosea prophesied that the children of Israel would yet be numbered as the sands of the sea, and it should be said unto them: "Ye are the sons of the living God."[5]

Isaiah continued this emphasis, saying that in the last days, "The Lord alone shall be exalted.... The idols he shall utterly abolish."[6]

When Hezekiah was threatened by the Assyrians he prayed, saying:

O Lord of hosts, God of Israel, that dwellest between the cherubim, thou art the God, even thou alone, of all the kingdoms of the earth; thou hast made heaven and earth. Incline thine ear, O Lord, and hear; open thine eyes, O Lord, and see; and hear all the words of Sennacherib, which he hath sent to reproach the living God.[7]

In the night the flower of the Assyrian army died. Sennacherib abandoned Jerusalem and returned to Nineveh.[8]

The unreality of the lesser gods was affirmed at every occasion of conflict with the prophets: Said Habakkuk,

What profiteth the graven image that the maker thereof hath graven it; the molten image, and a teacher of lies, that the maker of his work trusteth therein, to make dumb idols? Woe unto him that saith to the wood, Awake; to the dumb stone, Arise, it shall teach! Behold, it is laid over with gold and silver, and there is no breath at all in the midst of it.[9]

The declaration that God is living was an affirmation of God's authority and power, the breadth and continuance of his concerns, his personal responsiveness and his adequacy in changing circumstances. It was the prelude to God's universal concerns: He is a jealous God admitting no rivals, expecting and rewarding love and grateful service.

The proclamation of the living God has lost nothing of its importance down the generations. He is to be worshiped, and not the products of human enterprise: power, victory, skill, nor yet the wisdom or the glory of human acclaim.

Worship and Morality

Amos, who prophesied about 776-768 B.C., was the first of the "writing prophets." This was probably because a ban had been placed on his work by the priest of the royal sanctuary at Bethel.[10] He was called at a time when both the northern and the southern kingdoms were enjoying an exhilarating period of prosperity. The rich of both groups were living in luxury made possible by their oppression of the poor. Amos, himself probably a comparatively poor man, wrote in the name of God:

> For three transgressions of Israel, and for four, I will not turn away the punishment thereof; because they sold the righteous for silver, and the poor for a pair of shoes; that pant after the dust of the earth on the head of the poor, and turn aside for the way of the meek; and a man and his father will go in unto the same maid, to profane my holy name; and they lay themselves down upon clothes laid to pledge by every altar, and they drink the wine of the condemned in the house of their god.[11]

> I hate, I despise your feast days, and I will not smell in your solemn assemblies. Though ye offer me burnt offerings and your meat offerings, I will not accept them; neither will I regard the peace offerings of your fat beasts. Take thou away from me the noise of thy songs; for I will not hear the melody of thy viols. But let judgment run down as waters, and righteousness as a mighty stream.[12]

The prophetic ministry of Hosea followed that of Amos by a little more than a decade. He shared the spiritual discernment of the other prophets of the period. Concerning the manner of life which must underlie effective worship he wrote, "I desired mercy, and not sacrifice; and the knowledge of God more than burnt offerings."[13]

Isaiah struck the same note:

To what purpose is the multitude of your sacrifices unto me? saith the Lord; I am full of the burnt offerings of rams, and the fat of fed beasts; and I delight not in the blood of bullocks, or of lambs, or of he goats. . . . Bring no more vain oblations; incense is an abomination unto me. . . . I cannot away with; it is iniquity, even the solemn meeting. . . . And when ye spread forth your hands, I will hide mine eyes from you; yea, when ye make many prayers, I will not hear; your hands are full of blood.[14]

Micah, a younger and less cultured but discerning contemporary of Isaiah, wrote,

Wherewith shall I come before the Lord, and bow myself before the high God? shall I come before him with burnt offerings, with calves of a year old? Will the Lord be pleased with thousands of rams, or with ten thousands of rivers of oil? shall I give my first-born for my transgression, the fruit of my body for the sin of my soul? He hath showed thee, O man, what is good; and what doth the Lord require of thee, but to do justly, and to love mercy, and to walk humbly with thy God.[15]

The God of Justice

The minds and hearts of the prophets were illumined by their conviction that God is a God of justice. Abraham, for example, interceded with the Lord on behalf of Sodom and took as his basic premise that the judge of all the earth could be relied on to do right. But it was to Moses that the Children of Israel looked for the comprehensive affirmation of the righteousness of God:

I will publish the name of the Lord; ascribe ye greatness unto our God. He is the Rock, his work is perfect; for all his ways are judgment; a God of truth and without iniquity, just and right is he.[16]

The prophets of later years were of similar deep and perceptive social passion. They found the roots of the ills which beset their people in disregard of the covenant with its prevailing concern for fraternity under God. They said,

The Lord of hosts shall be exalted in judgment, and God that is holy shall be sanctified in righteousness.[17]

Zion shall be redeemed with judgment, and her converts with righteousness.[18]

Righteousness and judgment are the habitation of his throne.[19]

Jeremiah wrote,

Thus saith the Lord, Let not the wise man glory in his wisdom, neither let the mighty man glory in his might, let not the rich man glory in his riches; But let him that glorieth glory in this that he understandeth and knoweth me, that I am the Lord which exercise loving-kindness, judgment, and righteousness, in the earth; for in these things I delight, saith the Lord.[20]

Repentance and Forgiveness

Since the love and obedience of the chosen people were not constant, many of the prophetic messages were apparently denunciatory, but underlying the denunciation was a never-failing call to repentance. Jeremiah in a mood of both repentance and petition, prayed thus:

We acknowledge, O Lord, our wickedness, and the iniquity of our fathers; for we have sinned against thee. Do not abhor us, for thy name's sake, do not disgrace the throne of thy glory.... break not thy covenant with us.[21]

Isaiah said,

Wash ye, make you clean; put away the evil of your doings from before mine eyes; cease to do evil; Learn to do well; seek judgment, relieve the oppressed, judge the fatherless, plead for the widow. Come now, and let us reason together, saith the Lord; though your sins be as scarlet, they shall be as white as snow; though they be red like crimson, they shall be as wool.[22]

The way of repentance is always open to those who will look:

Seek ye the Lord while he may be found, call ye upon him while he is near; Let the wicked forsake his way, and the unrighteous man his thoughts; and let him return unto the Lord, and he will have mercy upon him; and to our God, for he will abundantly pardon.[23]

In character, Hosea wrote,

How shall I give thee up, Ephraim? How shall I deliver thee,
Israel?...mine heart is turned within me, my repentings are
kindled together [the Phillips translation renders thus: My heart
recoils within me, all my compassion is kindled]. I will not execute the fierceness of mine anger, I will not return to destroy
Ephraim: for I am God, and not man; the holy One in the midst of
thee.[24]

The Psalmist wrote,

The Lord is merciful and gracious, slow to anger, and plenteous
in mercy. He will not always chide; neither will he keep his anger
for ever. He hath not dealt with us after our sins nor rewarded us
according to our iniquities. For as the heaven is high above the
earth, so great is his mercy toward them that fear him....He
knoweth our frame, he remembereth that we are dust.[25]

Glory

In the Hebrew scriptures the word *glory* is often
translated *holiness* in such a way as to add a note of
visibility: glory is the holiness which is made known.
A great Jewish student, Edward Jacobs, has written,

Glory is what God can be seen as possessing in his own right; it is
a kind of totality of qualities which make up his divine power. It
has close affinity with the holiness which is of the nature of
divinity and it is a visible extension for the purpose of manifesting holiness to men.[26]

Glory is also related to the praise which recognition of the holiness of God evokes:

Give unto the Lord, O ye mighty, give unto the Lord glory and
strength. Give unto the Lord the glory due unto his name; worship the Lord in the beauty of holiness.[27]

I am the Lord; that is my name; and my glory will I not give to
another, neither my praise to graven images.[28]

Awareness of the deeper meaning of *glory* is important to students of the scriptures, for it is much
weightier there than is usual in modern conversation. Glory here is the reflection of the awe felt in the

presence of holiness. Its best known expression is probably found in Isaiah 6:1-3:

In the year that king Uzziah died I saw also the Lord sitting upon a throne, high and lifted up, and his train filled the temple. Above it stood the seraphim . . . and one cried to another, and said, Holy, holy, holy is the Lord of Hosts; the whole earth is full of his glory.

Isaiah was not the first to perceive the splendor of the glory of God. Abraham did so when he was told to leave his family and go to the land which the Lord would show him.[29] David, also, praised the Lord, saying:

Thine, O Lord, is the greatness and the power, and the glory, and the victory, and the majesty, for all that is in the heaven and in the earth is thine; thine is the kingdom, O Lord, and thou art exalted as head above all.[30]

The Remnant

The prophets were deeply aware of both the judgments and the mercies of God. They saw that in view of the faithlessness of the people, God must respond in judgment: his work in creation must go forward in righteousness. But they saw also that the Lord's mercy must win a "remnant" who would return to him, their faith refined through suffering. It is not surprising, therefore, that throughout the Old Testament there are indications of what came to be known as "the doctrine of the remnant." It probably went back as far as Noah and his family, who were saved from the flood and so made possible a new beginning strongly influenced by the principles of the covenant.

When Amos was confronted by the entrenched wickedness of the rich and powerful, he knew that this could not go unavenged forever. He found some comfort, however, in the thought of what might be saved through a remnant: "Hate the evil, and love the good, and establish judgment in the gates; it may be that the Lord God of hosts will be gracious unto the remnant of Joseph."[31]

Isaiah hoped for a remnant left in Jerusalem to see their true situation and mend their ways: "It shall come to pass, they that are left in Zion, and he that remaineth in Jerusalem, shall be called holy, even every one that is written among the living in Jerusalem."[32]

The expression "the remnant" occurs with some frequency in the writings of the Old Testament prophets. At times it refers only to those remaining after some activity has been concluded.[33] It was also used to indicate the condition of those who had been defeated in battle, or who themselves or their children had survived a pestilence. It dealt with both catastrophe and recovery, and so formed something of a bridge between judgment and mercy.

When his pleas went unheeded, however, Amos wrote in the name of God of coming catastrophe:

The city that went out by a thousand shall leave a hundred, and that which went forth by a hundred shall leave ten, to the house of Israel. For thus saith the Lord unto the house of Israel, Seek ye me, and ye shall live; But seek not Beth-el, nor enter into Gilgal, and pass not to Beer-sheba; for Gilgal shall surely go into captivity, and Beth-el shall come to nought.[34]

This was a continuance of the policy of Elijah.[35] It was echoed by Isaiah II, Micah, Jeremiah, and Ezekiel. Isaiah justified it in terms of its fulfillment of the covenant:

The remnant that is escaped of the house of Judah shall again take root downward, and bear fruit upward; For out of Jerusalem shall go forth a remnant; and they that escape out of Jerusalem shall come up upon Mount Zion; the zeal of the Lord shall do this.[36]

Jeremiah was given a vision of two baskets of figs

which were set out before the temple of the Lord. One basket contained ripe figs, about ready to be eaten. The other basket contained figs not fit to be eaten. Jeremiah was told that the good figs represented the captives who had been sent "into the land of the Chaldeans [Babylonia] for their good." The captives represented by the bad figs would be scattered among the nations, but eventually would be destroyed.[37]

In the Christian era the apostle Paul, who had taken the gospel to many of the descendants of the captives of Babylon who now formed the diaspora, wrote a letter to the saints in Rome in which he identified the Church as a remnant of Israel: "Esaias also crieth concerning Israel, though the number of the church of Israel be as the sand of the sea, a remnant shall be saved."[38]

The Book of Mormon contains several references to the remnant of Israel with essentially the same theme as the biblical references:

It shall come to pass in that day, that the Lord shall set his hand again the second time to recover the remnant of his people.... And he shall set up an ensign for the nations, and shall assemble the outcasts of Israel, and gather together the dispersed of Judah from the four corners of the earth.[39]

In 1832, long after the priesthood of the covenant people among the remnant had been forgotten, this further word was received through Joseph Smith II:

Thus saith the Lord unto you, with whom the priesthood hath continued through the lineage of your fathers, for ye are lawful heirs, according to the flesh, and have been hid from the world with Christ in God.... Therefore, blessed are ye if ye continue in my goodness, a light unto the Gentiles, and through the priesthood a savor unto my people, Israel. The Lord hath said it. Amen.[40]

REFERENCES

1. Isaiah 1:16-17.
2. I Kings 18:21.
3. I Kings 18:31-38.
4. Jeremiah 10:10.
5. Hosea 1:10.
6. Isaiah 2:17-18.
7. Isaiah 37:16-17.
8. Isaiah 37:37.
9. Habakkuk 2:18-19.
10. Amos 7:2-13.
11. Amos 2:4-6. See also Amos 6:6, 9, 11, 13, etc.
12. Amos 5:212-24.
13. Hosea 6:6.
14. Isaiah 1:11, 13, 15.
15. Micah 6:6-8.
16. Deuteronomy 32:3-4. See also Deuteronomy 16:18-20.
17. Isaiah 5:16.
18. Isaiah 1:27.
19. Psalm 97:2.
20. Jeremiah 9:23-24.
21. Jeremiah 14:20-21.
22. Isaiah 1:16-18.
23. Isaiah 55:6-7.
24. Hosea 11:8-9 KJ.
25. Psalm 103:8-11, 14.
26. See his *Theology of the Old Testament*, 1928, 79.
27. Psalm 29:1-2.
28. Isaiah 42:8.
29. Acts 7:2-3.
30. I Chronicles 29:11.
31. Amos 5:15.
32. Isaiah 4:2.
33. Amos 1:8.
34. Amos 5:3-5. See also Amos 3:12; Isaiah 17:17.
35. I Kings 19:17-18.
36. Isaiah 37:31, 32. See also Micah 5:7; Ezekiel 11:17, 19:20.
37. Jeremiah 24:1-10.
38. Romans 9:27.
39. II Nephi 9:126-127; III Nephi 9:49, 90-99; 10:1.
40. Doctrine and Covenants 84:3-4. See also Doctrine and Covenants 45:3, 4, 6d; 108:6-7.

As for God, his way is perfect:
The word of the Lord is tried:
He is our buckler to all that trust
    in him.
For who is God save the Lord,
Or who is a rock save our God?
It is God that girdeth me with strength
And maketh my way perfect.

—Psalm 18:30-32

Chapter 10

The Old Testament Prophets and History

The Old Testament prophets believed that God is the creator of all things and rules creation according to his own holy purpose. He is "from everlasting to everlasting"[1] and his counsel "standeth for ever."[2] Furthermore, God knows the end from the beginning, because he will bring it to pass. Isaiah wrote in his name:

I am God, and there is none else; I am God, and there is none like me. Declaring the end from the beginning, and from ancient times the things that are not yet done, saying, My counsel shall stand, and I will do all my pleasure.[3]

The prophets believed that the purpose of God in creation and in history is the redemption of humankind: "Thy mercy, O Lord, is in the heavens, and thy faithfulness reacheth unto the clouds. Thy righteousness is like the great mountains; thy judgments are a great deep."[4]

This declaration that God knows the end from the beginning has sometimes been thought of as limiting human agency. But the situation is like that of a master chess player who as a father teaches a son or daughter to play. He does not break the rules because of his affection, but his skill in applying them teaches their value. Both players know the meaning of checkmate, but the human player never achieves this except as God reveals what is truly important in the game of life, and the player accepts the divine instruction with gratitude and obeys it.

Sometimes it is difficult for the human player to understand and accept the divine wisdom. Isaiah has reminded us of the reason for this, saying this in the name of God:

My thoughts are not your thoughts, neither are your ways my ways, saith the Lord. For as the heavens are higher than the earth, so are my ways higher than your ways, and my thoughts than your thoughts.[5]

It is for this reason that we must seek God and listen:

Seek ye the Lord while he may be found, call ye upon him while he is near. Let the wicked forsake his way, and the unrighteous man his thoughts; and let him return unto the Lord, and he will have mercy upon him; and to our God, for he will abundantly pardon.[6]

At times this calls for faith when we cannot fully understand. Job expressed this in its classic form: "Though he slay me, yet will I trust in him."[7] When we have lost one who was infinitely precious many of us have had to fight through to this level of faith. The prophets knew this, and frequently called for trust in God:

Thou wilt keep him in perfect peace, whose mind is stayed on thee; because he trusteth in thee. Trust ye in the Lord for ever; for in the Lord Jehovah is everlasting strength.[8]

At its best such trust is based on experience with God. It was part of the Hebrew tradition that after their fathers had defeated the Philistines near Bethcar, Samuel took a stone and set it between Mizpeh and Shen saying "Hitherto hath the Lord helped us."[9] For those with eyes to see there is abundant evidence of the love of God in every stage of history.

The saving events of history have been the revelatory acts of God as these have been interpreted by the prophets:

Arise, shine; for thy light is come, and the glory of the Lord is risen upon thee. For, behold, the darkness shall cover the earth, and gross darkness the people; but the Lord shall arise upon thee, and his glory shall be seen upon thee. And the Gentiles shall come to thy light, and kings to the brightness of thy rising.[10]

Revelation through the prophets was known from the earliest times among the Hebrews, and came to its "golden age" about 800 to 650 B.C. It was apparently anticipated that it would continue. Amos said: "Surely the Lord God will do nothing, but he revealeth his secret unto his servants the prophets."[11]

The prophets were not appointed by popular vote, but were called of God, and in the assurance of this call they found their authority and strength. Each of them bore convincing testimony to his own call. They were witnesses rather than philosophers—proclaiming their messages and illustrating them rather than arguing about them. Since their ministry often involved denunciation, they were rarely popular in their times, but the generations vindicated them. They were sincere and impassioned. Although their words were distinctive, reflecting their personalities as well as the guidance of the Spirit of God, there was unity in their diversity. They spoke with one Spirit and one voice.

Every prophetic message centered in the God who acts. They dealt with what God is doing, with what he proposes to do, and with what he opposes. In so doing they revealed the nature of God. For example, the delivery of the Hebrew slaves from Egypt not only brought them out of their bondage, but also demonstrated the love of God which underlay his concern for them and the wisdom and power of God implements his will. The captivity in Babylon, hard as it was to understand and to endure, was so interpreted by Isaiah as to make it minister to the fulfillment of their calling.

Their experience with God and their consequent insight into the deeper meaning of events gave the prophets a point of departure for understanding history. It was not an insight common to all. There were elements of faith and hope in it. It involved personal contemplation, but—even more so—it was nourished in worship. They were keenly concerned with their times, but they did not isolate these times as is the usual tendency. They saw that the past is still potent in memories and traditions, and that these may be changed by the infusion of a new spirit and a new purpose. They saw the present as a time of opportunity having consequences beyond what anyone can see, and calling for direction toward the ultimate good of humankind rather than for the immediate satisfaction of temporary wants. And they saw the future as a time for which knowledge of God and experience in serving him is the best possible preparation.

The prophets knew from their own experiences that the only sure knowledge of God comes from experience with him. In this all their natural talents were called into play, or their agency would have been nullified. Judging history in terms of its divinely ordained end, they evaluated events by their contribution to this end—in terms of their moral and spiritual costs and consequences.

The prophets belonged to the times in which they

lived. They saw the events of those times not as others did but with insights born of the indwelling of the Spirit of God. Their declarations were twofold: revelation and judgment in the name of God, and God's call to repentance and righteousness.

The ways of life which they denounced had not developed in a moment, but had deep rootage in the pride and self-centeredness of the people, their resulting self-indulgence and hardness of heart. Moreover, these had been incorporated into social and economic practices, so that many of the common people accepted them without vigorous protest. The rich and powerful gave only lip service to the God of the Covenant, acting instead as though they were the rightful determiners of their destiny. It was this treason against their heritage which underlay the diverse elements of the denunciations of the prophets.

Although the prophets were Hebrews, the wickedness which they denounced was not confined to the Hebrews. Although the prophetic messages were directed to the Hebrews, and were of immediate importance to them, they were of worldwide and timeless significance for humanity in general. As was inevitable, the principles which the prophetic word embodied, although uttered in specific historical situations had authority for all people and forever. They belonged to history, but not to history as seen by their time-bounded compeers whose insight into events lacked the element of eternity which distinguished the prophets.

God is not a man, that he should lie; neither the son of man, that he should repent; hath he not said, and shall he not do it? or hath he spoken, and shall he not make it good?[12]

People of every age judge history in terms of the

passing scene. God judges the beginning from the end. The Covenant conditioned creation, God having redemption in mind in setting life before us. The prophets knew this, but the average person tended to ignore it. An ancient Hebrew proverb set forth this unpalatable aspect of human experience: "There is a way which seemeth right unto a man; but the end thereof are the ways of death."[13] Isaiah wrote, "The Lord of hosts hath purposed, and who shall disannul it? And his hand is stretched out, and who shall turn it back?"[14]

People judge events in terms of power and resulting dominion. They accept cosmic evil as though it is inevitable and final. But the prophets taught that the children of the covenant should serve the God of the covenant and rely on him for security and peace—not on the strength of their armies or those of their allies. They were the first in history to affirm that the reliance of nations on the strength of their armies is evil.[15]

Isaiah was too much of a realist to imagine that peace can be established by agreements which ignore the roots of conflict. But he saw clearly, as did other prophets, that war, being immoral, must be eliminated. And since war was so deeply entrenched it must be attacked at its roots. Peacemakers doing this must know something of the cost and be willing to pay it in the strength of their assurance of ultimate victory. Accordingly Isaiah and other prophets denounced the basic attitudes which engender war. Then—looking down the ages as though they were setting history right side up—they gave assurances that by the grace of God war shall be no more: "They know not to do right, saith the Lord, who store up violence in and robberies in their palaces."[16]

Isaiah took the king of Assyria as an example of the

arrogance and haughty pride characteristic of the major kings and generals:

I will punish the fruit of the stout heart of the king of Assyria, and the glory of his high looks. For he saith, By the strength of my hand I have done it, and by my wisdom; for I am prudent: and I have removed the bounds of the people, and have robbed their treasures, and I have put down the inhabitants like a valiant man: and my hand hath found, as a nest, the riches of the people: and as one gathereth eggs that are left, have I gathered all the earth; and there was none that moved the wing, or opened the mouth, or peeped.[17]

It appeared that no power on earth could turn aside the greed for conquest but the prophets looked beyond them and saw a time when war should be no more. Zechariah put it this way: "Not by might, nor by power, but by my Spirit, saith the Lord of Hosts."[18]

Isaiah wrote, "The work of righteousness shall be peace; and the effect of righteousness and assurance for ever."[19]

And, out of an assurance born of his knowledge of God:

Many people shall go and say, Come ye, and let us go up to the mountain of the Lord, to the house of the God of Jacob; and he will teach us of his ways, and we will walk in his paths; for out of Zion shall go forth the law, and the word of the Lord from Jerusalem. And he shall judge among the nations, and he shall rebuke many people; and they shall beat their swords into ploughshares, and their spears into pruning hooks; nation shall not lift up sword against nation, neither shall they learn war any more.[20]

The coming of peace, moreover, was not a local or Hebrew project. It was to be the fruit of the love of God to all who would turn to him. To this end he anointed Jeremiah to be "a prophet unto the nations."[21]

The ministry of the prophets was directed toward turning the children of God to him in gratitude and loving service. But there was no hope of their success so long as persons and nations continued to hate and rob each other. Before peace can be won the rich and powerful must cease using their might to oppress others, and the poor and needy must be free of resentment and conspiracy against their enemies. This was a long way from the situation in which the prophets lived, and the closer these men of God lived to their Lord the more concerned about it they became. Isaiah said, in the name of God: "The Lord is a God of judgment."[22] They knew, too, that the justice which the Lord seeks is not limited, but has its roots in his loving kindness, in his benevolence:

Righteous art thou, O Lord, and upright are thy judgments. Thy testimonies that thou hast commanded are righteous and very faithful.[23]

His work is perfect; for all his ways are judgment; a God of truth and without iniquity, just and right is he.[24]

He that oppresseth the poor reproacheth his Maker; but he that honoreth him hath mercy on the poor.[25]

At times the prophets felt the burden of injustices around them so deeply as to become impatient. Habakkuk, for example, wrote,

O Lord...why dost thou show me iniquity, and cause me to behold grievances? For spoiling and violence are before me; and there are that raise up strife and contention. Therefore the law is slacked, and judgment doth never go forth; for the wicked doth compass about the righteous; therefore wrong judgment proceedeth.[26]

But the prophets knew the direction in which justice lay, and the importance of keeping the people alert to this. Isaiah said, "Cease to do evil; Learn to do well; seek judgment, relieve the oppressed, judge [defend] the fatherless, plead for the widow."[27]

Righteousness was not a matter of casual concern. It was to be pursued. Isaiah said "Hearken unto me, ye that follow after righteousness; ye that seek the

112

Lord,"[28] and Zephaniah followed in a similar mood: "Seek ye the Lord, all ye meek of the earth, which have wrought his judgment; seek righteousness, seek meekness."[29] This pursuit is to be love-motivated, reflecting the love of God:[30]

The word of the Lord is right; and all his works are done in truth. He loveth righteousness and judgment; the earth is full of the goodness of the Lord.[31]

The righteous Lord loveth righteousness; his countenance doth behold the upright.[32]

Zion shall be redeemed with judgment, and her converts with righteousness.[33]

The prophetic awareness that God is Alpha and Omega, the beginning and the ending, was seen by many as meaning that he is the Lord of history. God is not a dictator but, rather, a director. He did direct the course of history, as when he chose Jeremiah before that prophet's birth to be his messenger to the nations (Jeremiah 1:5) or when he used Cyrus as his instrument of chastisement (Isaiah 54:2-3). But God's purposes are greater than those of even the wisest of humans, and these might cause him to permit things which mortals cannot understand except as they might be explained by the prophets. For example, God had ordered the sacrificial worship of the temple, but later permitted the victory of the Assyrians and the destruction of the temple, which canceled out that worship for the Jews of Babylon.

The meaning of history was a problem to many of the ancients. In their experience what seemed like an obvious procedure, and an enterprise undertaken with confidence, was frequently brought to naught by such unanticipated events as the appearance of David with his sling[34] or by the campaigns of Alexander the Great. So history was seen as a great circle of repetitious events propelled by blind chance. The prophets, however, saw beyond this, realizing that the lordship of God in history means that there is a wise and steady purpose behind seemingly inexplicable events. Something holy and of inestimable worth was being worked out.

Recognition of purpose in history does not solve all the problems which the contemplation of history raises. There is, for instance, the problem of human freedom. How real is it? Is it conceivable that we might have been so created as to be incapable of self-determination? But such creation could not produce persons of godlike stature. People must be free if they are to choose love and holiness as their way of life. And, having sinned, they must demonstrate their capacity for repentance before they can receive the grace of forgiveness. This repentance must be all-inclusive. It must eventuate in enlistment in the pursuit of truth and goodness and peace.

REFERENCES

1. Psalm 90:2.
2. Psalm 33:11.
3. Isaiah 46:9-10.
4. Psalm 36:5-6 KJ.
5. Isaiah 55:8-9.
6. Isaiah 55:6-7.
7. Job 13:15.
8. Isaiah 26:3-4. See also Isaiah 12:2; Psalm 18:2.
9. I Samuel 7:11-12. See also Joshua 6:11-20.
10. Isaiah 60:1-3.
11. Amos 3:7 KJ.
12. Numbers 23:19.
13. Proverbs 14:12.
14. Isaiah 14:27.

15. *The Prophets,* Abraham J. Heschel, p. 160.
16. Amos 3:10. See also Mosiah 9:4; Isaiah 14:5, 11, 17; Micah 6:12, 7:16.
17. Isaiah 10:12-14 KJ. See also Jeremiah 23:19-11.
18. Zechariah 4:6.
19. Isaiah 32:17.
20. Isaiah 2:3-4. See also Mosiah 1:7, 2-4, 20-21; Psalm 46:7-11.
21. Jeremiah 1:1-5; 25:30.
22. Isaiah 30:18.
23. Psalm 119:137-8.
24. Deuteronomy 32:4.
25. Proverbs 14:31. See also Proverbs 17:5.
26. Habakkuk 1:2-4.
27. Isaiah 1:16-17. See also Isaiah 1:18-20 and Jeremiah 7:5-6, 22-3.
28. Isaiah 51:1.
29. Zephaniah 2:3.
30. Psalm 99:4.
31. Psalm 33:4-5 KJ.
32. Psalm 11:7.
33. Isaiah 1:27.
34. I Samuel 17:40.

Jesus was the revelation to man not only of the power of God, but his merciful presence.

—Darian Cobb

Chapter 11

Judaism in the Time of Jesus

The religion of the Israelites was a revealed religion, and was the reason for their existence as a people. They thought of themselves as the Children of the Covenant. They were the inheritors of their fathers who had promised to live by the Covenant proposed by Yahweh at Sinai. The basic Covenant statement was part of their daily lives:

Hear, O Israel; the Lord our God is one Lord; And thou shalt love the Lord thy God with all thine heart, and with all thy soul, and with all thy might. And these words, which I command thee this day, shall be in thine heart; and thou shalt teach them diligently to thy children, and shalt talk of them when thou sittest in thine house, and when thou walkest by the way, and when thou liest down, and when thou risest up. And thou shalt bind them for a sign upon thine hand, and they shall be frontlets between thine eyes. And thou shalt write them upon the posts of thy house, and on thy gates.[1]

The Covenant was conceived in love, and the law was intended to implement this in the daily lives of the Israelites. But no matter how carefully law is stated, life lived toward God and expressed in love among others is beyond verbal phrasing. For those to whom the law was given, minute interpretation appeared to be called for. When the interpreters anxiously attempted to cover all the possible variations of meaning, this led to over-emphasis on minutiae rather than to balanced rendition in the spirit of love. So, for many, the law became a burden rather than a gateway to freedom.

At the time of the Babylonian captivity it was 150 years since the days of Amos and Hosea. During this interval their prophecies of the catastrophes which would overtake both the northern and southern kingdoms had been fulfilled. Israel had been scattered, and since 721 B.C. had been lost to history. The people of Judah were the victims of the later captivity. Their initial reaction was to blame God for their discomfiture, but both Jeremiah and Ezekiel pointed out that the people themselves had been unfaithful. The need now was for repentance, and after a time this was acknowledged by many. When this was achieved there was little point in dwelling on the past.

However, there were lessons to be learned, attitudes to be developed, and character to be refined and strengthened. These were such as could only be learned against a background of tragedy and pain. In this situation Deutero-Isaiah proved invaluable with his message of the suffering servant.[2] The vision of Deutero-Isaiah was more closely akin to the insights of Jesus than to any other prophet. But the coming of the Lord was 500 years away. Isaiah's message, having been sown in the minds of earnest men and women of spiritual caliber, must yet have time to germinate. For the present the need was for someone of God's own choosing who must proclaim again the priorities of righteousness and truth. Such a man was Ezekiel.

Ezekiel was a priest. Early in the captivity he was commissioned to speak out against the wickedness which was so prevalent and which others were taking more or less for granted. But when the battle with Assyria was lost, and he himself was among the prisoners, he rejoiced in the grace of God which came to him in comfort and guidance. His narrative of the valley of dry bones sounded an important warning of the need for the presence of the Holy Spirit if reconstruction was to be achieved.[3]

Against his personal and family background it was natural for Ezekiel to feel the importance of ordered religious life as a major spiritual factor in stable recovery. This was especially important for the immediate future. So we find the last nine chapters of the Book of Ezekiel concerned with rebuilding of the temple and the establishment of its ordinances.

While post-exilic worship as it now emerged was widely regarded as a continuance of what had gone before, and the law was considered central to the sound practice of daily life, there were marked differences. The quality of life was more sober and came to center more fully in the observance of the law. The eminence of the law gave dignity and authority to those who were considered to be experts in its analysis and interpretation. So, we begin to hear of the Pharisees. From our more liberal point of view it is easy to think of the Pharisees as a hair-splitting group of legal-minded autocrats. Some possibly warranted this description, but such is not fair to the earnest group of able and dedicated men who, unfortunately, often tended to over-emphasize the letter of the law and to lose sight of its spirit.

The Pharisees were deeply concerned with the restoration of the Jewish state. They sought to advance their cause by teaching strict obedience to the law as they saw it, together with such subservience to their political over-lords as the situation called for. In their rather narrow legalism they were not unlike the Puritans of later centuries. But, despite their limitations, their influence kept the spirit of the law as a living force among their local and more distant co-religionists. They encouraged the Jewish passion for knowledge, and their many contacts among the people made for progress of a limited sort.

The goal of the Pharisees was to raise the level of popular piety to a point consistent with that set for the priests in the ancient injunction: "Ye shall be unto me a kingdom of priests, and a holy nation."[4] They so interpreted the law as to extend its priestly requirements to the people also[5] and to carry into Jewish homes such temple ministries as would make these homes into domestic sanctuaries. Under their guidance attempts were made to make the requirements of the law the rules for governing personal and family life. They left temple rituals to the priests, but many of them served as preachers and teachers in the synagogues. Though surrounded by nations where many gods were worshiped, they were strictly monotheistic and this distinction had far-reaching significance on their moral and spiritual ministries.

After the passing of the great prophets, new types of literature appeared. Much of this was apocalyptic in that it expressed through visions and symbols the longing for the coming day when the hope for righteousness would be realized in all-encompassing victory. There is a strong apocalyptic element in the later part of Ezekiel, notably in the record of the conflict between Gog and Magog.[6] The last six chapters of Daniel are also apocalyptic. A major theme was what Amos had called "the coming day of the Lord." The Hebrews had lacked a strong sense of the importance of life after death prior to the exile, but now it developed. By the time of Jesus the belief was widely held among Pharisees and others.[7]

The Psalms are discussed in chapter 5, but it may be helpful in keeping sequences straight to remember that although some of the psalms were composed approximately a thousand years before the birth of Jesus, and some were even older,[8] the arrangement of the psalms from even earlier collections probably took place during the Babylonian period. The prophetic tone of some of the psalms indicates that the spirit of the golden age of prophecy had not fully departed.

Jesus began his ministry in Galilee, but soon went on to Nazareth, his hometown. He went to the synagogue, and when invited to address the assembly he read from Isaiah:[9]

The Spirit of the Lord is upon me, because he hath anointed me to preach the gospel to the poor; he hath sent me to heal the brokenhearted, to preach deliverance to the captives, and the recovering of sight to the blind; to set at liberty them that are bruised; To preach the acceptable year of the Lord.

Then he gave the book back to the minister, sat down, and said to them: "This day is this scripture fulfilled in your ears."[10]

It is probable that the Lord's ministry was accepted up to this point, for Luke goes on to write that "all bare him witness, and wondered at the gracious words which proceeded out of his mouth." But they had heard of his ministry in Galilee and in all probability were disappointed that no similar works were wrought among them. The situation was worsened when Jesus went on to emphasize the outreach implied in what he had read from Isaiah. Instead of confirming them in their national pride, he reminded them of the goodness of God to the widow of Sarepta[11] and of the healing of Naaman.[12] Both of these were Gentiles. This was too much for his hearers. They were "filled with wrath and rose up, and thrust him out of the city"[13] with the intention of throwing him down a steep cliff. But Jesus "passing through the midst of them," returned to Capernaum.[14] Here he continued his ministry of preaching and healing, and the people were again "astonished at his doctrine" and the power which he demonstrated.[15]

Opposition to Jesus continued. It came into focus, particularly, when he asserted his authority, as when he said the following:

Ye have heard that it was said by them of old time, Thou shalt not kill: and whosoever shall kill shall be in danger of the judgment: But I say unto you, That whosoever is angry with his brother without a cause, shall be in danger of the judgment; and whosoever shall say to his brother, Raca, shall be in danger of the council: but whosoever shall say, Thou fool, shall be in danger of hell fire.[16]

It was brought into even sharper focus when he said to the man sick of the palsy: "Thy sins are forgiven thee."

Seeing the disturbance this caused among the scribes, he said to them:

That ye may know that the Son of Man hath power upon earth to forgive sins. . . .

I say unto thee [the sick man] Arise, and take up thy couch, and go unto thy house.

And immediately he rose up . . . took up that whereon he lay, and departed to his own house.[17]

Both Jesus and the leaders of the Jews spoke constantly of the kingdom but, as soon became apparent, there was an underlying difference of spirit. Jesus was concerned that his hearers make the love of God and others their primary life force. The Pharisees and the scribes, however, had developed such an emphasis on the law that it was robbed of its basic love motivation. This made observance of their interpretation basic to salvation.

The formalism and legal aridity of the life of the Pharisees and their followers was the result of their failure to recognize that the covenant had been built on love, and should be maintained in love. The truly deadly sins, Jesus said, are not those which become visible in antisocial action, but the lack of love which underlies them: the attitudes and motives which are rarely considered sinful. He said,

Out of the heart proceed evil thoughts, murders, adulteries, fornications, thefts, false witness, blasphemies.[18]

Woe unto you, scribes and Pharisees, hypocrites! for ye make clean the outside of the cup, and of the platter; but within they are full of extortion and excess. Ye blind Pharisees! Cleanse first the cup and platter within, that the outside of them may be clean also.[19]

The righteousness to which Jesus called his disciples was not a refinement of what the Jewish leaders enjoined, but a different kind of life and thought. According to Jesus, the kingdom of God is reserved for those who love and serve God and others. Admission into the kingdom cannot be earned; its condition is overflowing love expressed in repentance, worship, and service.

In spite of our concern for Phariseeism in any age, we should remember that the Pharisees of the period, including the years immediately preceding the birth of Jesus, kept religion alive. It provided a body which enshrined the spirit of the Hebrew people and so preserved the possibility of its richer expression. In their maintenance of religious duties, in their consuming passion for knowledge in every field, in their courage under persecution, and in many other enriching ways the Jews have shown the potency of devotion to Yahweh and to his law.

Although Judaism was shackled by self-regarding tradition, an unwarranted isolationism, and a pervading sense of complacency, it was to the Jews that John was sent to prepare the way for the Lord Jesus. The work of the prophets and seers had not been entirely in vain. Paul was not the only Pharisee who later saw the light of God more fully.[20]

In discharging his God-given call to evangelize the world it was the custom of the Apostle Paul to appeal first to his fellow Jews and when many of them rebuffed him to turn to the Gentiles. Many of these were familiar with the Jewish religion and history, and Paul became expert in explaining the law to them. He drew on this experience when writing his epistles. In the Galatian letter he wrote that "the law was our schoolmaster to bring us unto Christ, that we may be justified by faith. But after that faith is come, we are no longer under a schoolmaster."[21]

The usual understanding of this has been that the law was preparatory, clearing the way for the gospel, which is final. This, however, writes C. H. Dodd,[22] is not quite what Paul meant. In the Greek communities of that time a well-to-do person might—and often did—leave an inheritance to a minor child who was not yet able to manage it. On the death of the testator the executors would appoint a trusted slave to watch over the heir. The slave was given authority to direct the life of the heir—determining his spending money, his social life, and his education. The slave was called the "pedagogue" of the heir, and guided him until he was mature enough to manage his own affairs. What Paul was saying when he called the law a "pedagogue" was that when the law was given the Hebrew people had not yet attained spiritual maturity, and needed wise guidance. But when maturity came they were expected to "put away childish things" and act as responsible persons.[23]

After he became a Christian, Paul taught that obedience to the ancient law held no promise of salvation. To the saints in Rome he wrote,

The righteousness of God without the law is manifested, being witnessed by the law and the prophets; even the righteousness of God which is by faith of Jesus Christ, unto all and upon all them that believe: for there is no difference: for all have sinned and come short of the glory of God; being justified freely by his grace through the redemption that is in Christ Jesus; whom God hath set forth to be a propitiation through faith in his blood, to declare his righteousness for the remission of sins that are past, through the forbearance of God. . . . Therefore we conclude that a man is justified by faith without the deeds of the law.[24]

And he admonished the saints in Galatia:

Stand fast therefore in the liberty wherewith Christ hath made us free, and be not entangled again in the yoke of bondage. . . . I testify again to every man that is circumcised, that he is a debtor to do the whole law. Christ is become of no effect unto you, whatsoever of you are justified by the law; ye are fallen from grace.[25] Your relation with Christ is completely severed: you have fallen out of the domain of grace.[26]

The basic problem of the Jewish leaders was that they had no adequate answer to the persistent fact of sin. No one—Jew or Gentile or Christian—could overcome sin alone. There was need for a redeemer—and not just any redeemer would do. Paul said that God had sent such a Redeemer and the growing testimony of the Christians affirmed this to be so in their own lives. As John wrote,

God so loved the world, that he gave his Only Begotten Son, that whosoever believeth on him should not perish; but have everlasting life. For God sent not his Son into the world to condemn the world; but that the world through him might be saved.[27]

The depth and vitality of the Christian experience

was in the sharpest kind of contrast with what the most devout of the Jews had hitherto known. John set this forth in words which have been treasured down the ages:

The word was made flesh, and dwelt among us (and we beheld his glory, the glory as of the Only Begotten of the Father,) full of grace and truth.... The law was given by Moses, but grace and truth came by Jesus Christ.[28]

The difference was beyond description. It had to be experienced to be believed.

REFERENCES

1. Deuteronomy 6:4-9.
2. Isaiah 40 to 55, especially Isaiah 53.
3. Ezekiel 37:1-14.
4. Exodus 19:6.
5. Exodus 30:17-21.
6. Ezekiel 34.
7. John 11:21-25.
8. Psalm 90.
9. Isaiah 61:1-2; Luke 4:18.
10. Luke 4:19.
11. Luke 4:26.
12. Luke 4:27.
13. Luke 4:28-29.
14. Luke 4:30-31.
15. Luke 4:32.
16. Matthew 5:21-22 KJ.
17. Luke 5:20-25.
18. Matthew 15:18; Mark 7:21-23.
19. Matthew 23:22-23.
20. Luke 11:37.
21. Galatians 3:24-25 KJ.
22. C. H. Dodd, *The Meaning of Paul for Today*, 78-80.
23. I Corinthians 13:10-11.
24. Romans 3:21-25, 28 KJ.
25. Galatians 5:1, 3, 4.
26. Galatians 5:4 New English Bible.
27. John 3:16-17.
28. John 1:14, 17 KJ.

If it be for naught, for nothingness
At last, why does God make the world
   so fair?
Why spill this golden splendor out across
The western hills, and light the silver
   lamp
Of eve? Why give me eyes to see, and
   soul
To love so strong and deep? Then, with
   a pang
This brightness stabs me through, and
   wakes within
Rebellious voice to cry against all death!
Why set this hunger for eternity
To gnaw my heartstrings through, if
   death ends all?
If death ends all, then evil must be good,
Wrong must be right, and beauty,
   ugliness.
God is a Judas who betrays His love,
And with a kiss, damns all the world
   to hell—
If Christ rose not again.

—Anon.

Chapter 12

Jesus and the Holy Spirit

It is not possible to understand the life and ministry of the Lord Jesus Christ without giving attention to the accompanying ministry of the Holy Spirit, for understanding Jesus is a spiritual experience. All references to the activity of the Holy Spirit in the New Testament are related, directly or indirectly, to the ministry of the Lord Jesus. The Spirit does not supersede the presence of Christ, but accompanies and continues it. The relationship between the Lord Jesus and the Holy Spirit is a cornerstone of the Christian faith.

The gospels were written by men who experienced the Holy Spirit, and they mentioned the presence and participation of the Spirit at every crucial point in the coming and the ministry of the Master. The birth of John the Baptist—the forerunner of Jesus—was announced by the Holy Spirit.[1] Later, by the same Spirit, came the annunciation to Mary of the birth of her son, Jesus,[2] and to Joseph the assurance that the child was "of the Holy Ghost."[3] Furthermore, when the aged Simeon took the child Jesus into his arms to bless him Simeon recognized through the testimony of the Spirit that the infant was indeed "the Lord's Christ."[4]

The boy Jesus received such a measure of the Spirit

as was appropriate to his age and needs. Luke recorded that after the visit of the family to the temple Jesus was "subject" to his parents and "increased in wisdom and stature, and in favor with God and man."[5]

It was by the Holy Spirit that Jesus was endowed after his baptism.[6] He was then led by the Spirit into the wilderness to be with God and to confront the temptations which would assail him as he sought to fulfill his calling.[7] It was then in the power of the Spirit that he returned to Galilee and taught in the synagogues[8] and then went to his hometown of Nazareth and announced his mission in the words of Isaiah.[9] Thereafter, Peter said, "God anointed Jesus of Nazareth with the Holy Ghost and with power, who went about doing good."[10]

No account of the teachings of the Lord Jesus, and of the occasions when his life was nurtured by the Holy Spirit, is enough to convey the full story of the impact of the Spirit in the Master's life. The Spirit set Jesus apart, as the Lord had said: "He shall glorify me; for he shall receive of mine, and shall show it unto you."[11]

All of the Lord's teachings proved to be windows through which we may look with dedicated imagination and sense the inner life—the Spirit from which they grew. The beatitudes, for example, stimulate faithful revelations of his inner self. To find the best possible guide to sound understanding of Paul's hymn of love[12] or, indeed, to any scriptures, we must have the Lord Jesus as a constant participant in our study. Our situation is akin to that of the two who walked with Jesus on the way to Emmaus and to whom he "expounded. . .the scriptures."[13]

The Lord Jesus illustrated and conveyed the meaning of the Holy Spirit by the quality of his life—his light, and truth, and power; his availability and warmth and consolation—rather than by any formal definition of the nature of the Spirit. What his disciples needed to know they derived from remembrance of the Lord's total personal impact. Every aspect of his life needed to be considered as they sought the deepest meaning of his teachings. Later the apostle Paul was to write that "the gospel of Christ...is the power of God unto salvation to every one that believeth."[14] The message was essentially "of Christ" and it was attested by the power of his Spirit.[15]

Jesus was the Son of God, the Messiah for whose coming the godly among the Hebrews had waited with patient hope.[16] Although this fact was made known to Simeon and to Anna[17] and, to some degree, to John the Baptist, and was possibly discussed among some who heard him and who saw his miracles, there was sound reason for refusing to noise it abroad.

One of the basic convictions of the Hebrew people, treasured for generations as a truth divinely committed to them, was of the majesty and splendor of God. If Jesus had announced his divinity, and they had believed him, they would have fallen on their faces in bewildered adoration. So, since they must know, there was only one thing to do. They must be shown the truth in such ways as would intrigue their perceptions. As F. J. Sheed wrote, "His method was not to tell them, but to bring them to a point where they would tell him."[18]

Jesus tried to do this when early in his public ministry he went to the synagogue in Nazareth and addressed the assembly.[19]

On another occasion a man who was sick of the palsy was brought by his friends to Jesus and, unable to get through the crowd, was let down through the roof. When Jesus saw their faith he said to the sick man, "Son, thy sins be forgiven thee."[20] Certain of the scribes considered this claim to forgive sins to be blasphemous, but Jesus, hearing this, said to them:

That ye may know that the Son of Man hath power on earth to forgive sins (he said to the sick of the palsy,) Arise, and take up thy bed, and go . . . to thy house. And he arose . . . and went forth before them all.[21]

Yet again, there was brought to him "one possessed with a devil, blind and dumb; and he healed him; insomuch that the blind and dumb both spake and saw."[22]

The Pharisees who heard this said, "This man doth not cast out devils, but by Beelzebub the prince of devils."[23]

Such a comment arose from their resentment of Jesus rather than from anything in the situation. Jesus therefore commented,

All manner of sin and blasphemy shall be forgiven unto men . . . but whosoever speaketh against the Holy Ghost, it shall not be forgiven him; neither in this world; neither in the world to come.[24]

On another occasion he said,

All things are delivered unto me of my Father; and no man knoweth the Son, but the Father; neither knoweth any man the Father, save the Son, and they to whom the Son will reveal himself.[25]

Yet again he said, "I have not spoken of myself; but the Father which sent me, he gave me a commandment, what I should say, and what I should speak."[26]

And, perhaps more conclusively:

My sheep hear my voice, and I know them, and they follow me;

and I give unto them eternal life; and they shall never perish, neither shall any man pluck them out of my hand. My Father, which gave them me, is greater than all; and no man is able to pluck them out of my Father's hand. I and my Father are one.[27]

It was after this that Luke reports, "Then the Jews took up stones again to stone him."[28]

Many of those who listened to the public ministry of Jesus came to regard him as a great teacher and even as a prophet.[29] But the Jews as a whole were convinced monotheists, and some who had been considered his disciples "went back, and walked no more with him."[30] Then Jesus said to the Twelve, "Will ye also go away?" and Simon Peter answered: "Lord, to whom shall we go? thou hast the words of eternal life. And we believe and are sure that thou art that Christ, the Son of the living God."[31]

This confession of Peter (in which the other apostles apparently concurred) marked a major point of development in understanding between Jesus and those who must soon be his witnesses in all the world. It affirmed that in Jesus was unique authority and truth. He was now seen as the earthly repesentative of his Father. More was yet to come, for the revelations of Calvary and Easter were yet ahead. But a further step was taken when Jesus and the twelve were together on the coast of Caesara Phillipi and Jesus asked about the popular opinion of himself and of his work. Peter answered, "Some say John the Baptist; some Elias; and others Jeremias; or one of the prophets."

But Jesus went on: "But whom say ye that I am?" And Peter answered and said, "Thou art the Christ, the Son of the living God."

Whereupon Jesus said, "Blessed are thou, Simon Bar-jona; for flesh and blood hath not revealed it unto thee, but my Father which is in heaven."[32]

Years later the apostle Paul echoed this when he wrote to the Saints in Corinth, "No man can say that Jesus is the Lord, but by the Holy Ghost."[33]

It is difficult to trace with precision and confidence just what steps led the disciples to accept Jesus on this high level. But we can note with profit some of the important factors in their growth.

When Peter told Cornelius that God had anointed Jesus "with the Holy Ghost and with power"[34] it is probable that a major factor in this conclusion was Peter's conviction of the Lord's utter sinlessness. He had heard the Lord denounce the sins of thought and word and deed of all manner of people, but his life gave no ground whatever for rebuttal. Peter had traveled all over the countryside but had seen in his Lord no sense of guilt and no situation calling for pardon or redemption. As the late Adolph Harnack wrote some years ago, "Jesus carried no scars of a frightful struggle."

Again, all those who had lived close to the Master knew that his life was nurtured in prayer. There are many evidences of this. For example, Luke recorded an occasion when Jesus was worn out and might reasonably have sought relief in sleep. Instead he "went out into a mountain to pray, and continued all night in prayer to God."[35] Another time after a day culminating in the healing of "many that were sick...in the morning, rising up a great while before day, he went out and departed into a solitary place, and there prayed."[36]

Particularly revealing was the experience Jesus shared with his disciples immediately after he came down from the Mount of Transfiguration. The nine who were awaiting those who had been away were somewhat disturbed because they had been unable to heal a lunatic boy. Jesus healed the lad, and the disciples asked why they had not been able to do so. Primarily, said Jesus, their failure had been due to unbelief. But he added, "this kind goeth not out but by prayer and fasting."[37] Evidently he had understanding and powers which they had not yet attained.

Another factor in the conviction that Jesus was endowed with the Holy Spirit was probably the apostles' growing recognition of his uniqueness and, gradually and with some apprehension, of his godlikeness. This involved searching reexamination of their earlier concepts of the nature of God. There was also the cumulative effect of sharing the life of the Lord and being challenged by its revealing excellencies. They probably pondered the attitude Jesus had toward children and the underprivileged in general, toward the woman of Samaria and the Samaritan group which refused to entertain him, toward those who would have made him king, and toward the ofttimes hypocritical rulers of the Jews. Time and time again they must have contrasted their own way of life with what they saw Jesus do, and felt the rightness of the Master's call to repentance.

Throughout their experiences with Jesus, Peter and others of the disciples had felt the presence and power of a Spirit peculiar to Jesus, the Holy Spirit. They did not know the fullness of the Spirit until after the resurrection, but they saw it in operation in all that the Master did as he overcame the forces of evil, ministered the Word, healed bodies and minds, opened the eyes of the blind (including their own spiritual eyes), and kept the faith at whatever cost was involved.

After Calvary and Easter there was an even stronger complex of evidences. The miracle of the resurrection threw new light on all they had seen and heard. They remembered, for example, Jesus saying that if he wished he could have the assistance of "more than twelve legions of angels"[38] and knew that this was no idle phrase. They saw two amazing things: Jesus could have done what he said, but he had refused to be rescued at the price of his sacrificial mission. Knowing now that he was the Son of God made flesh for their redemption, they were amazed at the humility with which he had accepted his role and savored again their pride in the friendship he had offered them. Years later the apostle Paul seems to have been especially impressed by this, and wrote to the saints in Philippi:

Let nothing be done through strife or vain-glory; but in lowliness of mind let each esteem other as better than themselves. Look not every man on his own things, but every man also on the things of others. Let this mind be in you, which was also in Christ Jesus; who, being in the form of God, thought it not robbery to be equal with God; but made himself of no reputation, and took upon him the form of a servant, and was made in the likeness of men; and being found in fashion as a man, he humbled himself, and became obedient unto death.[39]

Our reflection on the relationship of Christ and the Holy Spirit is enlightening in both directions. The Holy Spirit guides us toward understanding of Jesus in terms which have enriched many generations. And the life of Jesus has illustrated the character of the Holy Spirit as only the Lord himself could do. Paul declared this in his classic definition: "The Lord is that Spirit." Christ is our portrait of the Father. He is no less our portrait of the Holy Spirit.[40]

The revelation of God in Christ came to culmination in the earthly ministry of the Lord Jesus, his death and resurrection, and ascension. Thereafter the revelation was continued through the ministry of the Holy Spirit. What had happened before now took on new meaning and ripeness: what had been promise now was achieved fullness. But the revelation was not completed so much as it was more fully available as it took on significance in the lives of the faithful. God was freer to do what he had wished to do down the ages for he now had more polished tools. But he did not retire. What Jesus had said long ago was still true: "My Father worketh hitherto, and I work."[41] And the Saints proclaimed in a sentence which might well have been put on the banner under which they marched: "Jesus Christ the same yesterday, and today, and forever."[42]

The early saints did not think their gospel was essentially different from what they had known hitherto, only that it was now available in its fullness. The Father had moved in the morning of creation. The Son was fulfilling the vision of the prophets, and was himself the bringer of salvation. And the Holy Spirit was empowering and directing them in ways experienced by "holy men of old" but now having fullness which had not been possible when Joel foretold it.

Jesus was a person of disciplined courage who knew what had happened to his cousin, John the Baptist; yet when the time was ripe, "steadfastly set his face to go to Jerusalem" knowing what awaited him there. And, having arrived, he left his impress on the money changers in the temple by driving them out. Through it all, when the hour of his passion was come, he so conducted himself as to make even Calvary carry his message of the love and forgiveness of his Father, which he now showed to be his own.

Recognition that Jesus is the Son of God may have

been dawning on a few who were nearest to Jesus. But the fullness of understanding involved a tremendous leap which was not fully made until the resurrection and the endowment of the Spirit brought conviction.

It is at the heart of the Christian faith that the Lord who lived on earth in complete communion with his Father was in truth the Son of God who now lives and reigns with him, but who also abides among those who love and serve him, leading them to life eternal.

REFERENCES

1. Luke 1:13.
2. Luke 1:26-38.
3. Matthew 2:3.
4. Luke 2:26.
5. Luke 2:52.
6. Luke 4:14-15.
7. Luke 4:2-3.
8. Luke 4:15.
9. Luke 4:16-22.
10. Acts 10:38.
11. John 16:14.
12. I Corinthians 13.
13. Luke 24:25-27.
14. Romans 1:16.
15. Romans 8:9-11.
16. Luke 2:25.
17. Luke 2:36-38.
18. John Mackintosh Shaw, *The Gospel of the Fatherhood of God*, London, England: Hodder and Stoughton, 143.
19. Luke 4:16-30.
20. Mark 2:5.
21. Mark 2:8-9.
22. Matthew 12:18.

23. Matthew 12:20.
24. Matthew 12:26-27.
25. Matthew 11:28.
26. John 12:49.
27. John 10:27-30.
28. John 10:31.
29. John 3:2.
30. John 6:66.
31. John 6:67-68.
32. Matthew 16:15-18.
33. I Corinthians 12:3.
34. Acts 10:38.
35. Luke 6:12.
36. Mark 1:30-31.
37. Matthew 17:21.
38. Matthew 26:51.
39. Philippians 2:3-8.
40. B. H. Streeter, quoted from memory from a late book of B. H. Streeter.
41. John 5:17.
42. Hebrews 13:8.

Hast thou not known? hast thou not heard, that the everlasting God, the Lord, the Creator of the ends of the earth fainteth not, neither is weary? there is no searching of his understanding. He giveth power to the faint; and to them that hath no might he increaseth strength. Even the youths shall faint and be weary, and the young men shall utterly fall; but they that wait upon the Lord shall renew their strength; they shall mount up with wings as eagles; they shall run, and not be weary; and they shall walk, and not faint.

—Isaiah 40:28-31

Chapter 13

The Comforter

Vital as was the life and ministry of the Lord Jesus Christ to the salvation of humankind, the time came when it was "expedient" that he should return to his place at the right hand of God. When he neared the end of his earthly ministry, therefore, he said to his disciples,

I will pray the Father, and he shall give you another Comforter, that he may abide with you forever; Even the Spirit of truth; whom the world cannot receive, because it seeth him not, neither knoweth him; but ye know him; for he dwelleth with you, and shall be in you. I will not leave you comfortless; I will come to you. Yet a little while, and the world seeth me no more; but ye see me; Because I live, ye shall live also.[1]

This "other Comforter" would be to his disciples what he himself had been, providing ministries which the Lord himself had brought, except that the Spirit would abide forever.

The promised Spirit is not Christ[2] but would be sent in response to the prayer of Christ.[3] The Spirit, said the Lord, would continue his work, and to this end he would teach them all things, bringing to their remembrance whatever he (Jesus) had said to them.[4] Later, the Lord said that the Spirit would guide them "into all truth."[5] The Spirit, moreover, would testify of Jesus in order to make them effective witnesses.

"Reprove the world of sin, and of righteousness, and of judgment." . . . Speak what he receives. . . . "Make known things to come." . . . Glorify the Lord Jesus by making the Master's teaching available and clarifying its meaning.

John brought these together in this way:

When he, the Spirit of truth, is come, he will guide you into all truth, for he shall not speak of himself; but whatsoever he shall hear, that shall he speak; and he will show you things to come. He shall glorify me; for he shall receive of mine, and shall show it unto you.[6]

Difficult though it was for the twelve to accept the idea that Jesus needed to leave them, this was nevertheless so, for the bodily presence of their Lord was not without its disadvantages. The most evident was the possibility that they would be over-awed by the majesty of his person and would rely on him to solve all their difficulties and so stultify their growth. It was essential for their own maturation in spiritual understanding that he should no longer be available in the sense that a neighbor is available. Yet it was also imperative that the Lord should stay with them in the sense that his Spirit would abide with them forever. This the Lord promised should happen.

From the point of view of succeeding generations, who could not see Jesus in the flesh as the disciples did, the departure of the Lord and the coming of the Spirit was imperative. Without this, later disciples would have been dependent on the testimony of their predecessors. With it they could receive both the testimony and the Spirit which together make the gospel "the power of God unto salvation."[7]

The Greek word rendered as *Comforter* in the King James and Inspired Versions of the New Testament is *paraclete*. Modern translators have had difficulty in finding a translation of *paraclete* as adequate for today as was *Comforter* more than three hundred years ago. The Revised Standard Version uses "counselor." The Moffatt version uses "helper." In noting these slight differences of emphasis we need to remember that the translators were trying to render a term used in various ways and relating to One who was beyond their full understanding. With this in mind, I have found myself drawn to the J. B. Phillips version. Here *paraclete* is "someone to stand by you."

Some years ago I read of a meeting of Alcoholics Anonymous held near the campus of the University of Pennsylvania. It was a testimony meeting where some who had overcome their alcoholism sought to strengthen and encourage others who had not yet achieved the victory. One of the more or less successful ones started his testimony by saying, "I want Jack to come and stand by me." Then, when a big and friendly fellow came forward, the testifier continued:

You know, Jack came and lived with me twenty-four hours a day for four days. I had been having a bad time. But when Jack was with me I felt strong because I knew he had been strong and he was right there for me to see that I could win. Then, gradually, I found that I did not need Jack quite so much. And now I think I am beginning to get on my feet, although now and again I find that I still need help. Tonight I want to thank you men for what you have already done, and Jack for the special way in which he stood by me, but most of all God for the patience of his love.

It was a wonderful thing that Jack could act as "paraclete" to this man who had been unable to solve his personal problems by himself. It is this practice of being helper, strengthener, comforter, advocate, that lies at the heart of the success of Alcoholics Anonymous. But, infinitely more so, it is the reality of the experience of the paraclete, the Spirit of the Lord Jesus, in the lives of disciples down the ages, which has revealed God in his compassion and power and so has brought many from degradation to salvation.

The early saints were witnesses before they were theologians. Interest in doctrine and theology developed as they sought to explain their faith to others. Their formulation of doctrine concerning the Holy Spirit probably began with personal experiences they shared which merged into statements of belief which they shared with growing numbers of the disciples, and which soon were related to their worship patterns. They soon laid hold on the essentials: that the Spirit was given by God and was not of their own contriving, that it was manifest in diverse ways, that it included manifestations of insight and power and "love unfeigned," that it quickened their memories and made these memories meaningful. The refinement of their common testimony took years, but was itself Spirit-guided. Yet their attempts at definition were never fully satisfactory, for the Spirit was—and is—a living reality.

Although the saints found that the presence of the Holy Spirit was akin to the presence of Christ, it was important for them to observe the distinction between them. It was Jesus who had lived among them and had demonstrated the grandeur of the love of God. To this love of God and the truth of the testimony of Jesus "the Spirit...beareth witness with our spirit, that we are the children of God."[8]

Peter and John and their fellow ministers proclaimed the lordship of Christ as this had been made known in his life and death and resurrection and was now confirmed daily in the lives of the saints. The hearing of this testimony was the indispensible prelude to the growth of faith.[9] But this must be refined into assurance by the inner testimony of the Spirit.[10] That this was occurring in the lives of the rapidly growing number of disciples gave confirmation to the preached word. Believers were not immediately transformed but, as a modern Quaker was to say, there was ample evidence that "the evil was losing power, and the good was raising up."[11]

The scriptures portray the Holy Spirit as a person in the same sense as God, the Father, is so portrayed. Some have found this difficult to understand, probably because we usually think of persons as having physical bodies. But this connection is not fully necessary. While we treasure pictures of those we love, it is the love which makes the pictures important. When Oliver Cromwell was being posed for an official portrait he is said to have told the artist to show him "warts and all." But it is only occasionally that we remember the warts, and then in connection with Oliver.

Many references to the Holy Spirit represent the Spirit in terms like those used in relation to the Father and the Son, but distinct from them. The Spirit is expressly distinguished from the Father, for the Spirit "proceedeth from the Father."[12] The Spirit is also distinguished from the Lord Jesus, who called the Spirit "another Comforter."[13] He said, too, that the Spirit would testify of him.[14] The personal pronoun is used of the Spirit by Jesus: "When he, the Spirit of truth, is come. . . ."[15]

Further, acts of will and decision are attributed to the Holy Spirit. These are personal attributes. The Spirit is said to guide, to intercede, convince, reprove, and speak. The Spirit may also be blasphemed and grieved and lied to.

The Spirit is associated with the Father and the Son in the sacraments: baptism, communion, and what is known as "the apostolic benediction." The Spirit is associated with the Father and the Son who together are "One God, infinite and eternal, without end."

The Holy Spirit is a person of the same order as the Father and the Son, united with them yet having a distinctive function within the godhead. This is of great importance to us in the recognition of their unity as well as their diversity. Thus we know that the Spirit acts always in loving-kindness, and is holy.

An ancient psalmist—possibly David—has a most impressive picture for us in this connection. He wrote:

Whither shall I go from thy Spirit? or whither shall I flee from thy presence? If I ascend up into heaven, thou are there; If I make my bed in hell, behold, thou are there. If I take the wings of the morning, and dwell in the uttermost parts of the sea; even there shall thy hand lead me, and thy right hand shall hold me. If I say Surely the darkness shall cover me, even the night shall be light about me. Yea, the darkness hideth not from thee; but the night shineth as the day; the darkness and the light are both alike to thee.[16]

I think of this scripture frequently when in the opening prayer of a worship service the Father is asked to send his Spirit to lead and bless and empower us. The Lord Jesus has already promised to meet and abide with us whenever two or three are met in his name. "His name" means we meet for his purpose. When we meet in his Spirit we become his fellowship of disciples. Given these conditions, it seems that much of our praying should be by way of preparation.

REFERENCES

1. John 14:16-19.
2. John 14:17.
3. John 15:26; 16:7.
4. John 14:26.
5. John 16:13.
6. John 16:13-14.
7. Romans 1:16.
8. Romans 8:16.
9. Romans 10:16.
10. Hebrews 10:15-16.
11. John 15:26.
12. John 15:26.
13. John 14:16.
14. John 15:26.
15. John 16:13. See, also, John 15:26.
16. Psalm 139:7-12.

After that in the wisdom of God the world by wisdom knew not God, it pleased God by the foolishness of preaching to save them that believe.

For the Jews require a sign, and the Greeks seek after wisdom;

But we preach Christ crucified, unto the Jews a stumbling block, and unto the Greeks foolishness;

But unto them which are called, both Jews and Greeks, Christ the power of God, and the wisdom of God.

Because the foolishness of God is wiser than men; and the weakness of God is stronger than men.

—I Corinthians 1:21-25 KJ

Chapter 14

The Holy Spirit
and
Church Beginnings

A fundamental conviction of the early saints, born of their experience with Jesus and its fruition at Pentecost, was that God had sent his Son into the world for their salvation. When the earthly ministry of his Son was finished he had sent his Spirit to continue this work of salvation. They did not think of the Spirit as superseding the presence of the Lord Jesus, but as continuing it and making it more widely and personally available.

It is apparent at every stage in the New Testament record that there is no substitute for the Holy Spirit in the life of the church.

The major function of the Spirit was to testify of the Lord Jesus, as Jesus had promised his followers when speaking of his departure:

When the Comforter is come, whom I will send unto you from the Father, even the Spirit of truth, which proceedeth from the Father, he shall testify of me; and ye also shall bear witness, because ye have been with me from the beginning.[1]

When the promise was given it could not be fulfilled immediately, for the Lord's earthly ministry was not then completed and its culmination was to give distinctive meaning to all that had gone before. As John

149

had put it: "The Holy Ghost was not yet given; because that Jesus was not yet glorified."[2] But now the situation was changed: Calvary and Easter and Pentecost were history. Moreover, the resurrection was not just a fact—it was an earthshaking fact, the most outstanding and miraculous revelation of all times.

After the resurrection, the Lord Jesus appeared to the twelve and "through the Holy Ghost had given commandments"[3] to them, and thereafter was "seen of them forty days and speaking of the things pertaining to the kingdom of God."[4] He then commissioned them to be his witnesses "in Jerusalem, and in all Judea, and in Samaria, and unto the uttermost parts of the earth."[5] Luke recorded that, as they had been instructed, the eleven returned to Jerusalem after the ascension, and met in an upper room where "with the women, and Mary the mother of Jesus, and with his brethren all continued with one accord in prayer and supplication."[6] They probably continued the worship which had occupied them while returning.[7] It is also possible, though this is conjecture, that the leadership of the church in Jerusalem was discussed, for it was not long until James, the Lord's brother, became the first presiding officer of that group.

Later (we do not know just when except that about a hundred and twenty were present), Peter reported the death of Judas and suggested that

of these men which have companied with us all the time that the Lord Jesus went in and out among us, beginning from the baptism of John, unto that same day that he was taken up from us, must one be ordained to be a witness with us of his resurrection.[8]

It is not likely that Peter made such a suggestion without some prior consultation. This may have taken place at the earlier meeting. Or Peter may have been instructed what to do by the Lord Jesus. These possibilities are interesting, but we have no evidence except that one condition named was suggested in the statement of the Lord that the twelve were to be his witnesses. Joseph Barsabas and Matthias were recognized as meeting the requirements set forth. Prayer was offered. Lots were cast, and Matthias was selected. Thereafter he was "numbered with the eleven apostles."[9]

The Jews of the time of Jesus celebrated three major religious festivals: the Passover, the Feast of Tabernacles, and Pentecost. The Passover was celebrated in commemoration of the Exodus, the Feast of Tabernacles commemorated the wilderness tradition, and Pentecost was probably thought of originally in connection with the giving of the Law on Sinai. In the time of Jesus it was like a harvest festival, and was a time of gathering and rejoicing.

At the Pentecostal celebrations the reports of the resurrection had probably been a topic of discussion. It was natural that those interested should come together where the believers were known to be meeting, and Peter and his fellow apostles took advantage of this opportunity to bear their testimony. It is not clear from the record in Acts when the meeting spread from those who were there "with one accord" to include the huge crowd of onlookers. The speaking with tongues was at first within the house where they were sitting, but later probably moved outside where "the multitude... were confounded, because that every man heard them [the apostles] speak in his own language."[10]

It is not unlikely that some in the multitude felt disquietude as they remembered how they had yielded to the mob spirit and called for the crucifixion of one whom they had known as he moved among them doing good. To them and to others in the crowd, probably including many godfearers, Peter spoke with such confident boldness as to carry conviction. And, as the Spirit bore its inner confirming witness, they cried out, "Men and brethren, what shall we do?"[11] So the great campaign of witness and response was launched. The proclamation of Jesus, which the Jewish leaders hoped had been squelched by the Lord's crucifixion, was taken up by thousands. Judaism was being challenged on its home grounds.

The New Testament references to the church are first and foremost about Jesus Christ—then about those who followed him and so constituted the church. Of these the twelve were the most prominent, having been chosen to be with him and instructed as a group about the importance and conditions of their unity.[12] In his memorable upper-room address to them Jesus had said,

Henceforth I call you not servants; for the servant knoweth not what his lord doeth; but I have called you friends; for all things that I have heard of my Father I have made known unto you. Ye have not chosen me, but I have chosen you, and ordained you, that ye should go and bring forth fruit; and that your fruit should remain; that whatsoever ye shall ask of the Father in my name, he may give it you.[13]

What was contemplated was not a voluntary association of individuals who had come together to promote their best understanding of things spiritual. It was not to be established by popular vote; nor was its development to be shaped by common consent. It was to be established by the power and authority of God in order to express and proclaim the Lord's purpose as it had been made known by the prophets and especially by the Lord Jesus. It was to be maintained by the gift and power of God in the lives of his willing servants through their response to the indwelling of the Holy Spirit.

By the time the New Testament epistles and the gospels were written the structure of church organization was fairly uniform, although its development was somewhat uneven. In the growth toward uniformity the apostles gave important leadership.[14] Although the partcipation of the saints was sought and respected, the apostles gave authoritative direction where they felt this was needed. They regulated Christian doctrinal development and presided over Christian worship as this was progressively separated from that of the temple or of the local synagogues.[15] They bore responsibility for the admission of new groups into the church.[16] Some, at least, played a leading role in taking the gospel to distant peoples.[17]

Although the New Testament refers to the Twelve and Paul as apostles in a special sense, others are also called apostles. These include James, the Lord's brother;[18] and Barnabas.[19] Then, too, Andronicus and Junia are described as being "of note among the apostles"[20] and something akin to this is said of Silas and Timothy.[21]

Of note, also, among the ministers of the growing fellowship were those known as the prophets. Their influence was probably second only to that of the apostles.[22] This was a natural outgrowth of the prophetic nature of the ministry of the Lord Jesus and his high regard for the prophetic contribution of such earlier men of God as Isaiah.[23] It was anticipated, also, in Peter's reference to Joel in his sermon at Pentecost.[24] The New Testament references to the prophets are not clear but have been augmented in modern revelation. In the early Christian church some of the prophets may have exercised leadership functions.[25] Others, such as Agabus, Judas, and Silas may have been recognized as exercising prophetic gifts as directed by the Spirit, but without official status.[26]

Paul wrote, "He that prophesieth speaketh unto men to edification, and exhortation and comfort.... He that prophesieth edifieth the church."[27]

Several modern versions of Corinthians indicate that prophecy in this connection referred to preaching (Philipps, Norlie, Goodspeed, Twentieth Century New Testament, and others). It may well be that this version is sound where they use it, and that the word *prophecy* referred primarily to the exposition of the scriptures. It is also probable that in some situations prophecy involved the foretelling of coming events.[28] The nearest parallel in the Restoration appears to be to the evangelist-patriarchs. Certainly there is current need for essentially spiritual ministry unimpeded by administrative responsibilities, just as there is evident modern need for the ministry of apostolic testimony.

As the church grew, there was growing need for local ministries. Elders and pastors and teachers are mentioned in the New Testament, as are deacons. But some who served in one capacity might later fill another calling. Philip was one of the seven "deacons" in Jerusalem. Later he was a successful evangelist.[29]

It is clear that as priesthood were selected and commissioned, their natural capacities were considered. But their faith and their responsiveness to the guidance of the Holy Spirit were all-important.

This is noted in connection with the elders of Ephesus and the deacons chosen to distribute food to the needy in Jerusalem.[30] But there is no evidence of a marked distinction between ministers and members, such as was indicated in more modern times by the differentiation between clergy and laity.

The New Testament has no record of Christians who were not members of the fellowship of the disciples. It was taken for granted that believers were enlisted in the cause of Christ. Faith in God and in the mission of his Son was primary. With this, and almost inseparable from it, was their awareness of their part in the crucifixion of the Lord. This was recent and all-inclusive, and they had no defense against it. One sign of their readiness for church membership was that there seems to have been little attempt to justify what had been done. But there was a broadening of the sense of sin. It had taken something like the crucifixion to startle them awake. When this happened they soon saw their need to repent of the way of life which had led to such a tragedy. This they did, and bore evidence of it by submitting to baptism in the name of Jesus. This was symbolic of their renunciation of the past and their public avowal of their new allegiance. Their baptism was intended, and was accepted by others, as a public affirmation of faith and new discipleship. It was a sign of grateful acceptance of their forgiveness.

But baptism alone was not enough. Despite their cleansing, too much of their yesterdays was enshrined within them in the form of habits and attitudes. More than regret and good intentions were needed if they were to become contributing members of the new fellowship. They must become like the Master and example of them all and must live in and by and under a new Spirit. This was symbolized in the rite of confirmation by which the endowment of the Spirit was passed on to them as they became *members* of the church. As members, rather than sympathetic observers, they undertook to share the risks and burdens of discipleship in expectation of the Spirit of which other members testified.

The decision to become a Christian was to the early saints, as it should be to us—a decision to seek and accept the guidance of the Holy Spirit. The change from independence to enlistment which this entails is fundamental. It has been described as a change of heart, a change of mind, and a change of loyalties. Essentially it requires what Paul called a "newness of spirit."[31] It is only this newness of Spirit which can transform us into "saints"—not immediately perfect, but enriched and strengthened for life after God's own order.[32] Paul wrote,

Ye are not after the flesh, but after the Spirit, if so be that the Spirit of God dwell in you. Now if any man have not the Spirit of Christ, he is none of his. . . . for as many as are led by the Spirit of God, they are the sons of God.[33]

Furthermore, he wrote, "Your body is the temple of the Holy Ghost which is in you, which ye have of God, and ye are not your own."[34]

Believers are not saved in isolation, but in comradeship in kingdom endeavor. The New Testament bears witness to this. It reminds us that Jesus promised, "Where two or three are gathered together in my name, there am I in the midst of them."[35]

And Paul wrote,

God is faithful, by whom ye were called unto the fellowship of his Son, Jesus Christ our Lord.[36]

Let us do good unto all men, especially unto them who are of the household of faith.[37]

And John, "If we walk in the light, as he is in the light, we have fellowship one with another, and the blood of Jesus Christ, his Son cleanseth us from all sin."[38]

It is probable that the earliest brief statement of faith by the early Christians was "Jesus is Lord."[39] This is readily understandable as the key declaration of the new age of faith since it brings together all the other aspects of the newly perceived spiritual order. Luke cited it as part of Peter's sermon at Pentecost: "Therefore let all the house of Israel know assuredly, that God hath made that same Jesus, whom ye have crucified, both Lord and Christ."[40]

Stephen was sustained by this faith and, almost in his last words, prayed: "Lord Jesus, receive my spirit."[41]

The apostle Paul elaborated this somewhat when he wrote to the saints in Rome:

The word is nigh thee, even in thy mouth, and in thy heart; that is, the word of faith which we preach; that if thou shalt confess with thy mouth the Lord Jesus, and shalt believe in thine heart that God hath raised him from the dead, thou shalt be saved. For with the heart man believeth unto righteousness; and with the mouth confession is made unto salvation.[42]

This was of a piece with Paul's much-quoted statement in his first Corinthian letter: "No man can say that Jesus is the Lord, but by the Holy Ghost."[43]

During the periods of persecution which soon overtook the saints, a commonplace shortcut to determining whether an accused person was indeed a Christian was to require him to acknowledge Caesar as Lord and so to deny the Lordship of Christ. Some renounced their faith when put to this test, and since such renouncing meant that they were no longer accepted among the saints and their testimonies had lost conviction among enquirers, the Romans were usually satisfied. Many believed and stood firm, however, and these gave courage to others. The example set by Polycarp, the eighty-six-year-old Bishop of Smyrna, who was burned after refusing repeated pleas to acknowledge Caesar as Lord, was influential through the regions round about.[44]

Such acknowledgment of Jesus as Lord evidently had deeper rootage than mere opinion. I grew up believing that the needed testimony of the Spirit must come in clear and moving fashion, probably in some "spiritual gift." I cherished my membership in the church, and felt inner confirmation when such gifts were manifested occasionally in the local branch and more frequently in the district and mission conferences. But I was not fully satisfied. Fortunately, I took my problem to my father, who helped me to see that no brief and arresting experience is promised: only that the witness of the Spirit is available to those who live for it, and that it should grow (as he said) "here a little, there a little."[45] Somewhat slowly, I came to understand that the testimony which each of us needs must be related to our capacity to understand, and that this capacity is enlarged by "patient continuance in well-doing."[46] We have Paul's statement of faith: "He that soweth to the Spirit shall of the Spirit reap life everlasting," and his admonition, "Let us not be weary in well doing; for in due season we shall reap, if we faint not."[47]

Our testimony grows from faith to faith:

I am not ashamed of the gospel of Christ; for it is the power of God unto salvation to every one that believeth; to the Jew first, and also to the Greek. For therein is the righteousness of God revealed from faith to faith.[48]

REFERENCES

1. John 15:26-27.
2. John 7:39 KJ.
3. Acts 1:2.
4. Acts 1:3.
5. Acts 1:8.
6. Acts 1:14.
7. Luke 24:52.
8. Acts 1:21-22.
9. Acts 1:23-26.
10. Acts 2:6.
11. Acts 2:37.
12. Mark 9:32-37. See also John 13:12-17.
13. John 15:15-16.
14. I Corinthians 2:3-16; 5:1-5, and others.
15. Acts 2:42, and others.
16. Acts 8:10-11.
17. Acts 1:8.
18. Galatians 1:19; 2:9.
19. Acts 14:14; I Corinthians 9:5.
20. Romans 16:7.
21. I Thessalonians 2:6.
22. I Corinthians 12:28; Ephesians 4:11.
23. Luke 4:16-21.
24. Acts 2:16-21.
25. Acts 13:2.
26. Acts 11:28; 15:32; 21:1-11.
27. I Corinthians 14:3-4.
28. Acts 11:28, 21:9, 11.
29. Acts 21:8.
30. Acts 6:3 KJ
31. Romans 7:6.
32. II Corinthians 5:17; Galatians 6:15.
33. Romans 8:9-14. See also I Corinthians 3:16.
34. I Corinthians 6:19.
35. Matthew 18:20.
36. I Corinthians 1:9.
37. Galatians 6:10. See also Philippians 1:5; 2:1-4.
38. I John 1:7. See also John 1:3-5.
39. See Oscar Cullman, quoted in William M. Ramsay, *The Christ of the Earliest Christians*, John Knox Press, 1959, 54.

40. Acts 2:36. See also Acts 10:36.
41. Acts 7:59.
42. Romans 10:8-10.
43. I Corinthians 12:3.
44. *The Martyrdom of Polycarp.* The Apostolic Fathers, Harper and Brothers, 1950, 247.
45. Isaiah 28:10, 13.
46. Romans 2:7.
47. Galatians 6:8-9.
48. Romans 1:16-17.

Sanctify the Lord God in your hearts: and be ready always to give an answer to every man that asketh you a reason of the hope that is in you with meekness and fear.

—I Peter 3:15 KJ

Chapter 15

The Holy Spirit
and
Early Christian Witnesses

The Christian church was (is) built on testimony. In his plans for the future the Lord rested his cause on the testimony of those who loved him. John, one of those who knew and loved him best, wrote the following:

That which was from the beginning, which we have heard, which we have seen with our eyes, which we have looked upon, and our hands have handled, of the Word of life (for the life was manifested, and we have seen it, and bear witness, and shew unto you that eternal life, which was with the Father, and was manifested unto us;) That which we have seen and heard declare we unto you, that ye also may have fellowship with us, and truly our fellowship is with the Father, and with his Son Jesus Christ.[1]

The heart of the earliest Christian testimony was the proclamation of the resurrection of the Lord Jesus Christ. The first disclosure of the resurrection was to Mary Magdalene and Joanna and Mary, the mother of James, and to other women who went to the grave of Jesus together to anoint his body with spices they had prepared for that purpose.[2] They learned of the risen Lord from the messengers in shining garments whom they found there. Astonished they hurried back to where the eleven and other disciples were gathered, and reported what had happened. But no one except possibly Peter believed them. Peter ran to the grave, saw the discarded grave clothes, and "departed, wondering in himself at that which was come to pass."[3]

Some who were not of the eleven followed Peter, and confirmed the story which had been brought to them. Then two of them resumed their journey to Emmaus, and as they walked Jesus joined them and shared their conversation and, "Beginning at Moses and all the prophets, he expounded unto them in all the scriptures the things concerning himself."[4]

The two did not recognize the Lord at first, but when he accepted their invitation to eat with them it dawned on them who he was.

They rose up the same hour and returned to Jerusalem, and found the eleven gathered together, and those who were with them, saying, The Lord is risen indeed, and hath appeared to Simon.[5]

Then Jesus himself appeared and made himself known, but they "believed not for joy," and wondered.[6] Indeed, what had happened was almost too much to believe, and it was part of the strategy of divinity to give to this nucleus of followers time to come to grips with the two aspects of the resurrection to which testimony must be borne: testimony to the fact itself, and testimony in their lives as to what the resurrection meant to them. Jesus addressed himself to both of these. During forty days of post-resurrection ministry to the twelve Jesus "showed himself alive...by many infallible proofs, being seen of them forty days."[7]

The fact that he was "declared to be the Son of God with power according to the spirit of holiness, by the resurrection from the dead,"[8] attached the authority of divinity to all his commandments and to the guidance of the Spirit.

It is recorded further that "When they . . . were come together they [the eleven] asked of him, saying, Lord, wilt thou at this time restore again the kingdom to Israel?"[9]

It may have been in response to this initiative that the Lord spoke to them of "things pertaining to the kingdom of God."[10] Jesus had preached about the kingdom[11] but his words now carried the authority of the resurrection. It seems that he was concerned to lift their understanding from their earlier temporal and Jewish point of view, for their calling had been broadened. He answered, "It is not for you to know the times or seasons, which the Father hath put in his own power."[12]

Then finally, the Lord reemphasized their immediate task which would take its tone from their passion for the kingdom but be to all the world:

But ye shall receive power, after that the Holy Ghost is come upon you: and ye shall be witnesses unto me, both in Jerusalem, and in all Judaea, and in Samaria, and to the uttermost part of the earth.[13]

Here, at the beginning of the distinctively Christian evangel, the essential nature of the apostolic witness was affirmed. It was to center in the lordship of Christ. It was to be universal. It would be attested by the confirming witness of the Holy Spirit.

The campaign of verbal testimony to the resurrection probably began before Pentecost as believers shared the testimony of the apostolic circle with their families and friends, but it reached its early peak with Peter's sermon at Pentecost and the confirmation of the Spirit which accompanied it. Pentecost set the pattern for much of the subsequent preaching and for personal testimony.[14] Significant preparation had been made so that the coming growth could be guided aright from the beginning. Paul wrote the Corinthians that over five hundred of the brethren saw Jesus at once.[15] It is consistent with the thought behind the selection of the twelve as special witnesses that these too were selected for leadership centering in testimony.

We know the names and some of the areas of ministry of the most prominent of the witnesses—they were members of the apostolic council. But even here our information is far from complete. We know of the work of Peter and John and, later, of Paul. But, beyond these and, perhaps, James, we know more of a few who were not of the leading group, but were closely associated with them or with their work. Stephen was possibly the most influential of these. He was one of the first to grasp the universality of the Christian message, and when he was falsely accused of blasphemy he ignored his defense and seized the opportunity to contrast the positions of the Judaizers and the Christians.

Others who come to mind are Philip the evangelist, a fellow-"deacon" of Stephen. He is remembered most widely as the man who, responding to the guidance of the Holy Spirit, joined the treasurer of Queen Candace as this Ethiopian official was reading Isaiah 53, explained the meaning of the prophetic forecast of the ministry of Jesus, converted, and baptized him.[16] Tradition has it that the convert laid the foundations of Christianity in Ethiopia.

Acquila and Priscilla were evangelically minded. Acquila was a Jew of Pontus. Priscilla was a God-fearer. They came to Corinth after the Jews were expelled from Rome by Claudius, arriving a few months before Paul. They were already ardent Christians and welcomed Paul to their home. They were tent makers, as was Paul, and they worked together. Paul preached in the synagogue with phenomenal success. Then he went to Ephesus. Acquila and Priscilla accompanied him and stayed in Ephesus while Paul went on a tour to strengthen churches which he had established. While he was away Apollos came to Ephesus and preached in the synagogue. He was well informed in Old Testament teaching and had been baptized by John the Baptist, but did not know about Calvary and Easter, the Ascension and Pentecost. Acquila and Priscilla took him to their home "and expounded unto him the way of God more perfectly."[17] He was convinced, and when he continued his journey and came to Corinth he "helped them much which had believed through grace; for he mightily convinced the Jews, and that publicly, showing by the scriptures that Jesus was Christ."[18]

Apollos was a man of considerable distinction when he was converted through the testimony of Acquila and Priscilla. What we know of him comes from Luke[19] and Paul.[20] He was a fervent expositor of the message of John. Born in Alexandria, he had helpful Greek connections. His talents were such that he was welcome in the synagogue when he preached there.[21] After his more complete conversion he probably maintained his synagogue connections, but was sufficiently popular among the Christians who now met in the house of Acquila and Priscilla, that some of the saints preferred his ministry to that of Paul.[22] Nevertheless it appears that he and Paul were close friends and fellow ministers. Paul stayed in Ephesus for about three years and it became one of the major centers of evangelism for the region.

The Jewish colony in Philippi was small, and Paul and Silas joined a group of women who were meeting by a river where prayer was made. According to the record,

a certain woman named Lydia...which worshiped God, heard us; whose heart the Lord opened, that she attended unto the things which were spoken of Paul. And when she was baptized, and her household, she besought us, saying, If ye have judged me to be faithful to the Lord, come into my house, and abide there.

Thereafter Paul and his company, at her request, made the home of Lydia their headquarters.[23]

The country surrounding Philippi was the richest and most prosperous of the region. The purple stripe worn on the togas of Roman officials and the togas themselves were very expensive and were an important product of the area. It is supposed that Lydia, who was a seller of purple cloth, was a fairly wealthy woman.[24] Luke has drawn her portrait in Acts 16, but she is not mentioned elsewhere. It is possible that she died before Paul wrote his letter to Philippi.

It was at Philippi, subsequently, that Paul and Silas were imprisoned on charges that they were "teaching customs which it was not lawful for them (the people of Philippi) to receive." The brethren were scourged and put in the stocks in the prison. But during the night the doors of the prison were blown open by an earthquake. The panic-stricken jailor was on the point of suicide when he heard the prisoners "praying and singing praises unto God." Impressed, he went to Paul and Silas and said "Sirs, what must I do to be saved?"[25] It is not unlikely that what he had in mind was avoiding the punishment likely to follow the escape of his prisoners. Paul reassured him at this point, and then went on to proclaim a much wider salvation, speaking unto him the word of the

Lord, and reaching out to all that were in the house. The members of the household were convinced and were baptized.

We do not know how many were included in the "households" of Lydia and the jailor. The term may have included relatives or employees or friends. It is important to note, however, that in the early church it was taken for granted that religion was considered an affair to be shared with one's nearest and dearest.

These I have mentioned who were close to the apostles in the early testimony are named in the New Testament, but there were many more whose contribution deserves comment. The names of some can be found at a glance as we leaf through the final sentences of the epistles. And if we venture into the post-apostolic period there are many more, a high percentage of them being martyrs. The most prominent are probably those named as co-workers of the leaders, such as Paul and Peter. Among these were Barnabas the trailblazer for Paul who may have been either a later apostle or one of the seventy. Mark and Silas and Timothy were also missionary companions of Paul and Barnabas. Then there was Nicodemus, one of the Sanhedrin who had a significant conversation with Jesus, provided the burial place for him, and is named in fairly credible tradition as one of the seventy. We remember Tabitha (Dorcas) who was raised from the dead under the ministry of Peter, and Rhoda who knew Peter's voice, but could hardly believe that he was at the door. And we remember with particular gratitude James—the Lord's brother—whose wise conservatism helped so much in the Council at Jerusalem and in the endeavor to promote Jewish-Christian unity.

Of course, we also remember Judas, the man who

betrayed his Lord, and who it is so easy to despise if we can only forget our own guilt.[26] Also Ananias and Sapphira who agreed together to "tempt the spirit of the Lord," and Simon who tried to buy the power to confer the Holy Spirit.

The picture of the saints as a group shows them to have been men and women of faith and courage, prayerful and expectant, witnesses for God out of their own experience with God, growing in unity and spiritual awareness as they shared in the common life of the fellowship: studying the scriptures, sharing the sacraments, growing into the likeness of their Lord.

The spirit in which the early saints bore their testimony was a major factor in its effectiveness. What they imparted to their hearers was not mere news—it was news of God's dealings with people, and it had changed their lives. They were on fire with it, and they commended it with passionate concern for its liberating truth and with evident love for all sorts of men and women and children. They made no monetary or similar gains for its proclamation. The reason for their testimony was gratitude for the gifts of God to them: gifts given freely and to be dispensed with similar freedom. There was joy in their ministering.

There was also convincing power. Even their persecutors admitted this. When Peter and his fellow apostles were examined before the Sanhedrin in connection with the healing of the lame man "they saw the boldness of Peter and John, and perceived that they were unlearned and ignorant men, they marvelled; and they took knowledge of them that they had been with Jesus."[27]

Nicodemus, a member of the Sanhedrin had spoken much of the same testimony: "We know that thou art a teacher come from God; for no man can do these miracles that thou dost, except God be with him."[28]

Mark's gospel affirms this: "They [the apostles] went forth, and preached every where, the Lord working with them, and confirming the word with signs following."[29]

REFERENCES

1. I John 1:1-3 KJ.
2. Luke 24:1, 10.
3. Luke 24:12.
4. Luke 24:26.
5. Luke 24:32-33.
6. Luke 24:41-43.
7. Acts 1:3.
8. Romans 1:4.
9. Acts 1:6.
10. Acts 1:3.
11. Mark 1:14-15; Matthew 6:33 KJ.
12. Acts 1:7.
13. Acts 1:8.
14. Acts 4:4-20.
15. I Corinthians 15:6.
16. Acts 8:26-40.
17. Acts 18:26.
18. Acts 18:27-28.
19. Acts 18:24; 19:1.
20. I Corinthians 1:12; 16:12; Titus 3:13.
21. Acts 18:24-26.
22. I Corinthians 1:12; 3:3-6.
23. Acts 16:14-15.
24. Acts 16:13-14.
25. Acts 16:30.
26. Hebrews 6:4-6.
27. Acts 4:13.
28. John 3:2.
29. Mark 16:21.

Now unto him that is able to do exceeding abundantly above all that we ask or think, according to the power that worketh in us, Unto him be glory in the church by Christ Jesus throughout all ages, world without end. Amen.

—Ephesians 3:20-21

Chapter 16

The Holy Spirit and the Testimony of Group Life

It is probable that the most important evidence commending the faith of the saints to earnest inquirers was the invincible optimism of the believers. Peter called it "joy unspeakable and full of glory."[1] John Weiss called it "a mood of victorious, jubilant, happiness and self-confidence." He went on to say that "unless we understand this we cannot understand the primitive church." It was part of the business of being Christian, and had been so from the resurrection and Pentecost.

This joy was demonstrated by Jesus throughout his life. The writer of the Hebrew letter wrote that disciples of the Lord Jesus can find resources for courage in the midst of difficulties by

looking unto Jesus, the author and finisher of our faith; who for the joy that was set before him endured the cross, despising the shame, and is set down at the right hand of the throne of God.[2]

The joy of the saints was joy in the Holy Spirit: the inner joy which attends lives of discipleship, the sharing of the work of the Lord Jesus among others. But it was likely to be costly. Jesus warned of both the costs and the rewards:

Blessed are ye when men shall hate you, and when they shall separate you from among them, and shall reproach you, and cast out your name as evil, for the Son of Man's sake. Rejoice ye in that day, and leap for joy; for behold your reward is great in heaven; for in like manner did their fathers unto the prophets.[3]

The words of Jesus were fulfilled both as to the persecution and the accompanying joy of the sincerely and sacrificially committed. The saints took heart in this. They knew of the examination of the apostles before a hostile Sanhedrin for preaching Christ. And they knew, too, that after the apostles were released they resumed their preaching, were re-arrested, examined, punished, given further warning, and again released. The apostles repeated their testimony: "Rejoicing that they were counted worthy to suffer shame for his name."[4]

Years later the apostle Paul, unconcerned regarding his personal safety when "under the constraint of the Spirit," went toward Jerusalem after it had been prophesied that "bonds and afflictions" awaited him there, saying,

None of these things move me, neither count I my life dear unto myself, so that I might finish my course with joy, and the ministry, which I have received from the Lord Jesus to testify the gospel of the grace of God.[5]

Jude, the almost forgotten brother of James, felt a similar concern that the saints should maintain their faith amid the multiplying temptations around them. His brief letter ends:

Now unto him that is able to keep you from falling, and to present you faultless before the presence of his glory with exceeding joy, to the only wise God our Savior, be glory and majesty, and dominion and power, both now and ever. Amen.[6]

Three thousand of those present at Pentecost were baptized, and many others came into the church shortly thereafter. This was an extremely impressive gain which probably included many who had been attracted by the preaching of Jesus in recent months now brought to completion by the testimony of the resurrection. Jerusalem was a large city, however, and many who had joined in the demand for the release of Barabbas and the crucifixion of Jesus were still unconverted. Of these, many said, mockingly, "These men [the endowed disciples] are full of new wine."[7] There were enough of them that Peter answered them in his sermon.

It was against such opposition as this that the new movement began, but the nucleus of the believers were steadfast in their faith. After a time Paul wrote, "I am not ashamed of the gospel of Christ; for it is the power of God unto salvation to every one that believeth; to the Jew first, and also to the Greek."[8] John saw the whole world lying under the dominion of the evil one, but never faltered in his message that "God is light, and in him is no darkness at all." Despised and persecuted though many of them were, the early saints lived in the assurance of faith and their assurance carried weight.

Much of the joy of the saints was rooted in their conviction that their sins had been forgiven. When they realized the magnitude of their guilt in connection with the crucifixion of their Lord, it seemed that there was no solution to the problem. Peter made the situation fully clear and moved quickly to announce the solution, making it one keynote of the sermon at Pentecost. When the repentant Jews cried out, "Men and brethren, what shall we do?" he answered them: "Repent, and be baptized every one of you in the name of Jesus Christ for the remission of sins, and ye shall receive the gift of the Holy Ghost."[9] There was the answer in all its rich fullness. They must truly repent and must signal this by their enlistment in the cause of Christ, and they would be granted a new Spirit. Many of his hearers responded to this call.[10] Their experience justified one of the great messages of the Old Testament:

Blessed is he whose transgression is forgiven, whose sin is covered. Blessed is the man unto whom the Lord imputeth not iniquity, and in whose spirit there is no guile. . . . Many sorrows shall be to the wicked: but he that trusteth in the Lord, mercy shall compass him about. Be glad in the Lord, and rejoice, ye righteous: and shout for joy all ye that are upright in heart.[11]

Remembering his part in the death of Stephen, Paul referred to himself as the chief of sinners,[12] but knowing that this was known also to the church he wrote with the authority of personal experience:

There is . . . no condemnation to them which are in Christ Jesus, who walk not after the flesh, but after the Spirit. For the law of the Spirit of life in Christ Jesus hath made me free from the law of sin and death.[13]

Their joy in Christ was so characteristic of the early saints that it could not fail to be noticed by honest inquirers. It conveyed a group testimony as well as a number of supporting personal affirmations. It could be seen in the fellowship of the saints, and was often mentioned in their preaching and conversations. In the Philippian letter Paul is reported as writing, "Our conversation is in heaven."[14] But the Moffatt version is clearer, and still carries the ring of truth when it renders the passage; "We are a colony of heaven." The thought here is that heaven is the homeland of the saints: their native country. They rejoiced in its glories, and shared them in anticipation of greater glories yet to come.

The apostles, who knew the joy of forgiveness, made its announcement an integral part of their evangelistic message. Said Peter to the Sanhedrin:

The God of our fathers raised up Jesus, whom ye slew and hanged on a tree. Him hath God exalted with his right hand to be a Prince and a Savior, for to give repentance to Israel, and forgiveness of sins. And we are his witnesses of these things; and so is also the Holy Ghost, whom God hath given to them that obey him.[15]

Those who heard such preaching, and noted its joyous acceptance among the believers, saw it as a significant part of the joy they had seen in the fellowship. That this was so was confirmed again and again. Paul wrote to the Ephesians:

Grieve not the Holy Spirit of God, whereby ye are sealed unto the day of redemption. Let all bitterness, and wrath, and anger, and clamor, and evil speaking, be put away from you, with all malice; and be ye kind one to another, tender-hearted, forgiving one another, even as God for Christ's sake hath forgiven you.[16]

Peter in like fashion put together the living of the life of faith and the bearing of testimony:

Sanctify the Lord God in your hearts; and be ready always to give an answer to every man that asketh you a reason of the hope that is in you with meekness and fear: having a good conscience; that, whereas they speak evil of you, as of evil doers, they may be ashamed that falsely accuse your good conversation in Christ.[17]

The New English Bible substitutes "with modesty and respect" for "with meekness and fear" and the Knox version renders it "courteously and with due reverence."

The New Testament contains many indications of the effects of the Christian evangel. Mark says that Jesus himself called James and John, his brother, "the sons of thunder."[18] But the time came when John was known in the fellowship as "the disciple whom Jesus loved."[19] And Peter, who denied him, Jesus likened to a rock.[20] Something of these changes appears to have been in the mind of Paul when he wrote, "We all, with open face beholding as in a glass the glory of the Lord, are changed into the same image from glory to glory, even as by the Spirit of the Lord."[21]

I do not presume that enquirers went among the saints with a checklist of spiritual qualities. Rather, it is likely that any who were interested either accepted invitations to the meetings of the believers or just attended without invitation. All who were seriously interested were welcomed and were likely to be impressed by the joy so freely demonstrated. The sense of forgiveness was also felt deeply and was likely to be impressive, for the people of the apostolic age were more aware of the breadth and depth and seriousness of sin than their modern successors. The sobriety (temperance) and the goodness and gentleness which Paul listed for the Galatians as fruits of the Spirit,[22] would also be noteworthy. But probably deeper than these, and a source and stay for several of them, was "the peace of God which passeth all understanding."[23]

This peace was very precious to the early Saints, comforting them in their tribulations.[24] It found place in their remembrance of the Old Testament: "Thou wilt keep him in perfect peace whose mind is stayed on thee; because he trusteth in thee."[25]

With such a background, and in a time of such deep need, it found a habitual place in the salutations of their letters. In the Galatian letter, for example, Paul wrote: "Grace be unto you, and peace, from God the Father, and from our Lord Jesus Christ."[26]

The reference made by John is similar, but a little more elaborate: "Grace be with you, mercy and peace from God the Father, and from the Lord Jesus Christ, the Son of the Father, in truth and love."[27]

The Apostle Paul knew from his own experience that the peace of Christ is creative. So did the saints, and inquirers heard their testimonies. The one-time insecurity of those who did not know Christ had given place to love and confidence in the power of God. Paul admonished the saints of Colossae to let this peace rule in their hearts.[28] In the inner realm from which so much that is petty can issue thoughtlessly the balanced judgment which is born of confidence in the Lord Jesus is to be cultivated and trusted. So Paul wrote to his son in the gospel "God hath not given us the spirit of fear, but of power, and of love, and of a sound mind."[29]

And to his friends in Rome he wrote, "Now the God of hope fill you with all joy and peace in believing, that you may abound in hope, through the power of the Holy Ghost."[30]

Paul listed peace as a fruit of the Spirit, contrasting it with the works of the flesh.[31] It is unique: nothing else brings such assurances for time and eternity. Although it demands something of those who would enjoy it, it is, in the final analysis, beyond all human understanding.[32] It is a manifestation of the Spirit of God, and helps the believer to distinguish between the eternal values approved of God and those which are of the earth—time-bound and perishable.

Their experience of this peace, and their confidence in commending it to others opened their eyes to the powers of the gospel. It is altogether likely, for instance, that they saw depth in the statement of Peter at Pentecost that "he [Jesus] hath God raised up, having loosed the pangs of death; because it was not possible that he should be holden of it."[33]

Joy in the testimony of their redemption through Christ, and of the guidance and inner witness of the Holy Spirit, was of the life of the Christian fellowship. It was the atmosphere which the saints breathed. Peter wrote of Jesus Christ, "whom having not seen, ye love; in whom, though now ye see him not, yet believing, ye rejoice with joy unspeakable and full of glory."[34]

And Paul, remembering what his own conversion had meant to him, wrote to the saints in Corinth: "Thanks be unto God for his unspeakable gift."[35]

The leaders of the early church counted on the conversion of persons of diverse talents to guide the spiritual growth of later converts. Paul was especially blessed in bringing unity out of diversity. He wrote to the saints in Ephesus:

> To the praise of the glory of his grace...wherein he hath abounded toward us in all wisdom and prudence.[36]
>
> In whom also we have obtained an inheritance.[37]
>
> Through him we both have access by one Spirit unto the Father.[38]

So that we

> are no more strangers and foreigners, but fellow citizens with the saints, and of the household of God; and are built upon the foundation of the apostles and prophets, Jesus Christ himself being the chief corner stone; in whom all the building fitly framed together groweth unto a holy temple in the Lord; In whom ye also are builded together for an habitation of God through the Spirit.[39]

The calling of the saints is to

> walk worthy of the vocation wherewith ye are called, with all lowliness and meekness, with long-suffering, forbearing one another in love; endeavoring to keep the unity of the Spirit in the bond of peace.[40]

It is within the fellowship as thus conceived that "speaking the truth in love, [we] may grow up into him in all things, which is the head, even Christ."[41]

To this end we are counseled to

> let all bitterness, and wrath, and anger, and clamor, and evil speaking, be put away from you, with all malice; And be ye kind

one to another, tender hearted, forgiving one another, even as God, for Christ's sake hath forgiven you.[42]

This was written nearly two thousand years ago. It is still timely.

REFERENCES

1. I Peter 1:8.
2. Hebrews 12:2.
3. Luke 6:22-23.
4. Acts 3:1-9, 13-26; 4:1-31; 5:17-42.
5. Acts 20:24.
6. Jude 24-25.
7. Acts 2:13.
8. Romans 1:16.
9. Acts 2:38.
10. Acts 2:36-41.
11. Psalm 32:1-2, 10-11 KJ.
12. I Timothy 1:15.
13. Romans 8:1-2.
14. Philippians 3:20.
15. Acts 5:30-32. See also Acts 13:36-39; Colossians 1:14; I John 2:12.
16. Ephesians 4:30-32.
17. I Peter 3:15-16 KJ.
18. Mark 3:17 KJ.
19. John 13:23, 19:26, 20:2-10, 21:20-23
20. Matthew 16:19.
21. II Corinthians 3:18.
22. Galatians 5:22.
23. Philippians 4:7.
24. John 16:33; Romans 5:3, 12:12.
25. Isaiah 26:3; Psalm 119:165.
26. Galatians 1:3. See also I Timothy 1:2; II Timothy 2:1, 2; Titus 1:14.
27. II John 3.
28. Colossians 3:15.
29. II Timothy 1:7.
30. Romans 15:13. See also Romans 12:18; 15:33.

31. Galatians 5:22.
32. Philippians 4:7.
33. Acts 2:24.
34. I Peter 1:8.
35. II Corinthians 9:15.
36. Ephesians 1:6, 8.
37. Ephesians 1:11.
38. Ephesians 2:18.
39. Ephesians 2:19-22.
40. Ephesians 4:1-3.
41. Ephesians 4:15.
42. Ephesians 4:31-32.

"Outwitted" has been called the world's greatest social quatrain:

He drew a circle that shut me out—
Heretic, rebel, a thing to flout.
But Love and I had the wit to win;
We drew a circle that took him in!

—Edwin Markham

Chapter 17

The Fellowship of the Spirit

The birth of John the Baptist was announced to John's father, Zachaeus, by an angel who said,

He shall be filled with the Holy Ghost, even from his mother's womb. And many of the children of Israel shall he turn to the Lord their God; And he shall go before the Lord in the spirit and power of Elias, to turn the hearts of the fathers to the children, and the disobedient to the wisdom of the just, to make ready a people prepared for the Lord.[1]

This is an important scripture, and our purpose in citing it is to note that John was to prepare "a people." His mission would not be fulfilled by the conversion of a large number of individuals, but only as those converted were knit together in a fellowship reaching across the generations.

Other scriptures show that the building of a fellowship was preliminary to the fellowship of the Lord Jesus Christ. Paul, for example, wrote to the saints in Corinth, "Ye are the temple of the living God; as God hath said, I will dwell in them, and walk in them; and I will be their God, and they shall be my people."[2]

Toward the end of his long life John, the apostle of love, carried forward the same basic theme:

That which we have seen and heard declare we unto you, that ye also may have fellowship with us; and truly our fellowship is with the Father, and with his Son Jesus Christ.... If we say that we have fellowship with him, and walk in darkness, we lie, and do not the truth. But if we walk in the light, as he is in the light, we have fellowship one with another, and the blood of Jesus Christ his Son cleanseth us from all sin.[3]

There was nothing superficial about the unity which Jesus enjoined. He prayed that it should be of the same order as the love which he shared with the Father: "Holy Father, keep through thine own name those whom thou hast given me, that they may be one, as we are."[4]

And he prayed:

Neither pray I for these alone, but for them also which shall believe on me through their words; that they all may be one; as thou, Father, art in me, and I in thee, that they also may be one in us; that the world may believe that thou hast sent me.[5]

What God wills is not mere unity, but community. He seeks a community of love in which he reigns in every human heart and in every human relationship.[6]

After the ascension of the Lord, and the endowment of the Twelve with the Holy Spirit, the way was clear for the apostles to enter into their responsibilities as special witnesses of the resurrection and the builders of the church.[7] They did this under a high sense of commission, and it is altogether likely that in perfecting the organization they had to draw heavily on some of the "five hundred brethren" who had seen the Lord after his resurrection.[8]

The first public meeting under the direction of the apostles was on the day of Pentecost. The record of what happened at that time emphasizes the unity of the disciples under the guidance of the Spirit:

When the day of Pentecost was fully come they were all with one accord in one place. And suddenly there came a sound from heaven as of a rushing mighty wind, and it filled all the house where they were sitting. And there appeared unto them cloven tongues like as of fire, and it rested upon each of them. And they were all filled with the Holy Ghost.[9]

The New Testament bears repeated testimony to the strong sense of fellowship among the saints. A Greek word used frequently in this connection is *koinonia*. The word is important to us today because of its intrinsic meaning and because it is used so frequently in modern discussions of the nature of the early Christian church. *Koinonia* is one of a group of related words which have to do with the idea of fellowship. It is used fifteen times in the New Testament. One of the related words occurs ten times and means *companion* or *fellow-worker*.

Koinonia as used in the New Testament conveys these ideas: *A specially warm kind of sharing: fellowship within a group held together by a passionately shared common faith.* John wrote, "That which we have seen and heard declare we unto you, that ye also may have fellowship with us; and truly our fellowship is with the Father and with his Son, Jesus Christ."[10]

Sharing affectionately with the less fortunate, as did many Christians from distant places with the poor of Jerusalem. Paul wrote,

He hath given to the poor; his righteousness remaineth for ever. Now he that ministereth seed to the sower both minister bread for your food, and multiply your seed sown, and increase the fruit of your righteousness; (Being enriched in every thing to all bountifulness, which causeth through us thanksgiving to God).[11]

Partnership with Christ. Paul wrote to the saints in Philippi: "I thank my God upon every remembrance of you, always in every prayer of mine for you all making request with joy, for your fellowship in the gospel, from the first day till now."[12]

The fellowship of the saints is born of the Spirit. Paul emphasized this:

If there be therefore any consolation in Christ, if any comfort of love, if any fellowship of the Spirit, if any bowels and mercies, fulfill ye my joy, that ye be likeminded, having the same love, being of one accord, of one mind.[13]

The rich fellowship shared among the saints of the apostolic church is clearly evident in the New Testament epistles. In the Roman letter, for example, thirty-five persons are named as friends of Paul. Some references are quite specific, showing Paul's appreciation of past association and hope for its continuance. These references are all perfectly natural, and testify across the centuries of the spirit of the saints of the first generation. It has been equally characteristic of the saints of succeeding generations. It is a precious fruit of the Spirit. In our present situation the inclusion of the ten women mentioned in the letter throws an interesting light on the attitude of Paul when women were not usually highly regarded.

Several years ago my wife and I were returning from a field assignment when car trouble forced us to stay overnight in a small town. The car was not ready the next morning, which was Sunday, and we had no branch nearby, so we went to the Methodist church. The pastor was on vacation, and a retired minister preached. He began by saying, "I want to talk with you this morning about Brother Quartus." Then he went on to explain that the King James version of Romans 16:33 with its reference to Quartus as "a brother" is not supported by more recent translations, and should be rendered "brother" (Goodspeed has "our brother" and the American Revised Version "the brother"). Then the minister spent about fifteen minutes distinguishing between the coldness of "a brother" and the warmth of "brother" with its presumption of intimacy and friendship. Certainly "brother" fits in well with the other greetings of the letter. Now, as I write, I do not remember the name of that town, or of the minister, or of any other details of our stay. But I have a sense of brotherhood with Quartus and with his friend Paul, and with their friends from ancient Rome and Corinth, whence the epistle was probably written.

In his concern to convey the diverse values in church association Paul used many illustrations. Of these, the most fruitful has probably been his characterization of the church as the body of Christ[14] and the "habitation of God through the Spirit"[15] and the "household of God."[16] To the saints in Corinth Paul wrote: "Ye are the body of Christ, and members in particular."[17]

Consideration of the church as a body (an organism rather than an organization) is of major importance. Paul did not picture the saints as parts of a building in whose structure bricks and mortar and other materials are combined, but as living members of a body—a family—bound together and made one by their common experience of the Spirit. Though everyone who is born of the Spirit has a special calling, this calling is to be exercised to the intent that

speaking the truth in love [we] may grow up into him in all things, which is the head, even Christ; from whom the whole body fitly joined together and compacted by that which every joint supplieth, according to the effectual working in the measure of every part, maketh increase of the body unto the edifying of itself in love.[18]

It was out of concern for maintaining this high quality of church life that the author of the letter to the Hebrews wrote a few years later:

Let us hold fast to the profession of our faith without wavering...and let us consider one another to provoke unto love and to good works; not forsaking the assembling of ourselves together...exhorting one another.[19]

The early saints became members of the church through baptism and the endowment of the Holy Spirit. Paul emphasized this: "By one Spirit are we all baptized into one body."[20] They were no more "strangers and foreigners, but fellow citizens with the saints, and of the household of God."[21]

They were united in the communion of the Holy Spirit, so that one of Paul's wishes for them sounds perfectly fitting at the end of his second Corinthian letter: "The grace of the Lord Jesus Christ, and the love of God, and the communion of the Holy Ghost, be with you all."[22]

The young church was guided by the Holy Spirit, and its members were counseled by revelation: "He that hath an ear, let him hear what the Spirit saith unto the churches."[23]

The unity of the saints was especially evident when they rejoiced together in the goodness and power of God, and when they were clearly aided by the Spirit in achieving important decisions.[24] Paul took great satisfaction in this unity, as appears from a letter he wrote to the saints in Philippi: "Fulfill ye my joy, that ye be like minded, having the same love, being of one accord, of one mind. Let nothing be done through strife or vainglory; but in lowliness of mind."[25]

That this was a fundamental concern is shown in the conclusion of the Corinthian letter referred to.[26]

There were many other factors contributing to the maturing fellowship of the early Christian church. The saints shared a common faith and life which was probably most revealing in their worship. Almost all of those whose worship life was centered in Jerusalem were Jews who had been familiar with the words of the prophets and psalmists from childhood. It was natural, therefore, that much of the worship to which they now felt directed should be built on the Old Testament, which Jesus himself had loved. But these scriptures were read and sung and understood from a new vantage point, for they were seen in the light of the life and ministry of the Lord Jesus. Familiar language gradually took on richer meaning for their understanding of the nature of the Messiah was soon interpreted in terms of the suffering servant of Isaiah (Isaiah 53, and others). The doctrine of the atonement did not leap to the forefront of their consciousness, but its elements were thought and prayed about and received with deep gratitude long before any formal statement was set forth. Together, in the mood of adoration, the saints began to understand what Paul meant when later he wrote to the church in Ephesus:

We have redemption through his blood, and forgiveness of sins, according to the riches of his grace; wherein he hath abounded toward us in all wisdom and prudence; having made known unto us the mystery of his will.[27]

And to Timothy:

(. . . without controversy, great is the mystery of godliness,) God was manifest in the flesh, justified in the Spirit, seen of angels, preached unto the Gentiles, believed on in the world, received up into glory.[28]

This maturing of faith and of the love for God which accompanied it, laid a welcome burden on the worshiping saints. To pattern their lives on the life of the Lord Jesus was seen as requiring and inspiring them to share the sufferings which their leader had borne so courageously. So there grew up a devotion to the fellowship of the sufferings of Christ. Paul wrote to the Corinthians:

We are troubled on every side, yet not distressed; we are perplexed, but not in despair; persecuted, but not forsaken; cast down, but not destroyed....Though our outward man perish, yet the inward man is renewed day by day....We look not at the things which are seen; but at the things which are not seen, for the things which are seen are temporal; but the things which are not seen are eternal.[29]

There was deep spiritual reason for this optimism. These early saints knew what had happened to Jesus, and that what at first had appeared to be the most abject defeat had become the prelude to the most glorious victory. But, quite clearly, the victory was not yet complete. They saw this as their "tribulations" continued, and made it a means of grace, encouraging and supporting each other. Seemingly very ordinary persons joined in what Paul called "the fellowship of his sufferings"[30] and in his basic affirmation of faith: "Thanks be to God, which giveth us the victory through our Lord Jesus Christ."[31]

REFERENCES

1. Luke 1:15-17.
2. II Corinthians 6:16.
3. I John 1:3-4, 6-7.
4. John 17:11.
5. John 17:20-21.
6. John A. McKay, *God's Order*, MacMillan, 63.
7. Ephesians 2:20.
8. I Corinthians 15:6.
9. Acts 2:1-4.
10. I John 1:3.
11. II Corinthians 9:9-11.
12. Philippians 1:3-5 KJ.
13. Philippians 2:1-2.
14. Ephesians 1:22-23. See also Colossians 1:16-24.
15. Ephesians 2:22.
16. Ephesians 2:19. See also Galatians 6:10.

17. I Corinthians 12:27.
18. Ephesians 4:15-16.
19. Hebrews 10:23-25.
20. I Corinthians 12-13.
21. Ephesians 2:19-22.
22. II Corinthians 13:14.
23. Revelation 3:6, 13, 22.
24. Acts 11:19-26.
25. Philippians 2:1-3.
26. II Corinthians 13-14.
27. Ephesians 1:7-9; 3:3-5.
28. I Timothy 3:16.
29. II Corinthians 4:8-9, 16, 18.
30. Philippians 3:10.
31. I Corinthians 15:57.

Then spake Jesus again unto them,
saying. I am the light of the world; he
that followeth me shall not walk in
darkness, but shall have the light of life.

—John 8:12

Chapter 18

The Holy Spirit
and
The Expanding Church

From its beginning the saints believed the Christian church was the old Israel reconstituted according to the will of God, by the authority of the Lord Jesus, and empowered by the Holy Spirit.

Apparently Stephen had this in mind when he said to the Jewish leaders that Moses was with the church in the wilderness.[1] From a similar background Paul referred to the Hebrew leaders of an earlier time as "our Fathers."[2] It was the assumption of James at the great council of Jerusalem[3] and of Peter[4] and James.[5]

The insight which enabled the early Saints to recognize the preparatory nature of the guidance given the people of Israel brought them many rich blessings. The early evangelists, for example, could assume that their Jewish hearers already knew a great deal about the declarations of the prophets concerning the character and purpose of God. The Hebrew scriptures became their scriptures. Thus Paul wrote to the saints in Rome that "whatsoever things were written aforetime were written for our learning, that we through patience and comfort of the Scriptures might have hope."[6]

The majority of the saints in Rome at that time were converts with Gentile backgrounds, and the scriptures referred to were the books of the Hebrew canon.

Despite indebtedness to the ancient faith, the church as it was reconstituted under the leadership of the apostles had many distinguishing marks. Chief among these, of course, was the experience of the guidance and liberating power of the Holy Spirit, which quickened and vitalized the saints' memories of the life and ministry of the Lord Jesus Christ. This was emphasized in the apostolic preaching and the group fellowship in the Lord's Supper.[7]

The ministry of the Lord Jesus Christ and the constant presence of his Spirit were apparently taken for granted. From very early in the church life the personality and teaching of the Lord Jesus and the experiences spoken of by the disciples as "the outpouring of his Spirit" were commanding factors in the testimony and fellowship of the saints. Time has robbed us of the sharp awareness of the pioneers of the wonder and power of the resurrection.[8] But these initial witnesses knew that the Son of God had lived among them, and had died for them, and was now enthroned in glory with his Father. And they knew that the Spirit which Jesus had shown was now being felt among them.

A major factor in the rapid growth of the church membership was the proselyting of the missionary-minded Christians among the Jews whom they met in the synagogues. These centers of Jewish instruction and worship could be found in almost every city of any size throughout the eastern provinces of the Roman empire. The synagogues attracted many "God fearers" who did not become Jews but accepted much of the Jewish moral teaching. Of these were such men as Cornelius, a Roman centurion, and the Ethiopian treasurer who had been baptized by Philip.

The ministry available in the synagogues was deeply affected by the coming of the Christians. Just as the early preaching of Jesus in Nazareth had stirred the resentment of the patriotic Jews, so now the fullness of the gospel was regarded by many as incompatible with the Judaism and the teaching of the Law to which they had been committed hitherto. As many of the God-fearers were lost to the Christians the opposition of the Jews became stronger and better organized. The first significant opposition to the young church came from the Jews.

One of the outstanding leaders of the Christian forces other than the apostles was Stephen who was well known as one of those in charge of the distribution of food to the needy. He was described by Luke as "full of faith and power" who "did great wonders and miracles among the people."[9] It was not long until Stephen met the Judaisers in a public "dispute" where according to Luke they (Stephen's opponents) "were not able to resist the wisdom and the spirit by which he spoke."[10]

On the initiative of his opponents Paul was brought before the Sanhedrin and charged with having spoken against the temple and the Law.[11] Stephen saw that this was an excellent opportunity to set forth his faith before the most important council of his people. With great courage, therefore, he gave little attention to the specific charges brought against him. Instead he made a carefully reasoned presentation of the purpose of God in choosing Israel and its culmination in the life and ministry of the Lord Jesus. In support of

195

his thesis he pointed out that Moses was recognized as a great ruler and deliverer and had prophesied that "a prophet shall the Lord your God raise up unto you of your brethren, like unto me."[12]

Stephen then spoke of the building of the temple by Solomon, but he also recalled the prophetic word that "the Most High [who created all things] dwelleth not in temples made with hands."[13]

Stephen ended with a denunciation of the known current practices of both his judges and his accusers:

Ye stiffnecked and uncircumcised in heart and ears, ye do always resist the Holy Ghost; as your fathers did, so do ye. Which of the prophets have not your fathers persecuted? and they have slain them which showed before of the coming of the Just One; of whom ye have been now the betrayers and murderers. Who have received the law by the disposition of angels, and have not kept it.[14]

The indignation of his hearers had mounted, and now they "ran upon him with one accord, and cast him out of the city and stoned him" to death.[15] But Stephen

...being full of the Holy Ghost, looked up steadfastly into heaven, and saw the glory of God, and Jesus standing on the right hand of God, and said, Behold I see the heavens opened and I see the Son of Man standing on the right hand of God.[16]

Stephen's address was acclaimed among many of the Greek-speaking believers who were beginning to see the importance of the world mission of the gospel above the minutiae of the law by fulfilling the deeper meaning of the covenant. Their familiarity with the prophecies of Daniel[17] and the reference to the "Son of Man standing on the right hand of God" stressed the note of universality and opened up for them the great vistas of the spread of the word of salvation.

Saul (later known as Paul) held the clothes of those who stoned Stephen, and soon afterward resumed his journey to Damascus where he expected to continue his persecution of the Christians. But on his way the Lord Jesus appeared to him, converted him, and called him to be one of his special witnesses. Little is written in Acts about the details of this conversion experience. It is clear, however, that from it Paul emerged as a new man in Christ Jesus.

As we have noted, there was a remarkable increase in the number of disciples at Pentecost. The next great increase followed the persecution to which the saints were subjected after the death of Stephen.[18] Luke wrote that the believers were "scattered abroad" and

> traveled as far as Phoenice, and Cyprus, and Antioch, preaching the word to none but unto the Jews only. And some of them were men of Cyprus and Cyrene, which, when they were come to Antioch, spake unto the Grecians, preaching the Lord Jesus. And the hand of the Lord was with them; and a great number believed, and turned unto the Lord. Then tidings of these things came unto the ears of the church which was in Jerusalem; and they sent forth Barnabas, that he should go as far as Antioch. Who, when he came, and had seen the grace of God, was glad, and exhorted them all, that with purpose of heart they would cleave unto the Lord...and much people were added unto the Lord.[19]

One of the results of this dispersion was that the gospel was planted in Pisidian-Antioch, a number of the local Greek-speaking citizens being converted. When the news of these gains reached Jerusalem, the leaders there sent Barnabas, "a good man and full of the Holy Ghost[20] to survey the situation. Seeing the promise of growth in the evident local support, Barnabas went to see Paul in Tarsus, Paul's hometown, and persuaded him to join in an evangelical campaign reaching out from Antioch through all the surrounding region. At that time Antioch was the third largest city in the world (after Rome and Alexandria) and had a large Jewish community, among whom were many God-fearers. Paul and Barnabas stayed for a year, preaching, organizing, and strengthening the church and the leaders they discovered, to whom they gave local responsibilities.

One of the most noteworthy of the advances of this remarkable period centered at Caesarea, a modern port having easy access to many important regions which were later evangelized.

Cornelius, a centurion of the Italian band stationed at Caesarea, was "a devout man, and one that feared God with all his house, which gave much alms to the people, and prayed to God always."[21] He was a God-fearer, and probably an attendant at the synagogue services so that he was well informed concerning the teachings of Judaism. Cornelius had a vision at the ninth hour (about 3:00 in the afternoon) in which he was told that his prayers had been acceptable to God, and that he was to send to Joppa for Simon Peter.

After the vision closed, Cornelius sent two of his household servants to Joppa, as he had been instructed. As these men were approaching Joppa, Peter went to the housetop to pray. Here he was given a thrice-repeated vision which prepared him to acknowledge that "what God hath cleansed" he must not call "common."[22]

The men from Caesarea arrived when he was meditating on the meaning of the vision, and Peter went down to greet them, being assured by the Spirit that he should "go with them nothing doubting." By the time the greetings and explanations were over it was too late to start for Caesarea, so Peter arranged for the visitors to stay overnight. The next day they went to Caesarea.

When Peter and his party arrived he found Cornelius and his friends awaiting him. These had had prior contact with the Jews and, probably, with the Christian message. Peter's introductory statement, therefore, was not entirely new. He added his testimony of the crucifixion and resurrection of Jesus, of the apostolic commission to proclaim these things to every nation, and the forgiveness of sins to those who believed.

While Peter yet spake these words, the Holy Ghost fell on them which heard the word. And they of the circumcision which believed were astonished, as many as came with Peter, because that on the Gentiles also was poured out the gift of the Holy Ghost. For they heard them speak with tongues, and magnify God. Then answered Peter, Can any man forbid water, that these should not be baptized, which have received the Holy Ghost as well as we? And he commanded them to be baptized in the name of the Lord.[23]

The Holy Spirit is, with Christ, the creator of the church. But the Holy Spirit is not the creature of the church, for the Christian calling is obedience to the Father and to the Son and to the Holy Spirit. This was revealingly illustrated at the council of church leaders held at Jerusalem.[24] The council was called because the success of the missions to the Gentiles (notably by Paul and Barnabas and by Peter) had deeply disturbed some members of the church in Jerusalem. They feared that the rate of Gentile baptisms meant that soon there would be more Gentile Christians than Jewish Christians. Behind this was the thought that the coming in of those who lacked prior Jewish moral training would debase the Christian ethical appeal. This concern was not without importance, but if the proposal of the Jewish party had been adopted, Christian converts would have had to be circumcised and keep the law of Moses.

Peter and Paul and Barnabas were known to favor the admission of the Gentiles. Peter therefore made an introductory statement indicating the guidance of the Spirit in what had transpired, saying:

God, which knoweth the hearts, bear them [the Gentiles] witness, giving them the Holy Ghost.... And put no difference between us and them, purifying their hearts by faith. Now, therefore, why tempt ye God, to put a yoke upon the neck of the disciples, which neither our fathers nor we were able to bear? But we believe that through the grace of the Lord Jesus Christ we shall be saved, even as they.[25]

Then Paul and Barnabas added their testimonies of the power of God which had attended their ministry among the Gentiles, and James summed up and gave his decision. The decision itself was of great importance, but the method by which they arrived at it was of at least equal importance. It was announced, then approved by the council: "It seemed good to the Holy Spirit, and to us to lay upon you no greater burden."[26]

In weighing the factors of this crucially important decision the leadership of James, the Lord's brother, should be noted. He was a member of the Jerusalem congregation—quite possibly its presiding officer. He was probably familiar with the arguments raised by those who wanted to maintain the Hebraic tone of the spreading movement. Members of the congregation who were present at the council expressed their point of view, and listened while Peter told of his Spirit-guided experience at Caesarea. This was augmented by the testimony of Paul and Barnabas. When James announced his decision it appears to have been accepted unanimously, although there may have been some reluctance on the part of a minority. The procedure which made possible this unanimity was (a) the apparent openness of the discussion; (b) Peter's reminder that "God first visited the Gentiles to take out of them a people for his name"; (c) the confirming testimony of Paul and Barnabas; (d) the Spirit-guided decision of James; and (e) approval by those most directly concerned.

The Book of Acts reports a number of sermons preached in continuance of what had transpired at Pentecost. Of these four stand out:

The basic doctrinal statements of Peter after the healing of the lame man at the gate of the temple.[27]

Stephen's statement of faith before the Sanhedrin.[28]

Peter's address in the house of Cornelius.[29]

The approach and central emphases in these sermons and defenses were determined, in large measure, by the fact that they were addressed to Jews and/or to God-fearers who were acquainted with Judaism. There is one other sermon reported in Acts, however, which does not fall precisely into this pattern. This is the sermon preached by Paul before the Athenians assembled in the Areopagus.

Paul had been persuaded to go to Athens after being attacked at Lystra and Derbe. When his missionary companions had not yet caught up with him, and with nothing else demanding his attention, Paul walked round the city and "his spirit was stirred in him, when he saw the city wholly given to idolatry."[30] As was his custom he went to the synagogue on the sabbath. But, beyond that, day after day he went to the marketplace and joined the discussions carried on there by the Stoics and Epicurians. The Stoics advocated living as consistently as possible with nature, and laid great emphasis on self-sufficiency. At its best Stoicism was marked by great moral earnestness and a high sense of duty and courage in the face of adversity. Their rivals, the Epicurians, considered pleasure to be the chief end of life. They cultivated freedom from disturbing passions and from the fear of death. They placed great value on the life of tranquility. Both groups placed a high value on reason.

Paul's marketplace conversations attracted attention and he was invited to address the Areopagus. In this more formal assembly the audience lacked the background of understanding which could be expected among Jews or God-fearers, but some ground had been broken in his previous conversations. Apparently he was given respectful attention. He wanted to talk about God, and found a suggestive opening when he referred to their altar to "the unknown God." Noting the admission of ignorance which this indicated, he then told of his own faith in the "God that made the world and all things therein."[31] He concluded with an affirmation of the inevitableness of the judgment.

Although no great missionary success was achieved, the record of Paul's ministry in Athens provided helpful guidance for an almost completely new style of approach, one which became more and more important as the church moved into areas having little or no Jewish background. Here are the highlights of what Paul gave primacy:

• He set forth the inadequacy of pagan idolatry:

"God is not worshiped with men's hands, as though he needed anything, seeing he giveth to all life, breath, and all things."[32]

• He tied his presentation to a clear social necessity which their greatest thinkers had approached, saying:

"[God] hath made of one blood all nations of men for to dwell on all the face of the earth, and hath determined the times before appointed, and the bounds of their habitations."[33]

- He sets forth the reasons which indicate God's concern for their well-being, having ordered the common life so

"That they should seek the Lord, if they are willing to find him, for he is not far from every one of us."[34]

- He stated that there are the best of all reasons for this seeking:

"In him we live, and move, and have our being; as certain also of your own poets had said."[35]

These things have been evident from the beginning, Paul said, but have not been understood. God holds no resentment for this. But now that people had heard the truth they had become responsible. They would be judged by One who had lived among them, has died in order to manifest the depth of the love of God, and has been raised from the dead by the power of God.[36]

REFERENCES

1. Acts 7:38.
2. I Corinthians 10:1.
3. Acts 15:28.
4. Acts 10:44-48.
5. James 1:5-7.
6. Romans 15:4. See also II Timothy 3:16-17.
7. I Corinthians 11:23-26.

8. Philippians 2:10.
9. Acts 6:8.
10. Acts 6:10.
11. Acts 6:13.
12. Acts 7:37.
13. Acts 7:48.
14. Acts 7:51-53.
15. Acts 7:55-59.
16. Acts 7:55-56.
17. Daniel 7:13-14.
18. Acts 6:1; 8:1.
19. Acts 11:19-24.
20. Acts 11:24.
21. Acts 10:1-2.
22. Acts 10:15.
23. Acts 10:44-48.
24. Acts 15:1-29.
25. Acts 15:8-11.
26. Acts 15:28.
27. Acts 3:11; 5:2.
28. Acts 6:7-9; 7:60.
29. Acts 10; 11:2-18.
30. Acts 17:16.
31. Acts 17:24.
32. Acts 17:25.
33. Acts 17:26.
34. Acts 17:27.
35. Acts 17:28.
36. Acts 17:31-32.

I know not where His islands lift
Their fronded palms in air;
I only know I cannot drift
Beyond His love and care.

     —John Greenleaf Whittier

Chapter 19

The Grace of the Lord Jesus Christ

Long before the Christian era, when people wished to speak of beauty or to share their awareness of charm such as gave them pleasure, they were likely to use the equivalent of our modern word *grace*. By its incorporation into the Christian vocabulary it became one of the great words of Christian thought and experience.

The prophet-leaders of the children of Israel taught them that they had been delivered from slavery in Egypt and set on their way to becoming a great people by the free and unearned choice of God: his loving-kindness. This word *loving-kindness* was coined by Miles Coverdale to combine the thought of love with that of loyalty, and it was retained in many of the subsequent translations of the Bible to express the attitude of God when confronted by the repeated disloyalty of the Hebrews. Yet while the faithfulness of God to his part of the covenant was never broached, it was always kept in balance by awareness of his unfailing righteousness.

It was the faith of the prophets that grace, or loving-kindness, is a reflection of the nature of the God of the Covenant. In the final analysis it was beyond their understanding, just as the choice of Israel was beyond their understanding. It was a fact of their experience and, when at their best, they were grateful for it, knowing that it was pointed toward their well-being by a power greater than their own.

Though the grace of God is manifest in the Old Testament in his choice of the chosen people, and his continual regard for them despite their many lapses, it is set forth more fully in the New Testament. This is because God's grace is so rich that it cannot be adequately expressed in words. It calls for demonstration in life.

God's healing ministry had obvious values and opened many doors. On one occasion a blind beggar named Bartemaeus was near the Jericho gate when Jesus and a group of his disciples went by. Learning that Jesus was there, Bartemaeus cried out, "Jesus, thou son of David, have mercy on me." Jesus, calling him, said, "What wilt thou that I should do unto thee?" And the blind man answered, "Rabboni, that I may receive my sight." And Jesus said to him, "Go thy way; thy faith hath made thee whole." And straightway he received his sight, and followed him in the way.[1] The narrative gives no further details, but it is not difficult to visualize Bartemaeus telling of his healing as he joined the disciples on the way to Jericho, and having them tell of other healings by the grace of God for those who believed.

There are many other healings recorded in the New Testament. Students often classify them, but for our present purpose we will note only a few which help illustrate the grace of the Lord Jesus. Sometimes this grace is evident from the narrative of its demonstration. At other times it is less direct. Luke, for instance, tells of a healing apparently directly related to the love of a father for his daughter. It concerns Jairus, a ruler of the synagogue, apparently not known as a disciple of the Lord, who went to him in desperation because his daughter, a girl of twelve, seemed to be dying. Jairus sought out the Master, and fell at his feet, and besought him to come to his home and heal the girl.[2] It seems from the record that Jesus started out with Jairus without any debate, but that they were met on the way by a servant who said that the girl had already died. But Jesus encouraged Jairus, and they continued to his house. There Jesus healed the girl and restored her to her parents. Jesus saw that the faith of the father was sufficient to meet the need of the daughter.

John mentions another healing which was seemingly less likely than the healing of persons having faith. The person concerned was Malcus, a servant of the high priest, whose ear Peter cut off. Jesus rebuked Peter, and healed the attendant.[3] We never hear of Malcus again, but the incident is an interesting application of Jesus' principle of loving one's enemies.

Many of the Jews regarded Jesus as a prophet,[4] but we do not know how deep was their regard for him. Of the ten lepers who were healed by Jesus only one came back to acknowledge his debt.[5] Whatever the perception of the five thousand who were fed miraculously, we have no hint that any of them saw here an indication of the Lord's divinity. On the other hand, there may have been many for whom the Lord's life among them prepared the way for later grateful belief. We remember the comment of Nicodemus early in his interview with Jesus: "We know that thou art a teacher come from God; for no man can do these miracles which thou doest, except God be with him."[6]

The twelve saw more clearly, but not fully. When

Jesus talked with them above Caesarea Philippi, asking what was the popular opinion about him, Peter answered: "Some say John the Baptist; some, Elias; and others, Jeremias; or one of the prophets."

And when the Lord made his question more direct, asking, "Whom say ye that I am?" Peter answered, "Thou art the Christ, the Son of the living God."[7] What Peter said meant that he and his fellow apostles accepted Jesus as the anointed of God, especially commissioned to represent him. But Peter did not go as far as he would after the resurrection: he did not yet affirm the Lord's unique divinity.

The resurrection shed new light on all that had gone before. It deepened and enriched the understanding of many Jews of the nature and purpose of God, who soon came to be regarded as the God and Father of the Lord Jesus Christ. Paul regarded it as evidence of the all-inclusive love of Christ. He wrote to the saints in Corinth: "Ye know the grace of our Lord Jesus Christ, that, though he was rich, yet for your sakes he became poor, that ye through his poverty might be rich."[8]

John also: "And the same word was made flesh, and dwelt among us, and we beheld his glory, the glory as of the Only Begotten of the Father, full of grace and truth."[9]

The other apostles, too: "With great power gave the apostles witness of the resurrection of the Lord Jesus; and great grace was upon them all."[10]

And the saints: "They [the saints]. . . by their prayer for you, which long after you for the exceeding grace of God in you."[11]

The grace of God expressed the gradually won common understanding of the deeper aspects of the love of God which came to the saints under the guidance of the Holy Spirit. In their hearts and minds it was directly related to the solution of the problem of sin, for they saw that although sin is not God's problem he made it his problem. Thenceforth the work of human redemption was a joint affair.

Those responsible for the crucifixion of Jesus thought that his following would die away; the very reverse was true. Nothing has ever created such deep and serious thinking about ultimates than the cross of Christ has done. If what was done at Calvary could write *finis* to the life and work of such a person as was the Lord Jesus, then all the arguments for the achievement of character of his kind were futile. The average person had no answer to perplexing issues until the resurrection.

As the apostles and other believers talked of what had happened they had no carefully reasoned explanation of what they all felt. They had a sense of continuing comradeship with the living Lord; they felt free—as they had never been free before—of the shackles of sin. They were possessed of power which they associated with the indwelling of the Spirit of Jesus, filling them with hope and assurance and peace, and setting them apart for a worldwide campaign of testimony and faith. At first the meaning of what had happened was expressed in terms of what had happened to them both as individuals and in the fellowship. They had been prisoners of evil habits but now were free. They had been afraid of their civil and religious rulers, but now they were their own masters. They had been living in a bookkeeping relationship to God; now they were saying, "If God be for us, who can prevail against us?"[12] They had entered into a new life of power.

All this had happened because of the grace of the

Lord Jesus. He had taken the initiative for their redemption when they could not help themselves. In his own body he had shown what sin does to the innocent, and at the same time his sacrifice had demonstrated the wonder of the love of God. While this was a specific act in history, it was at the same time an illustration of the unfailing love of God. Paul was to write later:

Where sin abounded, grace did much more abound; that as sin hath reigned unto death, even so might grace reign through righteousness unto eternal life by Jesus Christ our Lord.[13]

This was a major theme of the apostolic epistles:

When we were yet without strength, in due time Christ died for the ungodly.... God commendeth his love toward us, in that while we were yet sinners, Christ died for us.[14]

Hereby perceive we the love of Christ, because he laid down his life for us.[15]

Our Savior, Jesus Christ, gave himself for us, that he might redeem us from all iniquity.[16]

As we have seen, those who saw Jesus in action had been given hints of the love of God throughout the Lord's ministry. But the fullness of the revelation of God in Christ was not available until Jesus was "declared to be the Son of God with power, according to the spirit of holiness, by the resurrection from the dead."[17]

After this the best known illustration of the grace of God probably was the healing and commissioning of Paul when he was on his way to continue his persecution of the Christians.[18] Paul never forgot this. Years later he wrote to Timothy, saying that "Jesus Christ came into the world to save sinners, of whom I am chief."[19]

And to the Corinthians:

By the grace of God I am what I am, and his grace which was bestowed upon me was not in vain; for I labored more abundantly than they all; yet not I, but the grace of God which was with me.[20]

Grace became a favorite term of the apostle, in whose epistles it appears no less than a hundred times. Grace guided his own ministry, as he wrote to the saints in Colossae:

When it pleased God, who separated me from my mother's womb, and called me by his grace, to reveal his Son in me, that I might preach him among the heathen; immediately I conferred not with flesh and blood.[21]

It was a recurring note in his epistles. He wrote to the saints in Ephesus: "Let no corrupt communication proceed out of your mouth, but that which is good to the use of edifying, that it may minister grace unto the hearers."[22]

To his "son in the gospel," he wrote, "Thou therefore, my son, be strong in the grace that is in Christ Jesus."[23]

To do this effectively they were to remember that "the weapons of our warfare are not carnal, but mighty through God to the pulling down of strongholds."[24]

The New Testament affirms repeatedly that we are saved by grace through faith. Paul wrote to the saints in Ephesus:

By grace are ye saved through faith, and that not of yourselves; it is the gift of God; not of works, lest any man should boast. For we are his workmanship, created in Christ Jesus unto good works, which God hath before ordained that we should walk in them.[25]

And to his fellow-minister, Titus: "The grace of God which bringeth salvation to all men, hath appeared."[26]

All of us who have been blessed by the grace of God, which is also the grace of the Lord Jesus Christ, are deeply grateful for this, and find joy and renewal in remembering our indebtedness:

212

God, who is rich in mercy, for his great love wherewith he loved us, even when we were dead in sins, hath quickened us together with Christ (by grace ye are saved;) and hath raised us up together, and made us sit together in heavenly places in Christ Jesus.[27]

The apostle Paul was clear that none can earn their own salvation, and he so preached. There appears to have been no thought in his mind that the freedom of believers from the law and its penalties would reduce the need for good works.[28] Although the grace of the Lord Jesus laid no burden of service on them, his followers nevertheless felt themselves bound forever. No one could pay adequately for the riches they enjoyed through Christ, and they did not attempt to do so—they merely practiced the grace of love. They did this as a way of life, without any calculation of profit and loss, in a spirit of inspired generosity.

There is little glad awareness of the grace of God except where we take our transgressions seriously, facing up to the facts of our selfishness, resentments, and pride in the spirit of repentance. Paul rejoiced in the plenitude of the grace of the Lord Jesus, writing to the Corinthians, and to us: "Every man according as he purposeth in his heart so let him give. . .for God is able to make all grace abound toward you."[29]

And to the Ephesians:

We have redemption through his blood, the forgiveness of sins, according to the riches of his grace, wherein he hath abounded toward us in all wisdom and prudence.[30]

The plenitude of grace is not to be exhausted, for it is of God and continues with him. "Unto every one of us is given grace according to the measure of the gift of Christ."[31]

Even among believers today there are many who find it hard to accept in all its fullness the wonder of the love of God, and the Father's truly divine generosity in doing for us what we could not do for ourselves. Our pride makes us want to pay our way, and to glory in the paying. The late L. Nelson wrote, "Rare, indeed, is the Christian who does not consciously or unconsciously harbor the feeling that in some measure he is earning his own salvation and therefore deserves to be saved."[32] But we are not working our way to heaven. Of course Christianity entails many costs, and at times these are very heavy. They are such costs, though, as grow out of the nature of the enterprise. They are paid gladly by those who have come to know the grace of God. As John wrote in his first Epistle: "We love him, because he first loved us."[33]

Sometimes Paul calls the grace experienced in forgiveness *justification* and affirms that through the grace of the Lord Jesus Christ the repentant sinner is declared to be righteous. Past misdeeds no longer separate the sinner from God. In the Roman letter Paul wrote:

To him that worketh not, but believeth on him that justifieth the ungodly, his faith is counted for righteousness.[34]

Being justified freely by his grace through the redemption that is in Christ Jesus: Whom God hath set forth to be a propitiation through faith in his blood, to declare his righteousness for the remission of sins that are past through the forbearance of God; to declare, I say, at this time, his righteousness; that he might be just, and the justifier of him which believeth in Jesus. . . . A man is justified by faith without the deeds of the law.[35]

The declaration that the repentant sinner is justified by faith alone has at times been thought unfair. This thinking does not take into account the personal factors in sin: God, the sinner, and the one sinned against. Of these our heavenly Father is most deeply sinned against, and he has set the meaning of repentance. He can judge the depth of the repentance offered as no one else can. He has the best right to forgive. The sinner who is truly repentant is eager to be restored to the family of God. And the one sinned against needs to come under the benediction of the principle of repentance/forgiveness, as do we all. Becoming party to the forgiveness of the repentant reveals the meaning of the principle from the inside.

When one-time sinners are forgiven and restored to fellowship, there is no point in giving their past sins undue attention. There is plenty of constructive work to be done and this will be found acceptable if it is done in the spirit of loving gratitude. This is not unlike the situation in which those found guilty of a civil offense are required to do a certain amount of work, except that the guilty persons are not "required." With their changed attitude they are eager to serve where they can.

The apostolic concern that this spirit of fraternity should permeate the assemblies of the saints is shown in the characteristic style in which they closed their letters:

The grace of our Lord Jesus Christ be with you all.[36]

I write to all who are in Rome, beloved of God, called saints; (grace to you, and peace, from God our Father, and the Lord Jesus Christ.)[37]

The grace of the Lord Jesus Christ, and the love of God, and the communion of the Holy Ghost, be with you all.[38]

Grace be with all them that love our Lord Jesus Christ in sincerity.[39]

And, in what was destined to be the last sentence of the New Testament: "The grace of our Lord Jesus Christ be with you all. Amen."[40]

REFERENCES

1. Mark 10:46-53.
2. Mark 5:22.
3. John 18:10.
4. Matthew 16:14.
5. Luke 17:12-19.
6. John 3:2.
7. Matthew 16:15-17.
8. II Corinthians 8:9.
9. John 1:14. See also John 1:16-17.
10. Acts 4:33.
11. II Corinthians 9:13-14. See also II Corinthians 8:1, 6, 7.
12. Romans 8:31.
13. Romans 5:20-21.
14. Romans 5:6, 8.
15. I John 3:16.
16. Titus 2:13-14.
17. Romans 1:4 KJ.
18. Acts 8:1-18.
19. I Timothy 1:15. See also Romans 3:24.
20. I Corinthians 15:10. See also Ephesians 3:1-9; Romans 15:15-16.
21. Galatians 1:15-16.
22. Ephesians 4:29.
23. II Timothy 2:1.
24. II Corinthians 10:4.
25. Ephesians 2:8-10 KJ.
26. Titus 2:11.
27. Ephesians 2:4-6.
28. Acts 10:38.
29. II Corinthians 9:7-8.
30. Ephesians 1:7-8.
31. Ephesians 4:7. See also Romans 12:6.
32. *Christianity Today*, July 1973, p. 33.
33. I John 4:19.
34. Romans 4:5 KJ.
35. Romans 3:24-26, 28 KJ.
36. Romans 16:24. See also I Corinthians 16:23-24.
37. Romans 1:7. See also Galatians 1:3.
38. II Corinthians 13:14.
39. Ephesians 6:24.
40. Revelation 22:21.

It is the Dawn! the Dawn! The nations
   From East to West have heard a cry,—
"Through all earth's blood-red
      generations
   By hate and slaughter climbed thus
      high,
Here—on this height—still to aspire,
   One only path remains untrod,
One path of love and peace climbs
      higher.
   Make straight that highway for
      our God."

—From the Epilogue to Alfred
Noyes's Poem "The Wine-Press."

Chapter 20

The Holy Spirit and the Kingdom of God

Early Christianity was above everything else the religion of the Spirit. To the first Christians the Spirit meant Jesus in spiritual presence, triumphant over death, come back to his friends as comforter and guide and energizer, filling them with wisdom and power, raising their whole being to a new level of insight and effectiveness for him.

Eternal life is the life of God in the human soul. It is possible for faithful disciples to enjoy a measure of eternal life while yet on earth. This is because one aspect of eternal life has to do with godly quality. It is life enriched and guided by the Holy Spirit. It is a life of preparation for the fullness of the best we now know. It is life pointed toward both the immediate and the ultimate building of the kingdom. This latter will transpire when our mortality shall have been swallowed up in immortality: Paul wrote, "As we have born the image of the earthy, we also shall bear the image of the heavenly."

And continued: "My beloved brethren, be ye steadfast, unmovable, always abounding in the work of the Lord, forasmuch as ye know that your labor is not in vain in the Lord."[1]

The early teaching and preaching of the Lord Jesus

Christ centered in the gospel of the kingdom of God. He ministered in terms of the present needs of his hearers, but he always viewed these needs against the background of eternity. He treated them, so far as the circumstances permitted, as what the Moffatt version of Philippians 3:20 rendered "a colony of heaven."

The early kingdom ministry of Jesus had been anticipated in part by many of the prophets and by John the Baptist. Matthew wrote in his gospel that "in those days came John the Baptist, preaching in the wilderness of Judea, and saying, Repent ye; for the kingdom of heaven is at hand."[2] Shortly thereafter John was put into prison, but Jesus continued his forerunner's work, saying: "The time is fulfilled, and the kingdom of God is at hand."[3]

It will be seen that for both John and Jesus the time was propitious and the kingdom was within their grasp. They were announcing its availability. Hitherto the coming of the kingdom had been delayed because of the preoccupation of the people with non-kingdom affairs. Now, if they truly hoped for the kingdom, they must turn their backs on the way of life which had prevented its coming. They must repent. There was no attempt to make the transition appear easy, but they must recognize that they could no longer serve God and Mammon.[4] This was so, even though Mammon was entrenched and had no intention of yielding.

Jesus set forth the nature of kingdom righteousness. How this declaration must have astonished the worldly minded among his hearers! Here it is:

Blessed are the poor in spirit; for theirs is the kingdom of heaven.
Blessed are they that mourn; for they shall be comforted.
Blessed are the meek: for they shall inherit the earth.

Blessed are they which do hunger and thirst after righteousness: for they shall be filled with the Holy Ghost.

Blessed are the merciful; for they shall obtain mercy.

Blessed are all the pure in heart; for they shall see God.

Blessed are all the peacemakers; for they shall be called the children of God.

Blessed are all they which are persecuted for righteousness sake; for theirs is the kingdom of heaven.

Blessed are ye, when men shall revile you, and persecute you, and shall say all manner of evil against you falsely, for my sake. For ye shall have great joy and be exceeding glad; for great is your reward in heaven; for so persecuted they the prophets which were before you.[5]

The kingdom of God is unlike any other. This was obvious to any who looked at the Roman officials or listened to the rulers of the Jews. It was evident to any who could listen in on a conversation which took place between Jesus and Pilate. Pilate asked,

Art thou the king of the Jews?. . . Jesus answered, My kingdom is not of this world; if my kingdom were of this world, then would my servants fight, that I should not be delivered to the Jews; but now my kingdom is not from hence.

But Pilate persisted:

Art thou a king then? Jesus answered, Thou sayest that I am a king. To this end was I born, and for this cause came I into the world, that I should bear witness unto the truth. Every one that is of the truth heareth my voice.[6]

In view of the promise of the Lord Jesus that he would come again, it was inevitable that the saints would be concerned about the coming life which they would share with him. They found a clue in the report of a conversation between Jesus and one of the two men crucified with him. The man said to Jesus: "Lord, remember me when thou comest into thy kingdom. And Jesus said unto him, Verily I say unto thee; To-day shalt thou be with me in paradise."[7]

It seems clear that this man was not a stranger to the ministry of Jesus, for he called him "Lord" and sought the Master's favor beyond the tomb. He knew of paradise, and whatever the actions which brought him to the cross, and which he admitted,[8] the Lord regarded him with kindness.

Paradise was a Persian term for a garden or a closed park and was regarded by the Jews as the abode of the blessed dead. Jesus possibly had this in mind when he talked to his fellow sufferer. In the Book of Mormon it is recorded that

the spirits of all men, as soon as they are departed from this mortal body; yea, the spirits of all men, whether they be good or evil, are taken home to that God who gave them life. And then shall it come to pass that the spirits of those who are righteous, are received into a state of happiness, which is called paradise; a state of rest; a state of peace, where they shall rest from all their troubles, and from all care, and sorrow.[9]

John the Revelator indicated that Paradise is a place of instruction[10] and this is understandable if those in Paradise are to learn from those who have already been instructed.

Growth that fits us for the kingdom of God requires the development of such spiritual powers as compassion, fraternity, and loyalty to the highest. Paul gave expression to the kingdom spirit when he wrote to the saints in Galatia: "Bear ye one another's burdens, and so fulfill the law of Christ."[11] This and similar laws must be inviolate, for the absence of such laws is what distinguishes the kingdom of God from the kingdoms of this world. Recognizing this, Paul wrote to the saints in Rome, "The kingdom of God is . . . righteousness, and peace, and joy in the Holy Ghost."[12]

The assurance of immortality which is given to many of the faithful in this life is augmented by the testimony of the apostle Paul concerning the glories of the life of the redeemed. These glories are fashioned according to the quality of those who enter there. Paul wrote:

[There are] also celestial bodies, and bodies terrestrial, and bodies telestial; but the glory of the celestial, one; and the terrestrial, another; and the telestial another. There is one glory of the sun, and another glory of the moon, and another glory of the stars: for one star differeth from another star in glory.[13]

There is a sense in which those consigned to these glories have earned their places, but I remember with appreciation a conversation between Elders Elbert A. Smith and A. B. Phillips where one of them said: "They are all glories; and they are the best that the Lord can do with what we have sent up to him."

The apostle Paul wrote of the highest order of eternal life as "celestial glory" and indicated that we shall enter into this glory

when this corruptible [body] shall have put on incorruption, and this mortal shall have put on immortality then shall be brought to pass the saying that is written, Death is swallowed up in victory.[14]

The earthly life of the saints will have been a preparation for this life of celestial quality. Jesus commended it to his hearers in his sermon on the Mount, saying, "Be ye therefore perfect, even as your Father which is in heaven is perfect."[15]

As Paul also explained, there are other glories in the hereafter. These are "glories" where life is suited to the spiritual stature of the inhabitants, which is inferior to that of the higher celestial order.[16]

The Lord Jesus does not cease to love us when we die. God is love. The condition of our lives in the hereafter are different from our earthly life, but the divine concern continues. Peter wrote,

Christ once suffered for sins, the just for the unjust, being put to death in the flesh, but quickened by the Spirit, that he might bring us to God. For which cause also, he went and preached unto the spirits in prison.[17]

Modern revelation has alleviated some of the fears and doubts which for many years accompanied preaching concerning hell. There were many who found it extremely difficult to reconcile the thought of the love of God with expectation of unending punishment after death for the wicked. Martin Harris was concerned about this because of the protestations of some members of his family. To him the word of the Lord came through Joseph Smith shortly before the organization of the church. Wrote Joseph in the name of God:

Behold, I am endless, and the punishment which is given from my hand is endless punishment, for Endless is my name; wherefore—Eternal punishment is God's punishment. Endless punishment is God's punishment.[18]

Questions about the possibility and meaning of life after death come up again and again as we grow older and as those we love pass over. Perhaps the attitude which has least to justify it but is held most widely is that we do not know, and must wait to find out. This ignores the testimony of some of the wisest persons who have ever lived. And it also ignores the contribution which preparation for the life to come would incline us to make now.

Those who believe in the purpose of God in the life to come, like Jesus the Lord, live today for the best possible tomorrows.

Jesus said to his disciples,

I go to prepare a place for you. And if I go and prepare a place for you, I will come again, and receive you unto myself; that where I am there ye may be also.[19]

Relying on this promise, thousands of his followers have lived in this present world so as to make it a fitting preparation for that which is beyond.

The conviction of life beyond death is essentially a spiritual conviction. Again we turn to Paul:

[God] hath saved us, and called us with a holy calling, not according to our works, but according to his own purpose and grace, which was given us in Christ Jesus before the world began; but is now made manifest by the appearing of our Savior Jesus Christ, who has abolished death, and hath brought life and immortality to light through the gospel.[20]

We are loose in a world where the blind are leading the blind and it would take very little to cause us to fall. This is not a recent development. We have been on the edge of a reign of terror for centuries. In the ninth century Pope Innocent issued an encyclical against a new and terrible weapon which he felt sure could exterminate the human race. So terrible was this weapon, he said, that compunction of conscience demanded that it be outlawed immediately.... It was the cross bow. A writer commenting on this a few years ago added a further tidbit of history. He said that when Alfred Nobel discovered T.N.T. in 1890 he made the prediction that his new and powerful weapon would make wars impossible. Then the writer added his own terse summary: "That is all he knew about human nature."

The need for guidance such as this world cannot give of itself has been affirmed many times. In a now famous editorial an American journal called the church to speak with the voice of authority, which is the voice of God:

Unless we hear such a voice men of this generation will sink down that spiral of depression about which economists speak. There is only one way out of this spiral. The way out is the sound of a voice, not our voice but a voice coming from something not ourself, in the existence of which we cannot disbelieve. It is the earthly task of the pastors to hear this voice, to cause us to hear it, and to tell us what it says. If they cannot hear it, or if they fail to tell us we are as lay men utterly lost. Without it we are no more capable of saving the world than we were capable of creating it in the first place.[21]

All people need God. We need him more than we need anything or anyone else, and this need is as deep for us as it has been for the people of any generation. It is just because so many of us do not realize our need, and live without seeking God, that our world is divided against itself, our lives are lacking in stable purpose, and our morals lack compelling authority. Despite our riches, we are seemingly effective for no good beyond the multiplication of these riches. Our goods have not brought us happiness. Unless we learn to seek more earnestly for the guidance of our Heavenly Father in every department of life, our civilization will continue to crumble until it perishes.

Francis Thompson, as he lay drunk on a seat on the Thames embankment in London, England, knew and confessed that he could not be true to his best self and keep trying to escape from God. He wrote:

I fled him, down the nights and down the days!
  I fled him down the arches of the years;
I fled him down the labyrinthine ways
  Of my own mind; and in the midst of tears
I hid from Him, and under running laughter.
     . . . . . .
From those strong feet that followed, followed after.

REFERENCES

1. I Corinthians 15:49, 58.
2. Matthew 3:27-28.
3. Mark 1:13.
4. Matthew 6:24.
5. Matthew 5:5-14.
6. John 18:33-36.
7. Luke 23:43-44.
8. Luke 23:42.
9. Alma 19:43-44. See also Moroni 10:31; II Corinthians 12:4.
10. Revelation 2:7.
11. Galatians 6:2.
12. Romans 14:17.
13. I Corinthians 15:40-41.
14. I Corinthians 15:54.
15. Matthew 5:48 KJ.
16. I Corinthians 15:38-50.
17. I Peter 3:18-19.
18. Doctrine and Covenants 18:2d, e.
19. John 14:2-3 KJ.
20. II Timothy 1:9-10.
21. Quoted from John A. Mackay, *A Preface to Christian Theology* (New York): The Macmillan Co., 1948, 18.

*For ears to hear the heavenly
   harmonies;*
*For eyes to see the unseen in
   the seen;*
*For vision of the Worker in the
   work;*
*For hearts to apprehend Thee
   everywhere;*
   We thank Thee,
      Lord.

—"A Little Te Deum of the Commonplace"
   by William Arthur Dunkerley (Better
   known as "John Oxenham")

Chapter 21

The Spirit of Light and Truth

The Holy Spirit is the spirit of light and truth. They belong together. Jesus once said of the Pharisees that they were "blind leaders of the blind" and added, "If the blind lead the blind, both shall fall into the ditch."[1]

The function of light is to promote discernment so that those who see shall walk with confidence. According to modern revelation "The glory of God is intelligence or, in other words, light and truth."[2]

Of this the apostles wrote. The apostle John, for example, wrote at a time of creeping apostasy: "God is light, and in him is no darkness at all."[3] Jesus, who came to bear witness of the Father,[4] said of himself, "I am the light of the world; he that followeth me shall not walk in darkness, but shall have the light of life."[5]

The Spirit of light is the spirit of revelation. It centers in Christ Jesus. Revelation, however, is a dual process; it is completed only when confirmed by the inner witness of the Spirit. Revelation must be apprehended by the insight of faith. The psalmist sang, "The heavens declare the glory of God; and the firmament showeth his handiwork."[6]

In doing so he disclosed something of his own spiritual nature; the light within bore testimony of the wonder above.

For many of us the experience of the light of the Spirit comes in the fellowship of worship, especially as the scriptures are opened to our understanding, or the call to repentance is quickened within us. We live by such disclosures and prompting. We shall do well to receive with gratitude such light as is granted us with equally grateful awareness of the further light which beckons us forward and upward. Paul has a word for us here:

We know in part, and we prophesy in part. But when that which is perfect is come, then that which is in part shall be done away.... Now we see through a glass, darkly; but then face to face; now I know in part, But then shall I know even as also I am known.[7]

The realization that, being human, there is always something awaiting us beyond what we already know is an important insight. It was eminently fitting that Pastor Robinson, addressing the Pilgrims as they were preparing to leave for the New World, told them that "God has yet more light and truth to break forth from his word." What the Pilgrims already knew opened the way to welcoming more truth with roots soundly embedded in what they already treasured.

The guidance which brought us this far on our way has further ministries of truth for us and our children. Receipt of this may well come from further study of what we already have, but have not yet fully apprehended. This happened among the exiled Jews who had to learn that God could and would speak to them in Babylon even though they were now far removed from Jerusalem where he had spoken to them hitherto. Later there was still more to come to them through the ministry of the Lord Jesus. And there is still more that we need before we understand the nature of the Spirit of stewardship and its eternal rewards.

The light of the Spirit shines, as did the living testimony of the Lord Jesus. This shining was so evident that even some of the servants of the Sanhedrin said "Never man spake like this man."[8] Describing Jesus, John said, "In him was life; and the life was the light of men. And the light shineth in darkness; and the darkness comprehended it not."[9]

Jesus and those he commissioned combined their teaching concerning the shining light of the saints with associated good works. Jesus said, "Let your light so shine before the world, that they may see your good works, and glorify your Father who is in heaven."[10]

God is light. In every field his grace serves a double function: he creates beauty and truth and goodness, and gives and nurtures capacities for enjoying them and, sometimes, copying them. Browning wrote out of cultivated experience:

We're so made that we love
First when we see them painted, things we have passed
Nor cared to see.[11]

And Tennyson wrote, "We needs must love the highest when we see it."[12]

Early Christians were admonished again and again to "walk in the light." In his last public address to the Jews Jesus said,

Yet a little while is the light with you. Walk while ye have the light, lest darkness come upon you; for he that walketh in darkness knoweth not whither he goeth. While ye have light believe in the light, that ye may be the children of the light.[13]

This was a continuance of the ancient prophetic admonition.[14] The apostles also carried the thought forward. Paul maintained the relation between walking in the light and being truly the children of the light.[15] He stressed the same thought in his first letter to the Thessalonians: "Ye, brethren, are not in darkness. . . .Ye are all the children of light, and the children of the day."[16]

Peter sounded this basic thought in his general epistle: "Ye are a chosen generation. . .a holy nation, a peculiar people; that ye should show forth the praises of him who hath called you out of darkness into this marvellous light."[17]

Isaiah expressed the divine concern for those who chose to live in darkness, relying on their own strength. He wrote,

Woe unto them that call evil good, and good evil; that put darkness for light, and light for darkness; that put bitter for sweet, and sweet for bitter! Woe unto the wise in their own eyes, and prudent in their own sight![18]

The problem here is not merely that the wicked walk in darkness, but that they do so deliberately. Jesus made this clear, saying: "This is the condemnation, that light is come into the world, and men love darkness rather than light, because their deeds are evil."[19]

Paul was acutely aware of the social impulses toward walking in darkness, and wrote,

See then that ye walk circumspectly; not as fools, but as wise, redeeming the time, because the days are evil.[20]

If God be for us, who can prevail against us. . . .Who shall separate us from the love of Christ? Shall tribulation, or distress, or persecution, or famine, or nakedness, or peril, or sword?. . .Nay, in all these things we are more than conquerors through him that loved us. For I am persuaded, that neither death, nor life, nor angels, nor principalities, nor powers, nor things present, nor things to come, nor height, nor depth, nor any other creature shall be able to separate us from the love of God, which is in Christ Jesus our Lord.[21]

The light of the Spirit is more than the feeling of acceptance and of calling which many of us have felt in the assemblies of the saints. It is the movement in our souls of the power of God which clarifies and informs our experience as part of his eternal purpose. It was by virtue of such light that persons who had once been "aliens" became in more than name, "the people of God." Of them Paul wrote,

Ye are no more strangers and foreigners, but fellow citizens with the saints, and of the household of God; and are built upon the foundation of the apostles and prophets, Jesus Christ himself being the chief corner stone; in whom all the building fitly framed together groweth into an holy temple in the Lord; in whom ye also are builded together...through the Spirit.[22]

The light of the Spirit, furthermore, is the constantly renewed evidence of our spiritual growth:

God, who commanded the light to shine out of darkness, hath shined in our hearts, to give the light of the knowledge of the glory of God in the face of Jesus Christ. But we have this treasure in earthen vessels, that the excellency of the power may be of God, and not of us.[23]

If we love one another, God dwelleth in us, and his love is perfected in us. Hereby know we that we dwell in him, and he in us, because he hath given us of his Spirit.[24]

Walking together in the light calls for unity of spirit rather than agreement concerning details. This was emphasized in the revelation of 1894:

Let nothing separate you from each other and the work whereunto you have been called; and I will be with you by my Spirit and presence of power unto the end.[25]

There are factors involved in the receipt of the Holy Spirit, and by observing these we prepare the way for endowment. It is fairly obvious that we are not so likely to be filled with the Spirit while watching a ball game as we are participating in a good prayer meeting, while reading a detective story as when studying a beatitude in search of its deeper meaning, in memorizing an earthy song as when taking our part in an Easter choir rehearsal. In essence, the Spirit is more likely to be known where his work is being done. This will often occur at church, but it does not have to be in church. It can be felt while feeding a hungry child, or while persuading a badly treated boy to control his temper, or in encouraging a sick and despondent friend. Doing what a little reflection will show ought to be done will be found more effective than planning what should be done when time permits.

The Spirit of truth stands for reality as against self-indulgent imagination and irresponsibility. On the mundane level on which most of us are tempted to spend our lives we need more than this: a power which will quicken us to perception and action in the spiritual realm. No truth in the abstract can do this. We need the impetus given by truth which is much more than an idea—the truth which is personal and persuasive. Paul stated this principle in relation to the resurrection:

If ye then be risen with Christ, seek those things which are above, where Christ sitteth on the right hand of God. Set your affection on things above, not on things on the earth. For ye are dead, and your life is hid with Christ in God. When Christ, who is our life, shall appear, then shall ye also appear with him in glory.[26]

The Spirit of truth bids us look at things, at events, at life itself with concern for their wholeness, for their ramifications and—most of all—for what they are in the sight of God and their influence in the lives of other persons.

Knowledge of the truth with which Jesus was concerned comes by way of commitment. Search for it is a spiritual enterprise beyond the search for facts, and as such it has much to do with worship. One of the great psalms of praise begins, "Bless the Lord, O my soul; and all that is within me, bless his holy name."[27] It is when we worship in this fashion that the awareness of the grandeur of the truth as it is in Christ Jesus takes hold of us.

When Jesus was preparing his disciples for his coming departure he promised to ask his Father to send someone to continue his ministry among them. He said,

I will pray the Father, and he shall give you another Comforter, that he may be with you forever; even the Spirit of truth; whom the world cannot receive, because it seeth him not, neither knoweth him, but ye know him; for he dwelleth with you, and shall be in you.[28]

The promised Spirit was not unknown to the disciples, for Jesus said "he dwelleth with you." And the promise was consonant with the Lord's earlier promise that he would abide with them. The difference which Jesus was announcing was that he would no longer be visible among them nor available for questions and discussions. But, said he, the ministry of the Spirit would be equivalent to his own. The Spirit would testify within them.[29] Later, the apostle Paul was to sense the closeness of Jesus and the Spirit by saying, "The Lord is that Spirit."[30]

The Father, Son, and Holy Spirit are the authors and final guarantors of the truth. In themselves they guarantee its consistency. Believers seeking the fullness of truth are guided in their pursuit by the Spirit of truth. But the fullness always beckons. The pursuit itself is the way of salvation. The gift of the Holy Spirit was the distinctive experience of the early saints and the secret of their triumph.

The early disciples referred to the Christian way of

234

life as "the way." This was consistent with the scriptures with which they were familiar. Jesus had said: "I am the way, the truth, and the life; no man cometh unto the Father, but by me."[31]

The prophets had anticipated such an emphasis. Isaiah wrote: "The way of the just is uprightness; thou, most upright, doth weigh the part of the just."[32]

The Holy Spirit was the spirit of the way. They found that faith is conviction by the truth as well as of the truth. As Pascal wrote, faith moves "from experiment to insight, from conjecture to worship, from theology to prayer." The more we persist in the life of faith the more fully his message is vindicated in the unique perfection of his character and the matching perfection of his teachings.

Truth is so. It is of God, and James has told us that in him there "is no variableness, neither shadow of turning."[33] The more the light shines on it, the brighter it shines. It is not determined by human choices, nor can it be amended to suit human convenience. One of the major functions of students is to compare insights based on new evidence, and to adjust the seeming infallibilities of the past to the understanding made possible by greater light.

The Spirit of truth guides and enlightens disciples, but it does not make them infallible. It does affirm to them that in the final analysis all things are spiritual. A modern prophet says in the name of God:

All things unto me are spiritual, and not at any time have I given unto you a law which was temporal, neither any man, nor the children of men.... My commandments are spiritual; they are not natural, nor temporal, neither carnal nor sensual.[34]

To those who take this counsel seriously all life becomes sacramental. The principle is fundamental to the practice of stewardship on a high level. It enlightens the believer to see the power of the Spirit manifest through all creation.

Truth is to be valued to the end that it shall be lived.[35] In the gospel of John the apostle quotes Jesus as saying, "He that doeth the truth cometh to the light, that his deeds may be manifest, that they are wrought in God."[36]

And in his letters John wrote, "If we say that we have fellowship with him, and walk in darkness, we lie, and do not the truth."[37]

Those who live according to the spirit of truth build for eternity, for truth abides in God.[38]

The Spirit of truth enlightens those who walk in the light. Jesus stated this quite clearly, but often only part of his statement is quoted. The full statement reads

My doctrine is not mine, but his that sent me. If any man will do his will, he [the doer of the will of God] shall know of the doctrine, whether it be of God, or whether I speak of myself.[39]

The same correlation of obedience and understanding was emphasized in a conversation with a number of Jews who believed in him: "If ye continue in my word, then are ye my disciples indeed; and ye shall know the truth, and the truth shall make you free."[40]

John returned again and again to emphasize the importance of this relationship: "Hereby we do know that we know him, if we keep his commandments. . . . Whoso keepeth his word, in him verily is the love of God perfected."[41]

In his inspired instructions to the church in Laodicea John quoted Jesus as reaffirming the principle of seeking to finding. He quoted the Lord as saying,

Behold, I stand at the door and knock; if any man hear my voice, and open the door, I will come in to him, and will sup with him, and he with me. To him that overcometh will I grant to sit with me in my throne, even as I also overcame and am set down with my Father in [on] his throne. He that hath an ear, let him hear what the Spirit saith unto the churches.[42]

Perception of God's unfailing faithfulness—his truth on which all other truth depends—lays special claim on us in worship, and is of particular significance in this day of widely accepted secular culture. This is the hour of amazing achievement and parallel lostness. The greater our victories in things earthly, the more apparent is our failure in things heavenly. Despite our marvelous conquests elsewhere, all the ancient sins are still with us. There is no hope for us except as we come to recognize the primacy of things spiritual and so of a power which we cannot command but which we are willing to obey in love.

As has been noted, the prophets were a significant factor in the spiritual maturing of the Hebrew people from the beginning. But what is called "the golden age" of prophecy is generally dated between about 800 B.C. and 650 B.C. It was near the beginning of this period that Amos declared, "Surely the Lord God will do nothing, until he revealeth the secret unto his servants the prophets."[43]

This expressed a point of view common to the chosen people.

The word *reveal* has a part of its core meaning in the idea of disclosure. Revelation involves much more than telling or showing. It has to do with conveying meaning. And this, in turn, is conditioned by the interest and capacity of the hearer.

When we think, furthermore, of the vastness of the secrets of God—his nature and his love and his purpose in our creation and redemption—we know that revelation in its fullness is beyond the reach of our unaided understanding. We need help from above. But we need not despair, for we have the testimony of the apostle Paul that although

eye hath not seen, nor ear heard, neither have entered into the heart of man, the things which God hath prepared for them that love him. But God hath revealed them to us by his Spirit; for the Spirit searcheth all things, yea, the deep things of God.[44]

We cannot understand the deep things of God until we see as he sees and feel as he feels. To do this is not the task of a moment. It involves us in a commitment for time and eternity. It calls us to adventure with God. It involves worship.

When we think of walking in the light, and do so soberly, it is not long till we realize that it implies deep faith accompanied by moral integrity. It implies also striving alongside others of "like precious faith" toward goals approved of God and treasured by his people. And it calls for building on the testimonies of the yesterdays toward the kingdom which is our common goal.

REFERENCES

1. Matthew 15:14.
2. Doctrine and Covenants 90:6a.
3. I John 1:5.
4. John 18:37.
5. John 8:12. See also John 1:8-9.
6. Psalm 19:1. See also Psalm 150.
7. I Corinthians 13:9, 10, 12.
8. John 7:46.
9. John 1:4-5 KJ.
10. Matthew 5:18.
11. Fra Lippo Lippi.
12. "Idylls of the King."

13. John 12:35-36.
14. Jeremiah 6:16; Isaiah 2:5.
15. Ephesians 5:8.
16. I Thessalonians 5:4-5. See also I Timothy 6:12.
17. I Peter 2:9.
18. Isaiah 5:20-21.
19. John 3:19. See also Colossians 1:12-13.
20. Ephesians 5:15-16.
21. Romans 8:31, 35, 37-39.
22. Ephesians 2:19-22.
23. II Corinthians 4:4-7.
24. I John 4:12-13.
25. Doctrine and Covenants 122:17b.
26. Colossians 3:1-4.
27. Psalm 103:1.
28. John 14:16-17.
29. John 14:17.
30. II Corinthians 3:17.
31. John 14:6.
32. Isaiah 26:7. See also Isaiah 55:7; Jeremiah 29:8.
33. James 1:17.
34. Doctrine and Covenants 28:9a, c.
35. John 12:36; Acts 8:37; 16:31.
36. John 3:21 KJ.
37. I John 1:6.
38. I John 4:6.
39. John 7:16-17.
40. John 8:31-32.
41. I John 2:3, 5. See also 2:16-17.
42. Revelation 3:20-22.
43. Amos 3:7.
44. I Corinthians 2:9-10.

*It fortifies my soul to know
That though I perish, truth is so;
That howsoe'er I stray and range,
Whate'er I do, Thou dost not change.
I steadier step when I recall
That, if I slip, Thou dost not fall.*

—Arthur Hugh Clough

Chapter 22

The Power That Makes for Righteousness

The last word of Jesus with his apostles before his ascension reasserted their commission and promised them the help they would need to fulfill it:

All power is given unto me in heaven and in earth. Go ye therefore, and teach all nations, baptizing them in the name of the Father, and of the Son, and of the Holy Ghost; teaching them to observe all things whatsoever I have commanded you; and, lo, I am with you alway, unto the end of the world.[1]

The power to which the Lord Jesus referred had animated him throughout his ministry. It was the power of God which makes for righteousness—the power to declare convincingly the love of God for all humankind. And it was promised as it was needed until the end of the world.

This power might be manifested in many ways—in peaching, teaching, guiding, healing, or in any way which might be needed. But, fundamentally, it was the power of God which makes for righteousness.

According to the scriptural record one of the major characteristics of the Master's use of this power was his restraint. It was part of the strategy of redemption. Disciples must be persuaded, not coerced or bribed. They must learn in experience the richness of the love of God and of his forgiving grace. And they must turn to him in loving gratitude. Their love of God, moreover, must unite them with other grateful children of God as brothers and sisters.

Although the Father had "given all things into his hand" the exercise of this power required Jesus to carry out the most courageous ministry the world has ever known. His life must match and illustrate his message. Meanwhile, some of those he was most eager to win were offended by outworn loyalties which they were not yet willing to disavow. This was illustrated at Capernaum on an occasion when Jesus had taught in the synagogue, declaring himself to be the "bread from heaven."[2] Some of his hearers, including some who had been considered his disciples, "murmured at" this and "from that time many of his disciples went back, and walked no more with him."[3]

In this extremity Jesus said to the twelve, "Will ye also go away?"

And Simon Peter, apparently answering for the group, replied, "Lord, to whom shall we go? Thou hast the words of eternal life, and we believe and are sure that thou art the Christ, the Son of the living God."[4]

During the remainder of his ministry the Lord continued to meet the evident needs of those who were sick: the woman who touched the hem of his garment,[5] the man with the withered hand,[6] the daughter of the Canaanite woman,[7] the centurion's servant,[8] the impotent man at the pool of Bethsaida.[9] In all of these healings some measure of faith was a factor. But when Jesus healed the man sick of the palsy Jesus called attention to it. The sick man had been brought to Jesus by four believing friends who could not get near the Master at first. So they climbed to the roof and let the sick man down to where Jesus stood.

Apparently without further inquiry, the Lord said to the sick man, "Son, thy sins be forgiven thee." Seeing this, the nearby scribes ignored the healing and reasoned among themselves that for Jesus to claim to forgive sins was blasphemous. But Jesus said,

Whether is it easier to say to the sick of the palsy, Thy sins be forgiven thee; or to say, Arise, take up thy bed and walk? But that ye may know that the Son of Man hath power on earth to forgive sins, (he saith to the sick of the palsy,) I say unto thee, Arise, and take up thy bed, and go thy way into thine house. And immediately he arose, took up the bed, and went forth before them all; inasmuch that they were all amazed and glorified God, saying, We never saw it on this fashion.[10]

For many, the preaching of Jesus was attractive but disturbing. As Matthew wrote, they "were astonished at his doctrine; for he taught them as one having authority, and not as the scribes."[11] But they were set in their traditions and, while recognizing Jesus as a prophet, were unwilling or unable to go further. The situation was illustrated in the report which John preserved of a private conversation between Jesus and Nicodemus, a ruler of the Jews. Nicodemus said "Rabbi, we know that thou art a teacher come from God; for no man can do these miracles which thou doest, except God be with him."[12]

The difficulty confronting Nicodemus was that to believe what the facts seemed to require him to believe (that Jesus was the Messiah) was to require him to abandon the way of life he had trusted from his youth. Jesus had seen the problem clearly and so, with affectionate compassion, he explained that to truly understand Nicodemus must be "born again." He must abandon the Pharasaic approach with its emphasis on the law and a multitude of minutiae, and listen to the word of God. Jesus himself was the living Word, an expression of deep importance to the best of the Jews.

The instruction set out by Jesus was not entirely new, for it had been a key part of the Lord's preaching. For instance: "Ye have heard that it was said by them of old time...but I say unto you."[13] And, when the Pharisees complained to him about his disciples eating corn which they had plucked on the sabbath Jesus said, "The sabbath was made for man, and not man for the sabbath."[14]

After Jesus had declared himself to be the Son of God by the prophetic quality of his teaching and his power over evil and disease, and after the rulers of the Jews had resolved to kill him, Jesus "steadfastly set his face to go to Jerusalem."[15] He was resolved to face the final test of his ministry there and show beyond doubt the wonder of the love and power of God. Meanwhile in Jerusalem wicked and corrupt rulers combined to do to him the worst that they could do.

The betrayal and crucifixion of Jesus, said Peter at Pentecost shortly afterward, was permitted by the "determinate counsel and foreknowledge of God."[16] It was allowed to take place because this was the clearest way to demonstrate the utter awfulness of sin and the wonder of the love of God. Anything less than this would have fallen short of the dual revelation which was needed. That it was allowed to take place was the ultimate demonstration of the power of God: power shown in the restraint which begets conviction. For the time it was beyond the understanding of even the wisest of the disciples. It seemed to portend the success of the rulers of the Jews, indicating their final authority as rulers and interpreters of the law. But the final word had not been spoken until Calvary was overruled by Easter.

Among the Jews, the feast of Pentecost was celebrated as the closing feast of the Passover, but from this time forward it took on new significance for the Christians. It was the culminating event of the endowment of the new believers, and followed soon after the forty days of instruction of the twelve by the Lord Jesus, the renewed commissioning of the twelve, and the ascension. Apparently the apostles were preparing for their mission. They and other disciples—about a hundred and twenty in all—were worshipping together when "the day of Pentecost was fully come."[17]

Their meeting was graced by the presence of the Spirit of God including a remarkable manifestation of the gift of tongues. When this was noised abroad the multitude came together and were amazed at what they saw and heard.[18] Then Peter, "standing up with the eleven" spoke with great courage of the foretelling of such an outpouring as they were now witnessing.[19] Then he launched out in citations of Old Testament preparation for the ministry of Jesus, who was now exalted at the right hand of God, who had made him "both Lord and Christ." Peter's hearers were deeply moved, and said to the disciples, "Men and brethren, what shall we do?" To this Peter replied:

Repent, and be baptized every one of you in the name of Jesus Christ for the remission of sins, and ye shall receive the gift of the Holy Ghost, for the promise is unto you, and to your children, and to all that are afar off, even as many as the Lord our God shall call.[20]

About three thousand were baptized and in the fervor of their faith sold their goods and devoted the proceeds so that the disciples "had all things in common...as every man had need."[21]

Peter's sermon was attended by a rich measure of the Spirit which moved many of his hearers to repentance. We do not know how fully the way had been prepared by the ministry of the Lord Jesus and the twelve and seventy.[22] But three thousand were added to the church at Pentecost and thereafter "the Lord added to the church daily such as should be saved."[23] As became more and more evident, a new day had dawned, calling for life firmly grounded in love and of power after the order of the Son of God. Believers did not immediately become perfect, but they set perfection in Christ as the goal of every endeavor.

The promise of power had been fulfilled at Pentecost, but this endowment was renewed again and again. It was power for righteousness made possible by the Spirit working within them. Paul wrote, "Our sufficiency is of God, who also hath made us able ministers of the new testament; not of the letter, but of the Spirit; for the letter killeth, but the Spirit giveth life."[24]

Preaching in the early church carried conviction because of its power in proclamation. It is probable that few of the preachers were eloquent, but they were forthright and very much in earnest. Paul reminded the saints of Thessalonia of this: "Our gospel came not unto you in word only, but also in power and in the Holy Ghost, and in much assurance."[25]

In a letter to the Ephesians he wrote,

Now unto him that is able to do exceeding abundantly above all that we ask or think, according to the power that worketh in us, unto him be glory in the church by Christ Jesus throughout all ages, world without end.[26]

And to the Corinthians he wrote,

I, brethren, when I came to you, came not with excellency of speech or of wisdom, declaring unto you the testimony of God. For I determined not to know anything among you, save Jesus Christ, and him crucified....My speech and my preaching was not with enticing words of man's wisdom, but in demonstration of the Spirit and of power, that your faith should not stand in the wisdom of men, but in the power of God.[27]

The power of the Holy Spirit was manifested among the early Christians, as it has been ever since, in terms of what Paul called "the power that worketh in us." It was demonstrated at every level of the Christian life. It led the Lord Jesus to pray from the Cross "Father, forgive them; for they know not what they do."[28] and, again: "Into thy hands I commend my Spirit."[29]

Fortified by this Spirit, Paul wrote to his son in the gospel, Timothy, "God hath not given us the spirit of fear; but of power and of love, and of a sound mind."[30]

In his letter to the saints in Rome he wrote, "I am not ashamed of the gospel of Christ; for it is the power of God unto salvation to every one that believeth."[31]

For Mary it meant treasuring up in her heart the announcement of the angelic messenger, while she trained Jesus so that he "increased in wisdom and stature, and in favor with God and man."[32] It led Stephen to forego his chance to defend himself before the Sanhedrin in order to tell the story of Jesus where it could not be hidden.

For John it meant sending out the word of victory from his prison on Patmos: "This is the victory that overcometh the world, even our faith."[33]

For Peter it meant following his Lord, no matter what John's calling turned out to be.[34]

Power is a stewardship to be recognized and exercised by all disciples of the Lord Jesus, in things temporal and in things spiritual. We wield power in all sorts of circumstances, and it is easy to come to regard it as our own. It is ours in the sense that it is entrusted to our care for the time being. At some time we must account for it. It is never intended to be used as though it is naked power.

REFERENCES

1. Matthew 28:17-19.
2. John 6:58.
3. John 6:61, 66.
4. John 6:67-69.
5. Matthew 9:26-28.
6. Mark 3:1-6.
7. Matthew 15:21-27.
8. Luke 7:2-10.
9. John 5:2-9.
10. Mark 2:9-12 KJ.
11. Matthew 7:28-29 KJ.
12. John 3:2.
13. Matthew 5:27-28 KJ.
14. Mark 2:25.
15. Luke 9:51.
16. Acts 2:23.
17. Acts 2:1.
18. Acts 1:1-12.
19. Acts 2:14-20.
20. Acts 2:38-39.
21. Acts 2:41-45.
22. Luke 9:1-4; 10:1-2, 17.
23. Acts 2:47.
24. II Corinthians 3:5.
25. I Thessalonians 1:5.
26. Ephesians 3:20-21.
27. I Corinthians 2:1-2, 4-5.

28. Luke 23:35.
29. Luke 23:47.
30. II Timothy 1:7.
31. Romans 1:16.
32. Luke 2:52.
33. I John 5:4.
34. John 21:20.

*I believe in the sun, even when it is not
   shining;
I believe in love, even when I feel it not;
I believe in God, even when He is silent.*

> —Words found written on the wall
> of a cellar in Cologne after
> World War II.

Chapter 23

The Holy Spirit and
The Gift of Faith in God

The early Christian church was an association of believers. The philosophers came later, and made important contributions, but their task was to explore the faith and the facts on which it rested. Two were primary: (a) the resurrection of the Lord Jesus, and (b) the newness of life demonstrated in the Spirit-quickened lives of the saints. These affirmations were based on internal and external evidence of the most compelling sort. The fact of the resurrection was affirmed on the basis of scripture and proclaimed by many witnesses whose testimony might cost them their lives—as for many of them it did. The presence and power of the Spirit were apparent in the courage and fraternity, the joy and hope of the new-born believers.

The faith of the early saints was not contrary to reason; it came from insights which reason could not give of itself. It illuminated one of their ancient proverbs:

Trust in the Lord with all thine heart;
And lean not to thine own understanding.
In all thy ways acknowledge him,
And he shall direct thy paths.[1]

Their faith was the gift of God for which the way

had been prepared by their trust in the apostolic testimony and the Spirit which accompanied it.

A historian of this period might have written that during the administration of Pontius Pilate in Palestine Jesus was crucified between two thieves. The believer adds, "He was wounded for our transgressions, he was bruised for our iniquities; the chastisement of our peace was upon him; and with his stripes we are healed."[2]

The believer, too, is narrating history—on a different level. This addition rests on the fact of the crucifixion, and reflects the verdict of the soul which only faith can give, and which is beyond the power of the earth-bound historian to negate. Paul wrote to the saints in Corinth,

We preach Christ crucified, unto the Jews a stumbling block, and unto the Greeks foolishness. But unto them which are called, both Jews and Greeks, Christ the power of God and the wisdom of God.[3]

While he was with them the Lord Jesus was known among his friends and followers as a prophet and teacher, but after his resurrection—when he had been seen by witnesses chosen before of God—he was known to be the Son of the living God.[4] Many wise and honest men and women of that day, and many more of subsequent ages have had experiences with the Lord Jesus and under the guidance of his Spirit have joined the ranks of believers.

The gift of faith which Paul cites in his Corinthian letter[5] is also mentioned by him as a fruit of the Holy Spirit in the Galatian letter.[6] He refers to its abiding quality, but emphasizes that it is contributory to charity: "And now abideth faith, hope, charity, these three; but the greatest of these is charity."[7]

Faith, then, is a gift of God which must be nourished by his Spirit and manifested in love as a continuing aspect of the Christian life.

Faith in God is not of our own contriving. Although believers have much to do with its place in the Christian life and fellowship, in the final analysis it is the gift of God. It is evidence which has an element of challenge, a requirement that its testimony be faced. We cannot evade this challenge. No one likely to read this book has been left alone by God. We cannot live apart from his blessing, and if we oppose or ignore him we come under his judgment. This was discussed by Paul in Athens[8] and in his letter to the Romans:

When the Gentiles, which have not the law, do by nature the things contained in the law, these, having not the law, are a law unto themselves; which show the work of the law written in their hearts, their conscience also bearing witness, and their thoughts the meanwhile accusing or else excusing one another.[9]

A revelation to the early saints of the Restoration reads, "In nothing doth man offend God, or against none is his wrath kindled, save those who confess not his hand in all things, and obey not his commandments."[10]

Faith is evidence. The letter to the Hebrew saints affirms this forthrightly: "Faith is the substance of things hoped for, the evidence of things not seen."[11]

Modern translators have struggled to make this abundantly clear. Their difficulty has centered in the rendition of two words *substance* and *evidence*. Sound faith is not a figment of the imagination. It has weightiness. Weymouth calls it "confident assurance"; the New Testament in Modern English identifies faith as "the title deed of things hoped for." For "evidence" Weymouth substitutes "a conviction," while the New English Bible says that "faith makes us certain of realities which we do not see"[12]

Evidence is of various kinds. The kind we are most familiar with is legal evidence which convinces a judge or a jury of the guilt or innocence of one who is on trial. There is also scientific evidence that a certain theory is true or false. The evidence with which we are concerned here is the evidence of the Spirit having sound persuasiveness among believers.

A person is most likely to be strong in faith who seeks fellowship with men and women of faith of the present and of ages past. Chief of these, of course, is the Lord Jesus who is described in the Hebrew letter as "the author and finisher of faith."[13] Some of the variant translations of this part of the letter are quite thought provoking. According to Mofatt Jesus is "the pioneer and perfection of faith," and in the New English Bible: "Jesus, on whom faith depends from start to finish."

The capacity for faith is part of the endowment given us in our creation, and is an essential aspect of our personhood. Palm trees do not grow from acorns. Only oak trees do this. This is because something of their future is involved in acorns from the very beginning. In like fashion, spiritual possibilities are built into us from our beginnings. These possibilities await development and enrichment, but they have promise which reaches into eternity.

Having made it possible for us to know him enough to trust him, our Heavenly Father does not leave us to find the remainder of our way without help. Although we must do our part, ultimately faith is quickened in us by the Holy Spirit. Paul wrote to the saints in Corinth: "Your faith should not stand in the wisdom of men, but in the power of God."[14]

Indeed, faith cannot stand if it has no support but

human wisdom, even our wisdom. As Frederick Dennison Morisson preached years ago: "My hope is not in my hold on God, but in God's hold on me." The gift of faith involves both giving and receiving, and God is active at every step. Once we understand, we do not merely *have* faith but live the life of faith in the closest possible touch with God.

Among the great treasures of the faithful has been the assurance of the truth which grows in the hearts and minds of the obedient. Many of those who have felt this assurance have found it supported by confirming scriptures. Isaiah wrote, "The work of righteousness shall be peace; and the effect of righteousness, quietness and assurance for ever."[15]

Paul wrote, "Our gospel came not unto you in word only, but also in power, and in the Holy Ghost, and in much assurance."[16]

And he wrote, "The natural man receiveth not the things of the Spirit of God; for they are foolishness unto him; neither can he know them, because they are spiritually discerned."[17]

A clever man may learn about God, but only a responsive person can actually know God.[18] Unfaith has no promise. It is rarely deeply held atheism but, rather, a superficial time-conditioned occupation with "the weak and beggarly elements" of this present world.[19]

The assurance of faith has to do with the assurance of light and guidance, the spirit of illumination. It is manifest in that clear vision which dissipates the fog in which we so often stumble. Assured faith in God makes for freedom to act in enterprises of spiritual significance. Among the early saints it made for stability and confidence among those who were beset by all the lures of idolatry. The early apostles had good reason to be greatly concerned at this point. Paul wrote to the saints in Ephesus about the purpose of God in the church:

He gave some apostles; and some, prophets; and some, evangelists; and some, pastors and teachers; For the perfecting of the saints, for the work of the ministry, for the edifying of the body of Christ: Till we all come in the unity of the faith, and of the knowledge of the Son of God, unto a perfect man, unto the measure of the stature of the fulness of Christ: That we henceforth be no more children, tossed to and fro, and carried about with every wind of doctrine, by the sleight of men, and cunning craftiness, whereby they lie in wait to deceive; but, speaking the truth in love, may grow up into him in all things, which is the head, even Christ.[20]

The decisive element in the life of faith is the will. It is the doer who comes to know.[21] Action is therefore a major factor in understanding. Obedience and doing are related words in this connection. Soren Kierkegaard may be of help here. One of his most-quoted observations was that, "We must relate ourselves absolutely to the absolute, but only relatively to the relative." This is a trifle abstruse. But what the Danish theologian was concerned about was that we must decide whether Jesus was a great teacher, but only a teacher, or whether he was in fact the Son of the Living God, and so in a class by himself. If we regard him as a teacher only, we may pass judgment on him contrasting our judgment with his. But if we acknowledge him to be the Son of God we make him our standard of judgment, and at every point seek to learn of him in order that we may obey him. Sound faith affirms that the Father and the Son, as made known to us by the inner assurance of the Holy Spirit, rightly command the most absolute devotion of which we are capable.

Faith becomes strong in the experience of living

faithfully in the fellowship of the faithful; but this should be augmented by participation in corporate and private devotions of which the keynote is love of God and others: "If any man love God, the same is known of him."[22]

Faith grows strong in those who have the heart to seek:

Thou shalt love the Lord thy God with all thy heart, and with all thy soul, and with all thy mind, and with all thy strength.[23]

If...thou shalt seek the Lord thy God, thou shalt find him, if thou seek him with all thy heart and with all thy soul.[24]

The search for God does not stop with the first clear intimation of his goodness and truth. It must be pursued constantly. Spiritual understanding is a gift related to our growing capacity for understanding. Even the Lord Jesus "increased in wisdom and stature."[25]

Spiritual understanding is morally conditioned. It is not an intellectual product, but emerges in the process of the best action of which we are yet capable.

It is of the nature of faith to look upward, and God has surrounded us with inducements to faith. Paul affirmed this to the pagan Athenians.[26] It was particularly true of the chosen people, and they were reminded of this in their religious festivals. It is true also of the millions to whom the gospel has been presented down the generations of this dispensation. The grateful response of those who have recognized these inducements has been to seek him. And to such as have sought him in spirit and in truth he has made himself known. The second Isaiah set this forth in classic fashion:

Ho, every one that thirsteth, come ye to the waters, and he that hath no money; come ye, buy and eat; yea come, buy wine and milk without money and without price. Wherefore do you spend money for that which is not bread? and your labor for that which satisfieth not? Hearken diligently unto me, and eat ye that which is good, and let your soul delight itself in fatness. Incline your ear, and come unto me; hear, and your soul shall live; and I will make an everlasting covenant with you, even the sure mercies of David.[27]

Our Heavenly Father's quickening of faith in us comes in the framework of all that he does for us and for others. Our response of faith is essentially a recognition and acceptance of his gifts by which we live. Thus faith leads to worship and service. It is a natural outcome of the love to which Paul is so eager to give priority.

Followers of Christ in all ages have affirmed that their powers have been augmented by another power, greater than their own. Paul wrote,

Ye are...the epistle of Christ...written not with ink, but with the Spirit of the living God; not in tables of stone, but in fleshly tables of the heart.... Not that we are sufficient of ourselves to think anything as of our selves; but our sufficiency is of God.[28]

This power which is not of ourselves, but is adequate to our most pressing needs, is of God. It is given us through the Son, and is a ministry of the Holy Spirit.

REFERENCES

1. Proverbs 3:5-8.
2. Isaiah 53:5.
3. I Corinthians 1:23-24 KJ.
4. Acts 10:41; I Corinthians 15:6.
5. I Corinthians 12:9.
6. Galatians 5:22.
7. I Corinthians 13:13.
8. Acts 17:27-30.
9. Romans 2:14-15.

10. Doctrine and Covenants 59:5b.
11. Hebrews 11:1 KJ.
12. Hebrews 11:1 NEB.
13. Hebrews 12:2.
14. II Corinthians 2:5.
15. Isaiah 32:17. See also Colossians 2:2.
16. I Thessalonians 1:5.
17. I Corinthians 2:14.
18. Jeremiah 24:6-7.
19. Galatians 4:9.
20. Ephesians 4:11-15 KJ.
21. John 7:17.
22. I Corinthians 8:3.
23. Mark 12:35.
24. Deuteronomy 4:29. See also Jeremiah 24:7; Jeremiah 29:13.
25. Luke 2:52.
26. Acts 17:22-30.
27. Isaiah 55:1-3.
28. II Corinthians 3:3, 5.

Be not afraid to pray, to pray is right.
Pray if thou canst with hope, but ever
  pray
Though hope be weak, or sick with long
  delay.
Pray in the darkness if there be no light.
                    —Harley Coleridge

Chapter 24

Christian Hope and the Holy Spirit

At the end of his matchless hymn of love the apostle Paul emphasized the importance of hope by associating it with faith and enlisting both faith and hope in support of the love of God: "Now abideth faith, hope, and charity, these three; but the greatest of these is charity."[1]

All of us live by hope. Indeed, we entertain all sorts of hopes which we know are temporary and often trivial. But even when they are ill-founded they may bring color which we need. About a hundred years ago Robert James Burdette wrote,

Our hope is ever livelier than despair,
  Our Joy
Livelier and more abiding than our sorrows are.

If well grounded, hopes may well be of great importance in promoting and sustaining courageous action.

In the Pauline epistles hope is mentioned about forty times and is frequently associated with the glory of God. To the saints in Colossae Paul wrote of "Christ in you, the hope of glory."[2]

And to the Romans he wrote, "Hope maketh not ashamed; because the love of God is shed abroad in our hearts by the Holy Ghost which is given unto us."[3]

There is a close relationship between Christian hope and prayer. Paul wrote to his friends in Rome an admonition which is pertinent: "We know not what we should pray for as we ought; but the Spirit itself maketh intercession for us with groanings which cannot be uttered."[4]

What makes this especially interesting is that Paul knew well that we should pray for the coming of the kingdom, for the triumph of the will of God on earth, for aid in our practice of forgiveness, for protection in times of temptation and for our deliverance from evil. Jesus had named these hopes and petitions in his pattern for our prayers. And Paul's own letters abound with requests for his mission to be remembered in the prayers of the saints, and with assurances of his prayers for his correspondents.

Although Paul says we do not know some of the things we should pray for, nevertheless we ought to pray for them. His concern seems to be that we often pray from the surface of our minds, whereas we should learn to pray from the bottom of our hearts. Prayer at this level is possible only if and when we are aided by a power greater than our own. This power we cannot command, but we can seek it in the spirit of devotion. It is the Spirit of God. Actually this Spirit has far-reaching concerns which we frequently forget. To hunger and thirst after righteousness has a great deal to do with the fulfillment of our baptismal covenant. Paul called attention to this: "We through the Spirit wait for the hope of righteousness by faith."[5]

Similarly, peacemaking is important in terms of fraternity. And righteousness and love are both keynote concerns of the Christian hope. We should pray for them with understanding and realistic hope.

Their hope in Christ was a significant aspect of the lives of the early saints. This hope, says the writer of the Hebrew letter, was both sure and steadfast:

God, willing more abundantly to show unto the heirs of promise the immutability of his counsel, confirmed it by an oath that . . . we might have a strong consolation, who have fled for refuge to lay hold upon the hope set before us; which hope we have as an anchor of the soul, both sure and steadfast, and which entereth into that within the veil.[6]

The Christian hope is, fundamentally, the spirit in which we face the tasks of our Christian enterprise: their pains as well as their promise. The ancient psalmists and prophets saw this:

Happy is he that hath the God of Jacob for his help, whose hope is in the Lord his God. Which made heaven and earth, the sea, and all that therein is; which keepeth truth for ever. . . . The Lord shall reign for ever, even thy God, O Zion, unto all generations. Praise ye the Lord.[7]

The prophet wrote in similar terms: "Blessed is the man that trusteth in the Lord, and whose hope the Lord is."[8]

The "sure and steadfast hope" of the saints of the apostolic age was rooted in their experience of the power and love of God. This is the only place where such assurance can be rooted. Paul wrote,

If God be for us, who can prevail against us? He that spared not his own Son, but delivered him up for us all, how shall he not with him also freely give us all things? . . . Who shall separate us from the love of Christ? Shall tribulation, or distress, or persecution, or famine, or nakedness, or peril, or sword? . . . Nay, in all these things we are more than conquerors through him that loved us. For I am persuaded that neither death, nor life, nor angels, nor principalities, nor powers, nor things present, nor things to come, nor height, nor depth, nor any other creature shall be able to separate us from the love of God which is in Christ Jesus our Lord.[9]

The perils enumerated here were not figments of

Paul's imagination. They were parts of his experience and some of them had been shared by those to whom he was writing. They were part of the price for the "lively hope" in which they rejoiced.

The New Testament epistles frequently associate patience and hope. Note, for example, Paul's letter to the Roman saints:

Whatsoever things were written aforetime were written for our learning, that we through patience and comfort of the scriptures might have hope.[10]

Being justified by faith, we have peace with God through our Lord Jesus Christ; by whom also we have access by faith into this grace wherein we stand, and rejoice in hope of the glory of God. And not only this, but we glory in tribulations also; knowing that tribulation worketh patience; and patience, experience; and experience, hope; and hope maketh not ashamed; because the love of God is shed abroad in our hearts by the Holy Ghost, which is given unto us.[11]

Part of Paul's emphasis on patience was due to his awareness that the fullness of the kingdom is not to be realized in a short time, or by the adoption of a socio-spiritual program to which we may be attracted. It is related, rather, to the completion of the apostolic witness in all the world.[12]

Christian hope provokes an alert expectancy. True disciples look for good things to happen, and work to make them happen. If we look with patience at the record of history we can see that many sound advances have been made because of Christian concern in extending education, in perfecting medicinal practice and improving associated healing arts, in the advancement of women, in the abolition of slavery, in exploration (e.g., David Livingstone in opening up Africa). William Carey's slogan, "Expect great things from God. Attempt great things for God" has had creative repercussions throughout the world.

One of the cherished memories of the apostolic group was of the unblemished purity of Jesus. Hope of being like him, nourished on this memory, could not fail to include the hope of like purity. Paul called attention to this in his second letter to the saints in Corinth: "We all, with open face beholding as in a glass the glory of the Lord, are changed into the same image from glory to glory."[13]

Our hope in Christ should be enjoyed gratefully.[14] We may nurture it, but its roots are in the grace of God. We should examine it from time to time in the spirit of worship, for only so can we be reasonably sure that we have not let some of our own hopes intrude and take the place which should be reserved for our Heavenly Father. A story of a wise old abbott may illustrate this. The story is that when he sent his monks out on a mission he gave them this counsel:

God was at work with these people, to help them, long before you heard his call.

He will go on with his work while you do yours.

He will continue after you have left.

Those who love God are called to serve him, but they are not called to take over. God issues his call, and indicates the way of approach and the ends to be sought. And he also is the guarantor of victory.

According to Peter, our hope must be lively as well as humble. When Peter wrote his first epistle the resurrection of the Lord Jesus was cited by the newly converted saints as the basic evidence that Jesus was indeed the Son of God. Peter and the other church leaders cited this seeming impossibility as grounds for believing that in the gospel is salvation in time and eternity. Peter put it this way:

Blessed be the God and Father of our Lord Jesus Christ, which according to his abundant mercy hath begotten us again unto a lively hope by the resurrection of Jesus Christ from the dead, To an inheritance incorruptible, and undefiled, and that fadeth not away, reserved in heaven for you.[15]

This lively hope was not reserved for funereal occasions when death appeared to be victorious, but was a triumphant aspect of the gospel of life and power. Paul preached it in Athens and made it a major theme in his epistles.[16]

The Christian hope is for life which never ends: life of high quality and security. This hope is based on the promise of the Lord Jesus who said to the disciples from whom he was about to be separated:

Let not your heart be troubled; ye believe in God, believe also in me. In my Father's house are many mansions; if it were not so, I would have told you. I go to prepare a place for you. And when I go, I will prepare a place for you, and come again, and receive you unto myself; that where I am, there ye may be also.[17]

This promise was confirmed at the resurrection. In the strength of the hope vindicated there believers learned to look for life in Jesus' life in the community of love. Their scale of values was transformed. They gave attention to the things that endure, to things of the Spirit which grow stronger whenever they are put to the test and survive. It was out of such experience that Paul wrote that "if in this life only we have hope in Christ, we are of all men most miserable."[18] (The American Standard Bible calls this "most pitiable.")

We know something of eternal life, but cherish the hope for it because of assurance which transcends our present understanding. We look for life which is free from the threat of death and secure in the love and wisdom of the Lord Jesus. It is life, and not mere existence. We feel sure that since it is "prepared" for those who love the Lord it will be better than our most exalted imagination. But the very excellence of what awaits us admonishes us to prepare the way of understanding, which is the way of righteousness.

Although glorying in the power and love of God was characteristic of the epistles of Paul, similar comments on the Christian hope can be found in other New Testament writings. Peter wrote,

Ye know that ye were not redeemed with corruptible things, as silver and gold...but with the precious blood of Christ, as of a lamb without blemish and without spot; who verily was fore-ordained before the foundation of the world, but was manifest in these last times for you; who by him do believe in God, that raised him up from the dead, and gave him glory; that your faith and hope might be in God.[19]

And again: "Sanctify the Lord God in your hearts; and be ready always to give an answer with meekness and fear to every man that asketh of you a reason for the hope that is in you."[20]

Evidently the hope of the saints was sufficiently well known to provoke inquiry:

If we shall endure, we shall be kept according to his promise, And we look for new heavens, and a new earth wherein dwelleth righteousness. Wherefore, beloved, seeing that ye look for such things, be diligent, that ye may be found of him in peace, without spot and blameless.[21]

John wrote,

Behold, what manner of love the Father hath bestowed upon us, that we should be called the sons of God; therefore the world knoweth us not, because it knew him not. Beloved, now are we the sons of God, and it doth not yet appear what we shall be; but we know that, when he shall appear, we shall be like him; for we shall see him as he is. And every man that hath this hope in him purifieth himself, even as he is pure.[22]

Some of our finest hopes are for friends and relatives rather than for ourselves. They can be dissipated in undue concern about trivia, or they can be conserved and nurtured so as to bring delightful fruit down the generations. The history of the church is full of the stories of persons who saw their friends and acquaintances as potential kingdom builders.

The New Testament writers do not give much information about Andrew, but what we do know has stirred the hearts of many missionary-minded persons down the generations. Andrew was a follower of John the Baptist, but recognized the greater light of the Lord Jesus and followed him and stayed with him overnight. Then, being convinced, he sought out Peter, his brother, and brought him to the Lord. Thereafter we do not hear much of Andrew, but we hear a great deal of Peter, who became the leader of the Twelve. Bethsaida was a small town, but Andrew and Peter came from there, and so did Philip. And when Philip was called by Jesus he looked up Nathaniel and brought him also to the Lord.

The church has always had an urgent need for men and women who see potential kingdom builders in their best friends and relatives. The spirit of their approach is of major importance, and is most effective when it denotes a deep desire to share what has been tested and found a major means of blessing. It is those who know the wonder of redeeming love who can testify of it attractively.

The Christian hope is not a quiet waiting for what lies beyond. As Peter wrote, it is "lively." Christian life is filled with great expectations born of the experience of celestial glory in the fellowship of the saints in this present life, and its richer manifestation in the life to come.

The Christian assurance arises from the experience of the Holy Ghost as power. The faithful find their lives changed toward godliness by the ministry of a power which is not their own. In the midst of a secular world order we find ourselves open to the transforming power of the Spirit of God. What we experience as individuals we see illustrated in the lives of the faithful, and know it to be prophetic of the life to come.

REFERENCES

1. I Corinthians 13:13.
2. Colossians 1:27.
3. Romans 5:5.
4. Romans 8:26.
5. Galatians 5:5.
6. Hebrews 6:17-19.
7. Psalm 46:5-6, 10. See also Psalm 130:6-8.
8. Jeremiah 17:7. See also 17:13.
9. Romans 8:31-32, 35, 37-39.
10. Romans 15:4.
11. Romans 5:1-5. See also Romans 8:24-25.
12. Matthew 24:32.
13. II Corinthians 3:18.
14. Romans 12:2.
15. I Peter 1:3-4.
16. Acts 17:31-32, 34.
17. John 14:1-3. See also Matthew 25:35; I Corinthians 2:9-10.
18. I Corinthians 15:19.
19. I Peter 1:18-19, 21.
20. I Peter 3:15.
21. II Peter 3:13-14.
22. I John 3:1-3.

I will sing of the mercies of the Lord for ever, with my mouth will I make known thy faithfulness to all generations. For I have said, Mercy shall be built up for ever; thy faithfulness shalt thou establish in the very heavens.

—Psalm 89:1, 2

Chapter 25

Gifts of the Holy Spirit—I

When persons change their attitudes toward God they change the direction of their lives. In a sense they are the same as before: their heritage, possessions, and professional skills are likely to remain substantially as they were. But in another sense they are entirely different: their motivations, objectives, and spirit are not what they were. They will now seek help, and receive it—placing themselves under the tutelage of divinity, serving God rather than seeking their own temporal ends.

The early saints rejoiced in the gifts of God. Of these, God's gift of his Son and the accompanying gift of the Holy Spirit which bore witness of both the Father and the Son, were the most important. The receipt and sharing of these gifts were the marks of true Christians. Together these gifts came to be known as the incarnation, and included the assurance of the divinity of the Lord Jesus, his life and ministry on earth, his Spirit and example, his death and resurrection, and ascension. The Father, the Son, and the Holy Spirit are all included. According to the gospel of John "God so loved the world, that he gave his Only Begotten Son, that whosoever believeth on him should not perish; but have everlasting life."[1]

And Paul wrote concerning Jesus, "Thanks be unto God for his unspeakable gift."[2] Jesus himself said, "The Son of Man came...to give his life a ransom for many."[3]

The knowledge that Jesus is the Lord comes by the Holy Ghost. Paul wrote, "No man can say that Jesus is the Lord, but by the Holy Ghost."[4]

In a further letter to Corinth, in terms which included both the Father and the Son as givers of infinitely precious gifts he wrote, "God, who commanded the light to shine out of darkness, hath shined in our hearts, to give the light of the knowledge of the glory of God in the face of Jesus Christ."[5]

Peter wrote in similar vein:

Grace and peace be multiplied unto you through the knowledge of God, and of Jesus our Lord, according as his divine power hath given unto us all things that pertain unto life and godliness, through the knowledge of him that hath called us to glory and virtue; whereby are given unto us exceeding great and precious promises; that by these ye might be partakers of the divine nature, having escaped the corruption that is in the world through lust.[6]

The gift of his Son for our salvation was itself a reason for expecting still further gifts from God. Paul wrote to the Romans, "If God be for us, who can prevail against us? He that spared not his own Son, but delivered him up for us all, how shall he not with him also freely give us all things?"[7]

We often refer to such gifts of the Spirit as are received by the saints as "the gifts." This designation is unfortunate if we allow it to limit our understanding of the range and the richness of the manifold gifts of God. In ways far beyond what we may suspect, we live on his bounty. James wrote,

Do not err, my beloved brethren. Every good gift and every perfect gift is from above, and cometh down from the Father of lights, with whom is no variableness, neither shadow of turning.[8]

Life in the Holy Spirit was a very real experience among the early Christians. There are at least seventy references to the Holy Spirit in the Book of Acts, leading some students to refer to the book as "The Acts of the Holy Spirit." Mention of the person, the gifts, and the work of the Spirit abound.

The basic gifts of the Spirit by which believers are enabled to share in the life of the Christian fellowship, are augmented from time to time by special gifts given according to the will of God and the needs of the body and members of the body. These are special gifts within the more all-encompassing gift of the Holy Spirit. They are beyond the normal powers of the persons receiving them, but are exercised with their grateful consent. Sometimes the sound expression of these gifts in the assemblies of the saints overtaxed the experience and judgment of local pastors. This occurred at Corinth.

When Paul and Barnabas had planted the work in Corinth they left it in the care of the local ministry. The church in Corinth was probably less than four years old when friends in Corinth wrote of difficulties over the gifts which were dividing the saints. It was against this background that Paul wrote what is now known as "The first Epistle of Paul to the Corinthians" (actually there had been an earlier letter). This First Epistle is our major source of scriptural guidance concerning the gifts of the Spirit.

There are diversities of gifts, but the same Spirit. And there are differences of administrations, but the same Lord. And there are diversities of operations, but it is the same God which worketh all in all. But the manifestation of the Spirit is given to every man to profit withal. For to one is given by the Spirit the word of

273

wisdom; to another the word of knowledge by the same Spirit; to another faith by the same Spirit; to another the gifts of healing by the same Spirit; to another the working of miracles; to another prophecy; to another discerning of spirits; to another diverse kinds of tongues; to another the interpretation of tongues. But all these worketh that one and the self-same Spirit, dividing to every man severally as he will.[9]

The gifts of the Spirit are interrelated. They all come of "that selfsame Spirit." Each one depends on the others to round out its full meaning. The gift of faith is basic to all of them, as is inspired discernment. Wisdom and prophecy have a natural kinship. So do healing and the working of miracles; also tongues and the interpretation of tongues. Moreover, the gifts enumerated by Paul are all dependent, in the total area of salvation, on the basic revelation that Jesus is the Christ, the Son of the living God. As such they have to do with the life and power and witness of the body. They support the ministry of the word, and are often an essential part of this ministry. It was not the eloquence of Peter which moved those who listened to him at Pentecost, but the inner witness of the Spirit. Paul recognized this principle and wrote to the Saints in Corinth:

My speech and my preaching was not with enticing words of man's wisdom, but in demonstration of the Spirit and of power; that your faith should not stand in the wisdom of men, but in the power of God.[10]

In studying the gifts mentioned keep these things in mind:
- They were most probably given expression in an assembly of the saints, and were judged there.
- Some of them would naturally be voiced through the recognized leaders, and might be regarded as inspired counsel to meet specific situations: e.g., wisdom, knowledge.

274

- The Spirit pervading the assembly tended to make them variants on a central theme.
- The varied "gifts" were scrutinized in the spirit of worship. The sense of the divine presence might well have been the "beginning of wisdom."

It will be noted that Paul stressed certain principles relating to the exercise of the gifts:

- "Concerning the spiritual gifts, brethren, I would not have you ignorant." He did not want to squelch the gifts, but he did want them exercised with appropriate wisdom and dignity.
- "There are diversities of gifts, but the same Spirit." There should be no occasion for dispute. The relation of the members of the fellowship should be one of "love unfeigned."
- "There are differences of administration, but the same Lord." Leaders do things in different ways, but the Lord is tolerant of them so long as the fellowship of the joint endeavor is maintained.
- "There are differences of operation, but it is the same God which worketh all in all." The ordering of worship and service is in the hands of fallible persons. They should be humble in their approach to worship, seeking the guidance of the Spirit.[11] They should be upheld by the saints, but this does not make them infallible.
- "The manifestation of the Spirit is given to every man to profit withal." The major enrichment of the saints is in the mutual Spirit-guided sharing of their several gifts.

To these Paul added in his letter to the Thessalonians, "Quench not the Spirit. Despise not prophesyings. Prove [test] all things; hold fast to that which is good."[12]

The conditions under which the gifts of the Spirit

are manifested have much to do with the value of the gifts. This is apparent in the confirmation of the Spirit when the scriptures are expounded in preaching or in teaching, or in the awareness of the sacramental significance of the ordinances as these are shared in worship. There are other ministries of the Spirit which must first ripen in prayer and study and service. The first evidence of the presence of these gifts in rich and moving demonstration may be more or less unexpected as when a worship leader lifts the assembly into the atmosphere of the eternal and all who have any measure of discernment recognize that the power is not the leader's own.

More of the less spectacular gifts are shared among the saints than is sometimes recognized. I am sure that this is often so when sick persons seek administration as an aid to facing the uncertain future as God wishes. A young woman once asked me, "Tell me what do you do as your part in an administration when you have been told you have cancer? I have asked for faith to be healed. And I have no doubt that God can heal me if this is what is best. But how do I know what is best? I am biased in favor of my recovery, but others die and I do not want to give God the appearance of saying that I must have a special blessing, or I will not play his game." So we talked about Jesus in Gethsemane, and finally agreed that in extremities there is no better approach than praying with fullness of heart, "If it be possible, let this cup pass from me. Nevertheless, not my will. . . . "

Many gifts of the Spirit can and should be enjoyed in our homes. The gift of loving guidance and discipline, of sound persuasion of *family* prayer and a large variety of others belong here. Surely this is an area where we can learn by experience how "the

Spirit also helpeth our infirmities."[13]

There are times when the public manifestation of the spiritual gifts is specially arresting. I was present in a prayer meeting held in London, England, in 1921 when Apostle J. A. Gillen said, in essence, "My heart is filled with gratitude to my Heavenly Father for his loving-kindness toward us. I would that I had the skills which would enable me to speak forth a psalm in his praise." Then, with no observable change of tone or posture, but clearly and movingly, he went on to express, as in a psalm, the adoration which filled and inspired him. To a major degree the experience was shared by Brother Gillen and the Spirit which moved him. But those present also shared it. After more than sixty years I find myself recalling it and being uplifted by it.

But there are also times when the manifestation of the spiritual gifts, though sound, is of purely local or individual significance. That this is so does not detract from their importance in the divine scheme of things. One manifestation which was given to a small and earnest group at Gloucester, England, early in August 1914, markedly influenced my own life. We had been together for our mission conference but then, partly because we had a little time and were still enjoying the Spirit which had graced our assembly, we came together for a concluding prayer meeting. In the forepart of this meeting Evangelist James Baty told of a recent occasion when his evening prayer had centered in his concerns regarding the Doctrine and Covenants. As he lay in bed afterward he continued to think and pray in the same mood, and as he did so he became aware of the presence of a person who talked with him about the principle of revelation and commented on the first section of the Doctrine and Covenants as he went. Then, before the experience closed, he affirmed that the teachings of the Book of Doctrine and Covenants were "of God." The saints were quietly attentive and after the meeting had closed many expressed appreciation of the testimony and the Spirit which accompanied it. It was a major factor prompting my lifelong interest in the Doctrine and Covenants and in the first section of that book in particular.

The Spirit is manifested in many ways. But the ultimate purpose of all these manifestations is the same as at Pentecost: to beget and deepen the conviction that the Lord Jesus is indeed the Son of God, the victor over death and hell, the Savior of all who put their trust in him.[14]

REFERENCES

1. John 3:16.
2. II Corinthians 9:15.
3. Matthew 20:28.
4. I Corinthians 12:3.
5. II Corinthians 4:6. See also Hebrews 1:2.
6. II Peter 1:2-4.
7. Romans 8:31-32.
8. James 1:16-17.
9. I Corinthians 12:4-11. See also Doctrine and Covenants 46:7.
10. I Corinthians 2:4-5.
11. Doctrine and Covenants 17:8f, 10d.
12. I Thessalonians 5:19-21.
13. Romans 8:26. See also Hebrews 4:15.
14. John 16:14.

There can be no spiritual progress, no growth of the Church, no victory over evil, without prayer. If faithful work is the steam that keeps the engines in motion, prayer is the sacred fire without which there is no steam.

—Unknown

Chapter 26

Gifts of the Holy Spirit—II

When Jesus commissioned his apostles he said to them,

Go ye into all the world, and preach the gospel to every creature. He that believeth and is baptized, shall be saved; but he that believeth not, shall be damned. And these signs shall follow them that believe; In my name shall they cast out devils; they shall speak with new tongues; they shall take up serpents; and if they drink any deadly thing, it shall not hurt them; they shall lay hands on the sick, and they shall recover.[1]

And they went forth and preached everywhere, the Lord working with them, and confirming the word with signs following.[2]

As is noted elsewhere, the word was indeed confirmed by many signs.[3] The saints with a Hebrew background did not find these things strange, remembering the counsel of their ancient scriptures:

If from thence thou shalt seek the Lord thy God, thou shalt find him, if thou seek him with all thy heart and with all thy soul.[4]

Seek ye the Lord while he may be found, call ye upon him while he is near.[5]

These were augmented in Paul's first Corinthian letter: "Concerning spiritual gifts, brethren, I would not have you ignorant....Covet earnestly the best gifts...."[6]

This counsel of the apostle Paul has been confirmed, moreover, in modern revelation with an important addition:

Seek ye earnestly the best gifts, always remembering for what they are given.... They are given for the benefit of those who love me and keep all my commandments, and him that seeketh so to do.... All these gifts come from God for the benefit of the children of God.[7]

About seventy years ago our Sunday school class spent considerable time discussing the instruction to "seek earnestly" and then what are the "best" gifts. The first of these was summed up by the pastor/teacher when he said that seeking earnestly meant doing so with passionate concern, out of love for the Father and the Son. Then he said, "I have thought that the best gift is the gift of wisdom or, possibly, faith." The class was ready to dismiss after that but one member said, "Before we leave, will any of you tell me why we cannot say that the best gifts are those we need in the changing situations of our lives? If the Spirit is to divide gifts to everyone according to that person's current needs, why do we not just trust the Spirit's judgment, seeking what we need and being grateful for the wisdom which directs us?" I do not remember many Sunday school lessons of seventy or more years ago, but I am inclined to think that my friend was on the right track, and that the best gift of all is the Spirit, no matter what the specific form.

As the presence of the spirit of persons is vital to physical life, so the presence of the Holy Spirit is vital to their spiritual life. There is no satisfactory substitute for the Holy Spirit.

The Spirit does not come merely in impressive visible form or events. The Spirit guides and empowers us in the process of response to the type of action he has initiated. There is no fanfare—only the enlightenment and/or empowering. The person who receives the Spirit is no more governed by self-centered appetites but is responsive to the guidance of the Lord.

All the services of the church should be permeated by the power of the Holy Spirit. This does not mean that they should be judged by the presence or absence of what have often been referred to as the "outward manifestations of the Spirit." The test of a meeting lies, rather, in the degree to which the assembly has been unified in love, is given an enhanced awareness of the divine purpose in the lives of the group and its members, and is moved to wiser and more committed awareness of the purpose of God beyond the spiritual satisfactions of those present.

The normal ministries of the church should not be unduly disturbed for the sake of special interjections which tend to emphasize the artistic rather than the spiritual. And no anxiety for the manifestation of the spiritual gifts should be allowed to detract from the carefully planned order of service, which may itself be a gift of God.

Paul was concerned about possible disruptions when he wrote to Corinth that those aware of their prophetic messages should await their turn and not interrupt one another. The Moffatt version of I Corinthians 14:29-30 is clearer than the King James version, which reads: "Let the prophets speak two or three, and let the other judge. If any thing be revealed to another that sitteth by, let the first hold his peace. For ye all may prophesy one by one."

Moffatt reads: "Let only two or three prophets speak, while the rest exercise their judgment upon what is said."

As a further safeguard, Paul set forth the principle that the spirit of the prophets is subject to the prophets. I have never known a situation where there was competition as to who might speak, but I have known more than one situation where an unwise person has claimed in self-defense after an alleged but uninspired manifestation, "I could not resist the Spirit."

Among the spiritual gifts, primacy belongs to love which points beyond the gift itself to the achievement of its purpose.

The first test for deciding the validity and worth of any gift is to consider whether it serves the common good. Thus, in the assembly of the saints, prophecy is to be preferred above tongues since it gives understanding, while tongues conveys no such understanding except when it is associated with the gift of interpretation.

In recent years there has been a worldwide renewal of interest in the gifts of the Spirit. In many situations this has been highly selective, attention being centered on the gifts which are most apparent and, at times, those which are most arresting. The gifts of tongues and of healing have tended to be stressed rather than wisdom and knowledge and faith. This is due in part to a desire for that which can be seen and identified with some scripture and accepted as evidence of "salvation." This emphasis will not stand scrutiny when considered in relation to the total balance of spiritual direction needed for growth in spiritual maturity. The guidance desired from the ministry is to the end that the Saints shall be

no more children, tossed to and fro, and carried about with every wind of doctrine, by the sleight of men, and cunning craftiness, whereby they lie in wait to deceive; but speaking the truth in love, may grow up into him in all things, which is the head, even Christ; from whom the whole body fitly joined together and compacted by that which every joint supplieth, according to the effectual working in the measure of every part, maketh increase of the body unto the edifying of itself in love.[8]

Enjoyment of the gifts of the Spirit ought not to be sought as an end in itself. The gifts should fit into the life of the body. Although a particular assembly may include some who are not likely to be together again, and special ministry may rightly be directed to them, the overall pastoral concern is with the growing spiritual life of the people. This was one of the major concerns of the leaders of the apostolic church. They were pushing the work into all the world, and their endeavors centered in winning men and women to the Lord Jesus and then making co-workers of those enlisted. In the Ephesian letter Paul lists some of the grades of ministry and then goes on to say that these are "for the perfecting of the saints." Thus far most of the modern translators agree, but thereafter the great majority of them say that this perfecting is for the work of ministering. It is to this end that many of the spiritual gifts are pointed.

Gifts of the Spirit are not substitutes for the exercise of gifts already given as part of our natural or acquired endowment. The counsel is to "seek...diligently and teach one another words of wisdom; yea, seek ye out of the best books words of wisdom; seek learning even by study, and also by faith."[9]

This calls for hard and discriminating work in the spirit of worship. But it does much to open our eyes to what may prove to be "the best gifts" in time to come. It is only to those who observe things that are lovely, and—most of all—who observe in the spirit of gratitude, that the riches of their loveliness is revealed.

All things bright and beautiful,
   All creatures great and small,
All things wise and wonderful,
   The Lord God made them all.

He gave us eyes to see them,
   And lips that we might tell
How great is God Almighty
   Who has made all things well.[10]

All of us need the ministry of the Holy Spirit as an abiding comforter, strengthener, and guide. This need sometimes appears to rise to a peak, notably when we are parts of the fellowship of believers. Two illustrations occur to me: The first of these has primary reference to the seventy, but the basic principle is valid elsewhere. The story is in Luke:

The Lord appointed other seventy also, and sent them two by two before his face, into every city and place where he himself would come. And he said unto them, the harvest truly is great, but the laborers few; pray ye therefore the Lord of the harvest, that he would send forth laborers into his harvest.[11]

The principle behind this seems clear: those who can pray most effectively are those who are themselves fully committed and yet know that they need help which only God can supply. The Lord gave no indication as to where the help would come from. Maybe it would come from some unknown source. But, probably, it would come from among the converts whose commitment would help to inform them of the needs of others, and whose ministry would bring them added conviction.

The other illustration has appealed to me, very possibly, because I have been familiar with the conditions prompting it. The revelation of 1894 (Doctrine and Covenants 122:13) authorized the calling of a joint assembly of the Presidency, Twelve, and Presiding Bishopric. It turned out to be a very important gathering and the minutes were printed in the Doctrine and Covenants from 1895 to 1970. It was not a revelation, and in view of this the World Conference of 1970 authorized its transfer to the Appendix. Those taking part were the leading men of the church. When drafting their report they acknowledged the direction they had received:

To God whose hand has led us and whose patience has borne with our infirmities, the generous praise of his church is due. May our renewed consecration under the better conditions his mercy has brought about, bring to him added glory and to his church prosperity and peace.[12]

The guidance of the Spirit which these men had shared was not a momentary experience such as we have been accustomed to call "a gift." But it was suited to the needs of those participating and of the church, and it was God-given.

Many values accrue from the wise and disciplined exercise of the spiritual gifts. When they are recognized for what they truly are (as, for example, in the heaven-blessed presentation of the scriptures) they can and do bring blessings of understanding which endure. Here are some which I have known down the years. There are many more.

Heartfelt awareness of the light of the Spirit gives a sense of the love of God which promotes understanding and power.

Experiences with the gifts of the Spirit edify the body, promoting unity in diversity. Those participating have windows opened toward understanding such as they would be unlikely to open themselves.

The Spirit sounds the note of eternity in time. Assurance is undergirded. Divinely approved priorities are justified.

Pride is humbled as we recognize the splendor of the operations of the Spirit in bringing unity out of discord.

The spiritual gifts provide impulsions toward faith and repentance.

Faith is energized and made current. Discipleship is seen as more important than opinions. Native gifts are quickened and directed.

The gifts of the Spirit make available for the work committed to all, powers beyond what can normally be commanded: the healing of the mind and of the body, perception of the encroachments of evil, etc.

John the Beloved wrote toward the end of his long life: "Beloved, believe not every spirit, but try the spirits whether they are of God; because many false prophets are gone out into the world."[13]

At the time John wrote, the church was troubled by the promoters of the Docetic heresy, which alleged that Jesus did not really die but only appeared to do so. It is probable that John had the Docetists in mind when he wrote this warning. Down the ages, however, there has been need to repeat the warning against false prophets whether deliberate or self-deceived.

Every excellence carries with it the danger of abuse. Education can be an aid or a curse. Judge Jackson said during the Nuremberg trials that in the modern world we do well to guard against the clever and cultured but immoral person more than against any others. With regard to the spiritual gifts persons of clearly good intentions who have mistakenly thought of themselves as able to foretell the date of the end of the world, or of some famine or pestilence, have done immeasurable harm. Jesus said,

There shall also arise false Christs, and false prophets, and shall show great signs and great wonders; insomuch that, if possible, they shall deceive the very elect.[14]

We betray ourselves and our fellows, furthermore, if we seek the gifts for secondary or unworthy purposes: to bolster faith cheaply, or to minister to our personal or denominational pride, or to emphasize "do not perish" rather than "have everlasting life."

We deny the Spirit whenever we limit the range of operation. To have regard for the gift of healing, but not for the gift of wisdom is to limit the healing gift as well as to forego such healing as may have been available.

We limit our enjoyment of the spiritual gifts whenever we restrict our expectancy to our own present small areas of concern as though this was also the total area of concern of the Spirit of God.

Two observations lifted from my notes on the gifts of the Spirit may be helpful at this point. The first is from the Conference of 1912 when the venerable President Joseph Smith III said: "Do not neglect spiritual things for the intellectual." And, later, "I trust that we shall be able to enjoy the spiritual gifts more than we have."[15]

The other comes from my notes of comments made by President John F. Garver at an assembly of appointee ministers held in October 1946. President Garver said,

The "outward gifts" should be exercised with extreme care:

Only under clear light.
Under unmistakable propulsion.
With definite assurance that there is guidance in their
  public expression.
Never by manipulation.

Then he added:

When controlled, cherished, conserved, restrained, and understandingly appropriated, these with all other gifts should build up reserve power, and are a sure source of vision, stimulation, and strength in Christian living.[16]

REFERENCES

1. Mark 16:14-19.
2. Mark 16:21.
3. Acts 2:22, 5:12, 14:3; Hebrews 2:4.
4. Deuteronomy 4:29.
5. Isaiah 55:6. See also Proverbs 8:34-35; Jeremiah 29:12-14.
6. I Corinthians 12:1, 31.
7. Doctrine and Covenants 46:4, 7f.
8. Ephesians 4:14-16. See also II Peter 1:5-11; 3:17-18; Doctrine and Covenants 46:7.
9. Doctrine and Covenants 85:36a.
10. *Hymns of the Saints*, 18.
11. Luke 10:1-2.
12. Doctrine and Covenants, Appendix E, Section 123:31.
13. I John 4:1.
14. Matthew 24:24.
15. Church History 6:445.
16. From my personal notes.

Behold,
  What manner of love the Father hath
  bestowed upon us, that we should be
  called the sons of God.

  —I John 3:1

Chapter 27

The Love of God, the Fruit of the Spirit

The Lord Jesus was greatly concerned that his disciples should show the fruits of their faith in their lives. He said to them,

I am the true vine, and my Father is the husbandman. Every branch in me that beareth not fruit he taketh away; and every branch that beareth fruit, he purgeth it, that it may bring forth more fruit....Herein is my Father glorified, that ye bear much fruit; so shall ye be my disciples.[1]

And he said, "By their fruits ye shall know them."[2]

Moreover, the Lord brought this teaching into sharp focus for the apostles when he said to them, "By this shall all men know that ye are my disciples, if ye have love one to another."[3]

The gifts of the gospel are given, in the final analysis, for the manifestation of the fruit of the Spirit in the lives of the saints, in the fellowship in general, and beyond. While specific gifts may be given to meet specific needs, the fruit of the Spirit is basically the product of the abidingness of the Spirit. Jesus said,

Abide in me, and I in you. As the branch cannot bear fruit of itself, except it abide in the vine; no more can ye, except ye abide in me....If a man abide not in me, he is cast forth as a branch, and is withered.[4]

In his letter to the saints in Ephesus the apostle

Paul wrote, "The fruit of the Spirit is in all goodness and righteousness and truth."[5]

Paul elaborated somewhat in his letter to the Galatians: "The fruit of the Spirit is love, joy, peace, long-suffering, gentleness, goodness, faith, meekness, temperance."[6]

In each letter Paul uses the singular, "fruit" and in the Galatian letter he gives first place to "love." Here is a hint of Paul's own life. Before his experience with Jesus on the Damascus Road the vigor with which he persecuted the Jews was, in all probability, a reflection of his own inner conflict. Thereafter, in Christ and under the Holy Spirit, he found inner unity and consequent power and love. So, when Paul used the word *fruit* in the singular I am inclined to think that he did so in an inclusive sense. The other fruit he mentioned had its life from this empowering and unifying source. What he was really doing was introducing to the Galatian saints the various members of the "love" family. The members have different surnames, but are all closely related.

The love of God is without parallel throughout history. It was manifested most uniquely in the life and death of the Lord Jesus, and was most unforgettably revealed at Calvary. Enoch, Moses, and other Old Testament prophets had known of the coming of the Lord and of his sacrifice. And it is a major theme of the Book of Mormon. When the event actually took place, and when its cause and meaning were explained in light of the apostolic witness and the accompanying testimony of the Holy Spirit, what had transpired demanded response from people of spiritual calibre.

Many who had been attracted by Jesus' ministries and many who knew of the miracles associated with his name, began to think of the revelatory sequence associated with Calvary...the resurrection...Pentecost...and the new life being manifested by believers. As they looked and thought, they were impressed by a single explanation underlying all that had happened. The apostle John wrote of it again and again:

God so loved the world, that he gave his Only Begotten Son, that whosoever believeth on him should not perish, but have everlasting life.[7]

The...word was made flesh, and dwelt among us...full of grace and truth.[8]

John also called attention to this sequence:

Beloved, let us love one another; for love is of God; and every one that loveth is born of God, and knoweth God. He that loveth not, knoweth not God; for God is love. In this was manifested the love of God toward us, because that God sent his only begotten Son into the world, that we might live through him. Herein is love, not that we loved God, but that he loved us, and sent his Son to be the propitiation for our sins. Beloved, if God so loved us, we ought also to love one another.[9]

Jesus lived among the people of Palestine in order to reveal to them the widespread and penetrating love of God. This was at the heart of his preaching. He was not content, however, to describe his Father in words and arresting phrases, for no verbal description of Almighty God will meet human need. The apostle Philip sensed this, and on a memorable occasion said to Jesus, "Show us the Father, and it sufficeth us."[10]

Jesus answered with a question which required Philip to look into his own soul:

Have I been so long time with you, and yet hast thou not known me, Philip? He that hath seen me hath seen the Father...Believest thou not that I am in the Father, and the Father in me? The words that I speak unto you I speak not of myself; but the Father that dwelleth in me, he doeth the works.[11]

In his remarkable chapter on the primacy of love the apostle Paul wrote, "Though I bestow all my goods to feed the poor, and though I give my body to be burned, and have not charity, it profiteth me nothing."[12]

"Charity is the pure love of Christ"[13] is one of the most familiar quotes from the Book of Mormon. There is nothing casual or trivial or temporary about the love of God. Its strength is in the character of divinity. We may know ourselves to be unworthy of it, but it is nevertheless offered to each one of us freely. Having benefitted by the grace of God's love, we are encouraged to emulate it.

The love of God is the major theme of the scriptures:

- It motivated creation.
- By it the bounds of our habitation were determined.[14]
- It is by the grace of God that we "live and move, and have our being."[15]
- It has inspired the ministry of prophets and apostles.[16]
- It was proclaimed by the Lord Jesus, and given meaning in his life and death and resurrection.
- It is quickened in believers by the testimony of the Holy Spirit.
- It is the guarantor of the kingdom and of life everlasting.

The spiritual quality of men and women is known in the fervor and consistency of their response to such love:

Herein is love, not that we loved God, but that he loved us, and sent his Son to be the propitiation for our sins.[17]

Behold what manner of love the Father hath bestowed upon us, that we should be called the sons of God. . . . And it doth not yet appear what we shall be; but we know that, when he shall appear, we shall be like him; for we shall see him as he is. And every man that hath this hope in him purifieth himself, even as he is pure.[18]

The weeks between the crucifixion and the day of Pentecost were a time of deep concern for many who had known Jesus. They could not refrain from wondering what the crucifixion of such a man really meant in terms of the power of God to protect those who loved and served him. At first, it seemed to mean that so far as this world is concerned Rome and her legions would have the last word, and that the rulers of the Jews were justified in working in harmony with this brutal overlordship. Then came the almost unbelievable news of the resurrection and the supporting testimony of too many witnesses to be ignored. For many, certain basic convictions emerged:

1. Peter was right when he said at Pentecost that the crucifixion was not a routine affair of Roman administration, but had transpired in accordance with "the determinate counsel and foreknowledge of God."[19]

2. This purpose was not momentary or centered in the current situation, but had been anticipated by the prophets down the generations. The crucifixion was rooted in the divine intention of salvation. It was much more than an event; it was a revelation of the love and wisdom and foresight of God.

The love of God for us does not depend on our attitude toward him. He makes the rain fall on the just and on the unjust. We are told that we must strive to love as he loves. In his prayer for his disciples Jesus pleaded that the love which he shared with his Father should also be shared among them:

Now I am no more in the world, but these are in the world, and I come to thee. Holy Father, keep through thine own name those whom thou hast given me, that they may be one as we are.[20]

When our thoughts turn to the New Testament testimony of the love of God we tend to think first of the hymn of love.[21] Here Paul describes a love which is vastly different from that of the world, including the great poets and novelists of our race. Confronted by this, translators have rendered the Greek *agape* as *charity*, which they borrowed from the Latin. As noted earlier one of the earliest translators into English, Miles Coverdale, called it *loving-kindness.*

We should cherish the Corinthian hymn, but its beauty of expression should not distract us from considering other gems. Here is a related section from the Ephesian letter:

I bow my knees unto the Father of our Lord Jesus Christ, of whom the whole family in heaven and earth is named, that he would grant you, according to the riches of his glory to be strengthened with might by his Spirit in the inner man; that Christ may dwell in your hearts by faith; that ye, being rooted and grounded in love, may be able to comprehend with all saints what is the breadth, and length, and depth, and height; and to know the love of Christ, which passeth knowledge, that ye might be filled with all the fulness of God.[22]

The love of God which enriches and unites disciples of the Lord Jesus is born of the Spirit of God. Paul wrote of this to the Saints in Rome:

The love of God is shed abroad in our hearts by the Holy Ghost which is given unto us. For when we were yet without strength, in due time Christ died for the ungodly. For scarcely for a righteous man will one die; yet peradventure for a good man some would even dare to die. But God commendeth his love toward us, in that, while we were yet sinners, Christ died for us.[23]

Love such as this is generated in the study of the life of Jesus and matured in worship and service. It is

the family love of the children of God, and its possession is the primary evidence that we truly belong to
that family.

The prevalence of the love of God in all that he
does has been lauded down the centuries by poets
and psalmists who have depicted it with deep emotion, but have had difficulty describing it. Perhaps
the musicians come nearest. It is an attitude, a Spirit-
prompting action, so that we come to know it best in
worshipful recall of the mighty acts of God. This recall lifts worshipers to praise. It is because worship
is so basic in both Judaism and Christianity that the
Book of Psalms—the Hebrew book of praise—is the
best known and most frequently consulted book of
the Old Testament: The psalmist wrote: "His praise
shall be continually in my mouth."[24] "Praise is
comely for the upright."[25]

Praise is the consummation of joy. In it God communicates his transforming grace to the worshiper
and, most particularly, when the worship is a chorus
rather than a solo.

The love of God which Jesus proclaimed was of a
more elevated order than the most discerning of his
hearers realized when they first heard him. Their
minds and hearts and ways of life needed to be
stretched toward expanding understanding. The
love of which he spoke, and which he demonstrated,
was love for people as people, including the seemingly undeserving. His judgment of justice was
forward-looking, concerned with the justice which
might be achieved rather than the application of law
to what had happened. He illustrated this in his par-
able of the man who hired laborers to work in his
vineyard, and paid the man who worked only one
hour as though he had worked all day. Obviously he

297

did not pay according to the requirements of any local union, but according to the worker's own need. He absorbed any loss because of his generosity, standing for the moment where the worker stood, and recognizing the worker's need to have money to pay for the day's supplies.[26]

As we read that we should love God with all our hearts we should keep in mind that the Hebrew people of that time thought the heart had to do with the inner life as a whole. The reference does not have to do with feeling alone (as modern usage seems to imply) but to the lover's way of acting. It presupposes no distinctive attractiveness on the part of the one loved—only a deep sensitivity to the beloved's needs which the lover hastens to satisfy because of love.

In stories like that of Zacchaeus, the lost sheep, the lost coin, and—perhaps the most appealing of them all—the Prodigal Son, Jesus made it clear that there is something in the human soul which God regards as precious for its own sake. Distinctions of race, class, and condition are unimportant to him. He had demonstrated this many times by the inclusive outreach of his love.

In the love of God, believers find their major and stable reason for believing in the dignity and worth of the common person. The age-long endeavors of our Heavenly Father for our redemption attest both his patient concern for us and his knowledge that there are those who will respond. Even in the sinner and the rebel he sees beyond what we can see of the power of his grace to reach and transform. What happened to Saul (Paul) can have many counterparts: "If any man live in Christ, he is a new creature."[27]

It is inevitable that believers who lose loved ones by death will be concerned about the life that these loved ones now live. There are many things we shall not understand until we share them. But there are others of which we can have a high degree of assurance. The righteous dead are enjoying eternal life. This, we have reason to believe, is life of a high quality removed from many of the strains of life on earth.

Jesus said to the thief being crucified with him, who apprarently believed in him, "Today shalt thou be with me in paradise."[28] There are two other references to paradise in the New Testament. One is from Paul's second letter to the saints in Corinth. Here he told of a man he had known who was "caught up into paradise."[29] Probably Paul was using the word *paradise* as did the rabbis of his day. They taught that paradise is a garden—not unlike Eden—having the tree of life near its center. This, they said, was the abode of the righteous dead. The third reference is from the Book of Revelation: "To him that overcometh will I give to eat of the tree of life, which is in the midst of the paradise of God."[30]

Jesus differentiated between the abodes of the righteous and the unrighteous dead. Of those who failed to help their needy neighbors he said, "These shall go away into everlasting punishment." He continued, "but the righteous into life eternal."[31]

John wrote, "He that believeth on the Son hath everlasting life: and he that believeth not the Son shall not see life; but the wrath of God abideth in him."[32]

Toward the end of his long and fruitful life the apostle John wrote, "Behold, what manner of love the Father hath bestowed upon us, that we should be called the sons of God."[33]

John's "behold" was a reflection of his entire personality and ministry. He might have written, "You who have eyes to see, stop, and look and listen." It is not unlikely that he remembered Andrew's similar invitation which won Peter.[34] Certainly more than a passing glance is needed. Because so many of us fail to understand the love of God, or build on it, we often describe it in shallow fashion. We need to give serious thought of what it has meant in the lives of prophets, martyrs, and saints who sought to open people's eyes to the wonder of the love of God and urged them to respond and be transformed by it.

This love has nothing casual about it. It is the gift of God by which we are called and enabled to become like him. John wrote,

We have known and believed the love that God hath to us. God is love; and he that dwelleth in love dwelleth in God, and God in him. . . . We love him because he first loved us. . . . And this commandment have we from him, that he who loveth God love his brother also.[35]

REFERENCES

1. John 15:1-2, 8.
2. Matthew 7:29.
3. John 13:35.
4. John 15:4, 6. Note the emphasis in I John 2:2, 10, 14, 17.
5. Ephesians 5:9.
6. Galatians 5:22-23.
7. John 3:16.
8. John 1:14.
9. I John 4:7-11.
10. John 14:8.
11. John 14:9-11.
12. I Corinthians 13:3.
13. Moroni 7:52.
14. Acts 17:26.
15. Acts 17:28.
16. Amos 3:7.

17. I John 4:10.
18. I John 3:1-3.
19. Acts 2:23.
20. John 17:11.
21. I Corinthians 13.
22. Ephesians 3:14-19.
23. Romans 5:5-8.
24. Psalm 34:1.
25. Psalm 33:1; 147:1 KJ.
26. Matthew 20:2; 10-15.
27. II Corinthians 5:17.
28. Luke 23:44.
29. II Corinthians 12:4.
30. Revelation 2:7.
31. Matthew 25:47. See also Mark 10:29-39.
32. John 3:36 KJ.
33. I John 3:1.
34. John 1:40-42.
35. I John 4:16, 19, 21.

Though we walk in the flesh, we do not war after the flesh (For the weapons of our warfare are not carnal, but mighty through God to the pulling down of strongholds). Casting down imaginations, and every high thing that exalteth itself against the knowledge of God.

—II Corinthians 10:3-4

Chapter 28

Life in the Spirit

In his Galatian letter Paul contrasted the works of the flesh[1] with the fruit of the Spirit.[2] He then wrote: "If we live in the Spirit, let us also walk in the Spirit."[3]

Paul affirmed this principle frequently, as in the Roman letter:

If ye live after the flesh, ye shall die: but if ye through the Spirit do mortify the deeds of the body, ye shall live. For as many as are led by the Spirit of God, they are the sons of God.[4]

The people of God are called to live in the Spirit, and the Spirit is concerned with them as a people:

By one Spirit are we all baptized into one body, whether we be Jews or Gentiles, whether we be bond or free; and have been made to drink into one Spirit.[5]

There is one body, and one Spirit, even as ye are called in one hope of your calling.[6]

The strength and vigor of the church depend on the spiritual vitality of her people. There is no substitute for this.

Disciples of the Lord Jesus Christ believe in the primacy of spiritual forces in the world: of love over hate, of cooperation over conflict, of service over acquisition. Attitudes, they know, are more important than things, for attitudes govern the creation and use of things. Disciples do not think of themselves more

highly than they ought. They find fulfillment in to-
getherness. Paul wrote of this to the saints in Rome:

I say, through the grace given unto me, to every man that is
among you, not to think of himself more highly than he ought to
think, but to think soberly, as God hath dealt to every man the
measure of faith. For as we have many members in one body, and
all members have not the same office; so we, being many, are one
body in Christ, and every one members one of another.[7]

Those who are spiritual accept and live within the
divine revelation of their true nature: their creaturehood. They therefore seek fulfillment under God in
worship, in the fellowship of the faithful, and in personal and group service.

Disciples of the Lord Jesus share their Lord's passionate concerns. As Spinoza said long ago: "Passion
must be met with passion. Only a higher passion can
quench a lower." Jesus lived by this principle,
demonstrating the power of love which will not be
denied. Of concern for little children he said, "Whoso shall offend one of these little ones which believe
in me, it were better for him that a millstone were
hanged about his neck and he were drowned in the
depth of the sea."[8]

As his followers share the passionate concerns of
their Lord they feel deeply about things which rob
the poor or about strength which glories in the
inequities imposed on the weak.

In the minds of the early Christians the Holy Spirit
was regarded as the Spirit of the new age. It was the
power of the age which the greatest of the prophets
had glimpsed, of which Joel had spoken, and which
Peter had proclaimed in his sermon at Pentecost.
When scoffers accused the spiritually endowed believers of being drunk Peter said,

Be this known unto you, and hearken to my words; for these are not drunken, as ye suppose, seeing it is but the third hour of the day. But this is that which was spoken by the prophet Joel; And it shall come to pass in the last days, saith God, I will pour out of my Spirit upon all flesh; and your sons and your daughters shall prophesy, and your young men shall see visions, and your old men shall dream dreams; and on my servants and on my hand-maidens I will pour out in those days of my Spirit.[9]

In the minds of the believers the power which they enjoyed was the first installment of that which was yet to come. Paul wrote in this fashion: "[God] hath also sealed us, and given the earnest of the Spirit in our hearts."[10]

And to the saints of Ephesus, "Grieve not the Holy Spirit of God, whereby ye are sealed unto the day of redemption."[11]

Life in the Spirit is life in Christ. Paul wrote to the saints in Colossae of a mystery which, he said, had been hidden for ages and for generations, but now was being made manifest to the saints: "Christ in you, the hope of glory."[12]

The motive power in the lives of the saints was the Spirit of Christ within them. It was not just a set of rules to remind them of the requirements of the Christian way of life. It can well involve rules, but only as reminders. The lively hope of the saints was in the Spirit of Christ within them.

Among the early saints, life in the Spirit was regarded as life guided by God who was present in the Spirit of the risen Christ and manifested in the lives of twice-born persons: Paul wrote, "If any man live in Christ, he is a new creature; old things are passed away; behold, all things are become new."[13]

This indwelling of the Holy Spirit was not regarded as the intrusion of an alien Spirit, wholly foreign to the true nature of the disciple. Rather the new nature was seen as the true nature, coming into its own. The "I" of the repentant sinner had been "crucified with Christ." Paul put it this way:

I am crucified with Christ; nevertheless I live; yet not I, but Christ liveth in me; and the life which I now live in the flesh I live by the faith of the Son of God, who loved me, and gave himself for me.[14]

The indwelling of the Holy Spirit enabled the saints to face life with the assurance of the support of a power greater than their own. Paul prayed:

I bow my knees unto the Father of our Lord Jesus Christ...that he would grant you, according to the riches of his glory, to be strengthened with might by his Spirit in the inner man: That Christ may dwell in your hearts by faith; that ye, being rooted and grounded in love, may be able to comprehend with all saints what is the breadth, and length, and depth, and height; and to know the love of Christ, which passeth knowledge, that ye might be filled with all the fulness of God. Now unto him that is able to do exceeding abundantly above all that we ask or think, according to the power that worketh in us. Unto him be glory in the church by Christ Jesus throughout all ages, world without end.[15]

Both inspiration and striving are involved in the endeavor to cultivate life in the Spirit. Standards are important. Habits carefully considered and developed, which the faithful have set up as guides to excellence, help the believer to maintain the life of the Spirit and set patterns for coming generations. Habits which enriched the lives of our parents need to be renewed from time to time to safeguard them from the erosions of secularism. I am inclined to believe that the importance of habits in life in the Spirit prompted the psalmist to write the following:

Judge me, O Lord; for I have walked in mine integrity; I have trusted also in the Lord; therefore I shall not slide. Examine me, O Lord, and prove me; try my reins and my heart. For thy loving-kindness is before mine eyes; and I have walked in thy truth.[16]

Life in the Spirit is a life of humility before God: of

demonstration without fanfare of the fruit of the Spirit. It is a life of cheerfully accepted responsibility for setting family and community patterns of right relations: of fellowship, integrity, and peace.

Life in the Spirit is a life of stewardship; this involves accounting but is much more than that. Accounting is a means to a cherished end. At its heart it is joy in responding to the love of God. It is prompted by the love to which John called attention out of his own experience:

Behold, what manner of love the Father hath bestowed upon us, that we should be called the sons of God.[17]

Whosoever will come after me, let him deny himself, and take up his cross, and follow me. For whosoever will save his life shall lose it; but whosoever shall lose his life for my sake and the gospel's shall save it. For what shall it profit a man, if he shall gain the whole world, and lose his own soul? Or what shall a man give in exchange for his soul?[18]

Though we walk in the flesh, we do not war after the flesh (For the weapons of our warfare are not carnal, but mighty through God to the pulling down of strongholds). Casting down imaginations, and every high thing that exalteth itself against the knowledge of God.[19]

Life in the Holy Spirit is life integrated around the conviction of the lordship of Jesus. This integration is concerned with the central conviction, but may not yet have achieved maturity. Paul was converted and commissioned by the Lord Jesus and "straightway he preached Christ in the synagogues, that he is the Son of God."[20] Thereafter he went into Arabia and then to Damascus, but he did not go to Jerusalem for three years when he went to confer with Peter and the Lord's brother, James. It was fourteen years before he went to Jerusalem again, this time by revelation, and after consulting with James, Cephas (Peter), and John received their approval of his mission to the Gentiles. Apparently these years were spent in perfecting his insight into the meaning of the central fact of Christ.[21]

What Paul sought in Arabia and throughout his life thereafter was the meaning of life in Christ. There is more than a hint of biography in his letter to the Corinthians:

The Spirit searcheth all things, yea, the deep things of God. For what man knoweth the things of a man, save the spirit of man which is in him? even so the things of God knoweth no man, except he has the Spirit of God. Now we have received, not the spirit of the world, but the Spirit which is of God; that we might know the things that are freely given to us of God.[22]

Something of the same thought of the centrality of Christ was apparently in Paul's mind when he wrote the saints in Philippi:

I count all things but loss for the excellency of the knowledge of Christ Jesus, my Lord; for whom I have suffered the loss of all things, and do count them but dung, that I may win Christ. . . . Brethren, I count not myself to have apprehended; but this thing I do, forgetting those things which are behind, and reaching forth unto those things which are before, I press toward the mark for the prize of the high calling of God in Christ Jesus.[23]

Paul was willing to suffer "the loss of all things" as though they were of no value, in order that he might have the mind of Christ within him. For, he said, "It is God which worketh in you both to will and to do of his good pleasure."[24] When the saints heeded this inspired counsel they shared eternal life in the midst of time.

To live on this level is not just to share an intellectual understanding of things spiritual, although it may include this. It is, rather, to share the fullness of the life of the Lord: to see as he sees, to feel as he feels, to love as he loves. We should test the fullness of our spiritual experiences at this point, for the experience points beyond itself toward kingdom life. It is not complete until it enlarges that life in terms of love and service. It may be that it was something of this that Paul had in mind when he wrote, "Be not conformed to this world; but be ye transformed by the renewing of your mind, that ye may prove [test] what that good, and acceptable, and perfect will of God is."[25]

The late Elder Gomer Wells wrote an article in the *Saints' Herald* many years ago. It came at a troublesome time in my high school debating, and helped me so much that I have never ceased to feel grateful to Gomer. I do not remember the specific title of the article, but it may well have been something like "The Next Step in Creation."

The theme was to the effect that there is no believable promise for world salvation in human longevity, or comfort, or vigor. These may be achieved, and may make the lives of our great-grandchildren more comfortable and more secure. But, he wrote, this line of investigation does not deal with our deepest problems. Our need is for persons of spiritual quality. This can happen only if and as persons capable of success in the present order of social achievement apply themselves to life after a new order.

To the early saints this meant the presence of the Spirit in their personal and group lives: the evident changes which the Spirit made possible pointed unmistakably to the coming of a new age. Peter put it this way: "If ye be reproached in the name of Christ, blessed are ye; for the Spirit of glory and of God resteth upon you."[26]

Paul wrote that the new knowledge and power of which they were aware were but an earnest of that which was to come, a foretaste of the Spirit of the kingdom.[27]

Life in the Spirit is life made joyous by the sense of acceptance with God. Paul wrote in one of his most powerful letters,

There is no condemnation to them which are in Christ Jesus, who walk not after the flesh, but after the Spirit. For the law of the Spirit of life in Christ Jesus hath made me free from the law of sin and death.... They that are after the flesh do mind the things of the flesh; but they that are after the Spirit, the things of the Spirit. For to be carnally minded is death; but to be spiritually minded is life and peace.... Ye are not in the flesh, but in the Spirit if so be that the Spirit of God dwell in you.[28]

It was not Paul who created the sense of assurance indicated here but the Spirit of God. Paul wrote that the Spirit came "not...in word only, but also in power, and in the Holy Ghost, and in much assurance."[29]

It was in this awareness that the Thessalonians accepted it.[30] And with this Peter fully agreed.[31]

Those who live in the Spirit live in the spirit of praise. We are moved to worship at specific moments, but to be deeply effective our worship must reflect the tone of our lives as a whole. This happens when we take time to meditate on the wonder of the love of God as did the Twelve on their way back to Jerusalem after the ascension of their Lord, and as did the disciples who hurried back to tell of the resurrection, saying, "Did not our hearts burn within us, while he talked with us by the way, and while he opened to us the scriptures?"[32]

This is our day of opportunity on the highest possible level. More truly than ever before we live in one world, every part of which is quickly accessible from other key parts. But, strangely, its parts are widely separated by racial and political and religious barriers. However, none of these barriers are absolutely impenetrable, and they are being breached every day. Some of these interpenetrations are with evil intent and need to be safeguarded against, but others are in the nature of things. It is probable that the arts are most helpful. People are much less mutually antagonistic than are their governments. Modern inventions such as automobiles, planes, cameras, and printing plants all have their place in movements toward mutual completion and achievement if those who would use them for evil purposes could be controlled, or if more of such persons see the futility of their way of life.

The threatening problem of our times is in the men and women now alive and in their children who are learning from their forebears the evil power of self-assertive sovereignty. As Joseph Smith wrote more than a hundred and fifty years ago,

Every man walketh in his own way, and after the image of his own god, whose image is in the likeness of the world, and whose substance is that of an idol, which waxeth old and shall perish.[33]

The antidote is in the prophetic word which reaches our day from the apostolic age:

I saw another angel fly in the midst of heaven, having the everlasting gospel to preach unto them that dwell on the earth, and to every nation and kindred, and tongue, and people. Saying with a loud voice, Fear God and give glory to him; for the hour of his judgment is come; and worship him that made heaven, and earth, and the sea, and the fountains of waters.[34]

REFERENCES

1. Galatians 5:19-21.
2. Galatians 5:23-24.
3. Galatians 5:25.
4. Romans 8:14 KJ.
5. I Corinthians 12:13.
6. Ephesians 4:4 KJ.
7. Romans 12:3-5.
8. Matthew 18:5.
9. Acts 2:14-18.
10. II Corinthians 1:22.
11. Ephesians 4:20.
12. Colossians 1:27.
13. II Corinthians 5:17. See also John 3:3; II Corinthians 3:18.
14. Galatians 2:20.
15. Ephesians 3:14, 16-21.
16. Psalm 26:1-3.
17. I John 3:1.
18. Mark 8:34-36 KJ. See also II Corinthians 8, 9.
19. II Corinthians 10:3-4.
20. Acts 9:20.
21. Galatians 1:17 - 2:9.
22. I Corinthians 2:10-12.
23. Philippians 3:8, 13-14.
24. Philippians 2:13.
25. Romans 12:2.
26. I Peter 4:14.
27. II Corinthians 5:5.
28. Romans 8:1-2, 5-6, 9 KJ.
29. I Thessalonians 1:5.
30. I Thessalonians 2:13.
31. I Peter 1:12.
32. Luke 24:31.
33. Doctrine and Covenants 1:3e.
34. Revelation 14:6-7.

Wherefore we receiving a kingdom
which cannot be moved, should have
grace, whereby we may serve God
acceptably with reverence and godly
fear: for our God is a consuming fire.

—Hebrews 12:28-29

Chapter 29

The Falling Away

The Christian Church was established under the authority of the Lord Jesus Christ who said to Peter, "I will build my church."[1]

It was the divine intention from the beginning that Christ should be the chief cornerstone. Later Paul was to write to the saints in Ephesus,

Ye are no more strangers and foreigners, but fellow citizens with the saints, and of the household of God; and are built upon the foundation of the apostles and prophets, Jesus Christ himself being the chief corner stone.[2]

The local activities of the church were guided by "overseers" (probably elders). Paul evidently took the work of these presiding officers quite seriously, for he called those from Ephesus to meet him at Miletus for a final word of counsel:

Take heed therefore unto yourselves, and to all the flock, over the which the Holy Ghost hath made you overseers, to feed the church of God, which he hath purchased with his own blood. For I know this, that after my departing shall grievous wolves enter in among you, not sparing the flock. Also of your own selves shall men arise, speaking perverse things, to draw away disciples after them.[3]

Paul wrote in similar fashion to the saints at Thessalonica[4] and to Timothy.[5] Peter wrote out of like foreknowledge,[6] and John, too.[7]

One of the most pressing problems which confronted the leaders of the apostolic age as they grew older was discovering and commissioning leaders who would continue their work. Only the Holy Spirit could supply this basic need. Leaders must be found who were wise, humble, and filled with the Spirit. Some were found and enlisted, but the volunteers were never sufficiently numerous or willing or qualified.

A factor which made for unity and common understanding among the members of the early Christian church was the ministry of the prophets. Paul mentioned them as next to the apostles in building the foundations of the church, writing to the Ephesians that the church was "built upon the foundation of the apostles and prophets, Jesus Christ himself being the chief corner stone."[8]

As the church grew more carefully prepared, narratives became available and the work of the itinerant prophets was not in such urgent demand. The local ministers and, possibly, many of the saints, felt that the transition from the guidance of the prophets to that of resident ministers would make for stability of purpose, and that money given to the itinerant prophets could be saved and applied to urgent local needs. So, the number of the traveling prophets diminished, and the freedom and spontaneity of their type of ministry was never fully recaptured. Lacking local leadershp, it is not unlikely that the body of the saints did not fully realize what was happening and just "strayed."[9]

At first the membership of the church was comparatively small, but in a surprisingly short time it became widely diversified. Persons of some local importance were found among them. Barnabas and Nicodemus seem to have been men of business.

There were members of Caesar's household among them.[10] Lydia was seemingly a successful dealer in Roman uniforms. Increase in the membership and in its diversity continued without abatement. And the influence which accompanies growth did not escape the attention of some onlookers whose interest was in business and in politics rather than in religion. Occasions arose when prominence in the church opened doors to bribery (simony) and to nepotism (the preferential treatment of relatives). These corruptions did not become evident all at once, but by the time that they were apparent they were generally entrenched.

The first persecutors of the Christians were the Jews. These were soon joined by various groups of the pagans. After a time, opposition became chiefly political. The Christian way of life was such that it was not difficult to make their celebration of the sacraments appear anti-social. Then, too, the Christians would not pay homage to Caesar, and this seemed disloyal. Under various forms of persecution which had but one real cause, the saints showed remarkable faith and courage. Gradually it dawned on Caesar and his advisors that here was an asset which should not be dissipated. So Caesar legalized the church, seeking thereafter to use it as an arm of government. There was nothing spiritual about this. Sacerdotalism and nepotism continued with little thought of reform. But the faith of the apostolic age was increasingly more difficult to find and to practice.

Groups within the church such as the Montanists sought to stem the tide. Montanus, a recent convert from paganism, protested the loss of the Holy Spirit and proclaimed the imminent return of the Lord

Jesus. His movement was strongest between about 135 A.D. and 160 A.D. and then lapsed. After a time, the major points of emphasis were revived by the Novatians, and through them remained influential into the fifth century. Even after the central strength of the protestors lost its appeal, there were many who still felt that all was not well. But, despite their concern, the people lacked the fullness of power which would make this concern effective. Their suggestions were born of their memories and hopes, not of a recommitment of spiritual vigor.

The fight for the purity of the faith was not all one-sided. A major difficulty was that many of those who protested against one deviation were already the victims of another. Those protesting against the temporal claims of the popes, for example, might be handicapped by their acceptance of the papal claims for authority over the administration of the sacraments. Nevertheless the rebuttal was sometimes very important. Creeds (short statements of elements of the faith) were first used in the struggle against pagan heresies. Later they were refined and became official statements of basic faith. In periods when so many of the people were unable to read they formed starting points for discussions and explanations and for disagreements which in themselves were helpful.

Beyond the local struggles for power just noted were city-wide, nation-wide and, in time, worldwide struggles of the same type but of progressively larger scope. At the highest levels, both military and political forces were actively involved. The key principles involved were known as "sacerdotalism" and later, as "sacramentalism." Sacerdotalism may be defined very roughly as *priestcraft*, but it was priestcraft of dictatorial proportions. It centered in certain rites

317

held to have healing power in themselves which could be administered or denied by priestly authority only. In time it came to be related to penance rather than repentance as the means of forgiveness: penance being related to punishment and retribution. Since the minister could set such punishment as his judgment advised this gave him unlimited power.

References to sacerdotalism came to be replaced by the word *sacramentalism*, having direct relation to baptism and communion. The punitive word used was *excommunication*. This denied an offender the right to receive any sacrament or to be present when the sacraments were administered to others. A related word was *interdiction*. This was akin to excommunication except that it was related to the community. By it the church building and its ministries were closed to the person under interdiction except for infant baptism and extreme unction. If the civil authorities were so inclined, they could use the interdiction to justify civil action.

It was hardly to be expected that rulers and other men of power would submit to the application of such penalties against them. Even as the power of Rome personified in the reigns of the great popes seemed to be more secure, opposition grew. Philip of France resisted some of the papal claims and was excommunicated, whereupon he seized the pope and imprisoned him in France. This led to a succession of seven French popes and the selection of enough French cardinals to give the French a majority of the cardinals of the church. Attempts to correct the situation led to the appointment of two popes at once. Since no one knew which was the true pope it made for uncertainty all down the ministerial line (1378 to 1409). To make matters worse, an attempt to correct the situation led to the selection of a new pope. Once in office the new pope decided to stay, and since the other two were intrenched politically and refused to resign, this resulted in three popes (1409 to 1415).

The struggle for papal supremacy was, in fact, a struggle for world power. In such a struggle all sorts of weapons were used. To illustrate this I call attention to two documents which were used for many years to consolidate and extend the power of the popes.

The first of these was probably produced about 754 A.D., and was known as "The Donation of Constantine." It asserted that when Constantine moved his capital to Constantinople he donated sovereignty over the Western world to the pope, and ordered the clergy to be obedient to him. Continued study of the Donation showed that it included awareness of events which did not take place until long after the date of its publication. But the popes had come to rely on it and they continued to do so.

The other influential but forged document was known as "The Pseudo-Isodorian Decretals." The forgery sought to magnify the office of the pope in contrast with the claims of the archbishops and metropolitans who opposed him. This, too, was important in the struggle over papal power. The Holy Spirit's guidance was presumed, but the evidence was hardly visible. This, of course, became apparent when the fraudulent background of the Decretals was recognized.

The Moslems invaded Spain in the eighth century, and were soon followed by many Arabic scholars. Their influence spread throughout Europe in a remarkably short time and, among other things, the study of antiquities became the vogue. As part of this emphasis, the Hebrew and Greek foundations of the Christian scriptures were studied. Over the centuries the church had kept the scriptures from the people. But in the general upheaval John Wycliffe, William Tyndale, Miles Coverdale, and others in England made and distributed translations of the Bible in English and these were paralleled on the continent. Almost simultaneously came the invention of the printing press, and in about fifty years copies of the scriptures could be found almost everywhere.

Dissent spread rapidly all over Europe. In addition to the opposition felt to the civil rule of the papacy, there was correspondence between many whose primary concern was religious. This revealed considerable uniformity in opposition to infant baptism, to the sale of indulgences, the doctrine of transubstantiation (that in the process of its consecration the bread and wine of the communion are transformed into the actual body and blood of the Lord Jesus), to the merit of prayers to the saints. Almost without exception those opposed to the Catholic position affirmed the authority of the Bible as opposed to that of any other standard of authority.

The Lutheran revolt was important, but it was not the sole factor in the division of Christendom. Other leaders such as Ulrich Zwingli of Zurich, John Calvin of Geneva, and their associates played important parts, but their differences were deep enough that before long the Lutherans and the Calvinists were joined by the Anabaptists, the Puritans, the Anglicans, the Quakers, and others.

Even while the non-Catholic world was recovering from the excesses of papal domination another widely and deeply felt cause for resentment arose. This was the establishment of the Inquisition, possibly intended originally for the suppression of internal dissent. But the valor of the Inquisitors was such that they soon spread their efforts far and near, and the cruelties visited on all types of captives who came into their hand were such as to make this a major reason for rejecting papacy without much further inquiry.

Even after a review of the progress of apostasy as brief and as concentrated as this has had to be, one wonders at the blindness which made it impossible for those chiefly responsible to see what they were doing and its inevitable consequences. Superstition is rampant wherever it is not controlled by the assurances of truth and light. But even in the midst of the sixteenth century, when their kind of world was breaking up all around them, church leaders acted as though more of what had brought them to such an impasse would correct their many ills. So the Council of Trent passed up its opportunities, and postponed its sittings until 1559. No constructive work toward unity was done thereafter.

The good intentions of many of the Catholics were made evident in the support given the monastic movement. This came under the work done by the several monastic orders, the Benedictines being chief of them. The Benedictine monks secured large areas of land which were cultivated under their direction, providing work and sustenance for the poor. In connection with the most successful of these schools, considerable important scholastic work was done. But the excellence of the work led to many donations of money and land and implements. The monks had sworn a vow of poverty, but they controlled the wealth of the orders and functioned in this relation about as other owners did.

With the passing of the years innovations piled on innovations until it became almost impossible to recognize the apostolic church in the newly available records. The central problem was that although the direction of the Holy Spirit was often alleged, it was difficult to find evidences of the Spirit in the official actions of the hierarchy. The ministry were regimented more and more closely.

The availability of the scriptures in the languages of the people, however, became a major factor leading to inquiry and understanding. The scriptures won their way into the hearts of the people before their production was given official approval.

Another potent factor making way for understanding and richer worship was the sharing of evangelical hymns. This took time, and the exchanges often included doctrinal adjustments before they were widely accepted. (Our hymn "Faith of our Fathers" once began with "Faith of our fathers, Mary's prayers.") But some became the common possession of many denominations. Among these the best known is Bernard of Clairvaux's hymn:

Jesus, the very thought of thee
With sweetness fills my breast
But sweeter far thy face to see,
And in thy presence rest.

Other ancient hymns in the *Hymns of the Saints* are "All Creatures of Our God and King," Francis of Assisi, 1182-1226 (72); "All Glory, Laud, and Honor," Theodolph of Orleans, 760-821 (23); "Of the Father's Love Begotten," Aurelius Clemens Prudentius, 348-413 (220); and others less readily identified.

REFERENCES

1. Matthew 16:19.
2. Ephesians 2:19-20.
3. Acts 20:28-30.
4. II Thessalonians 2:3.
5. II Timothy 4:2-3.
6. II Peter 3:1-3.
7. I John 4:1-3.
8. Ephesians 2:20.
9. Doctrine and Covenants 1:3d.
10. Philippians 4:22.

This spirit shall return to Him
   Who gave it heavenly spark;
Yet think not, Sun, it shall be dim
   When Thou thyself art dark.
No. It shall live again and shine
   In bliss unknown to beams of thine,
By Him recalled to breath
Who captive led captivity,
Who robb'd the grave of victory,
And took the sting from death.

               —Thomas Campbell
                 (Inscribed on the memorial
                 in Westminster Abbey).

Chapter 30

Immortality and Eternal Life

We tend to think of our modern world as better in every way than the world of our ancestors. In many ways this is true. No one wants to go back to the ignorance and superstition and pain of even the not-so-remote centuries. However, not all the changes which the ingenuity and struggle of the intervening years have brought have been unqualifiedly good. One of the very costly catastrophes of recent years has been the loss of the sense of immortality and eternal life which has overtaken us as we have become more and more deeply involved in the secular outlook of our times. The loss has been consequent on our neglect of the Holy Spirit which Paul said "searcheth all things, yea, the deep things of God."[1]

This loss has been both costly and unnecessary. Costly because it has resulted in disregard of the moral issues confronting us, even though our moral quality is the most important thing about us. And unnecessary, because—unless we reject it—nothing can separate us from the love of God which is in Jesus Christ our Lord. Paul wrote of this in his Roman letter.[2]

In this chapter we discuss immortality and eternal life, and it will be well to begin by distinguishing between these two terms. Immortality is "the survival of personal individuality after physical death."[3] Whether immortality is to be desired or not depends on the kind of persons we have been during our life on earth. I remember Elbert A. Smith preaching on life after death and after commenting on the wonder of the life of the redeemed saying, "Hell is to be with evil people and to know that you belong there."

Immortality is security from the onslaughts of death. It is important as the safeguard of righteousness, and is part of the abidingness promised by the Lord Jesus. While it has no reference of itself to the quality of the life beyond, it does have an important bearing on the life that it continues, subject only to the will and power of God. Paul affirms this.

The dead shall be raised incorruptible, and we shall be changed. For this corruptible must put on incorruption, and this mortal must put on immortality.[4]

Of those raised, immortality and eternal life is promised:

To them who by patient continuance in well doing seek for glory and honor and immortality, eternal life; but unto them that are contentious, and do not obey the truth, but obey unrighteousness, indignation and wrath, tribulation and anguish, upon every soul of man that doeth evil.[5]

Paul wrote to Timothy that the Lord Jesus

Who hath saved us, and called us with a holy calling, not according to our works, but according to his own purpose and grace, which was given us in Christ Jesus before the world began. But is now made manifest by the appearing of our Savior Jesus Christ, who hath abolished death, and hath brought life and immortality to light through the gospel.[6]

The Christian conviction of immortality is supported by many considerations which have been valued by believers. They are not so convincing as to silence all questions, but they strongly support the testimony of the Spirit. Actually, they often enrich our awareness of the truth on which they are built.

One of these supporting considerations requires that we consider the moral splendor of God and its concomitants: what follows his unfailing love, his holiness, his truth, his justice. These are all of a piece with his guarantee of immortality. Against them the plea that we do not know is very feeble and leads to no victories.

In our concern for immortality, it is important that we shall stand as near as we can to our Heavenly Father and his point of view. We isolate ourselves from the truth when we insist on deciding our attitude toward it while we are bowed down with grief. We can be helped by wise and experienced counselors. But in the long run the deep healing which we need can come only from God who loves and understands us. This calls for prayer of a unique sort.[7] Prayer which centers in recital of our griefs may and does bring relief. At times, however, it augments our distress. What we need, basically, is to kneel within the radiance of God's love. We can do this when we remember what God suffered when he gave his Son to the agony of the cross for our sake, and that he has shared the pains of all the prophets and martyrs down the generations.

Eternal life is life patterned on that of the Lord Jesus. We are not able to describe it satisfactorily in words, for even the scriptures are tainted in our use of them. This occurs both because of our own lack of understanding and the divergent meanings given to our words by our hearers. What is needed is that indwelling and prompting of the Holy Spirit which John Rushton used to call "the vocabulary of the redeemed." With such enlightenment both from above and from within communication becomes a genuinely spiritual experience, and the sharing of that experience becomes a foretaste of the fullness of life which awaits the faithful. Paul wrote of this, saying that Christ "hath also sealed us, and given us the earnest of the Spirit in our hearts."[8]

In his letter to the saints in Ephesus he said that they "were sealed in the Holy Spirit of promise which is the earnest of our inheritance."[9]

He defined the Spirit by telling the Romans that "The gift of God is eternal life through Jesus Christ our Lord."[10]

There can be such commitment by devout believers to living the life eternal that they are indifferent as to whether they do so with Christ in this present world or in the life to come. Paul was aware of his limitations, but could nevertheless write this to his close friends in Philippi:

For me to live is Christ, and to die is gain. But if I live in the flesh, this is the fruit of my labor; yet what I shall choose I wot not, for I am in a straight betwixt two, having a desire to depart, and to be with Christ; which is far better.[11]

Eternal life was the goal and the reward of all the endeavor of the Lord Jesus among his disciples.

The abundant life to which Jesus called his disciples can be known in this present life to a convincing degree. Jesus made this clear throughout his own life, constantly enriching his followers' thought of God. The knowledge of God of which Jesus spoke is that by which Jesus himself lived. Apostle J. Arthur Gillen used to describe it as "knowledge beyond a superficial acquaintance," for it is born of shared life. Jesus himself holds the key to this knowledge, and is its living exponent.

We tend to think of death as a destructive enemy

because it does not consult our wishes. It robs us of our friends and loved ones and co-workers. But death is really a friend. To live in a world without death would be to live where the care of the aged and infirm would require the time and strength of the majority of able and skilled workers. It would deprive them of the best products of their maturity, and in time would rob both old and young.

Some deaths are beyond our understanding. Nor does the ravaging intensity of our grief add to our understanding. Our only hope is for love and strength which will bless those who are no longer with us and do for them what we cannot do. If we think of death as Jesus and Socrates and other great spiritual leaders have done, it can be known as a friend. It may be an open door to life of larger dimensions, of truth and beauty and goodness such as we have never known hitherto. Paul's writing to the Corinthians has brought comfort to untold millions:

Eye hath not seen, nor ear heard, neither have entered into the heart of man, the things which God hath prepared for them that love him, but God hath revealed them unto us by his Spirit.[12]

Hope and courage to face the adventure of death are the frequent fruitage of life given to pursuits which require eternity for their fulfillment.

Death does not mean extinction; it may well mean invitation. If we have made our investments as Jesus advised us to do, death opens the way into a new order which is not entirely strange if we have already savored that which is now beckoning. By the grace of God, when we die we pass into the arena of eternal life, not eternal death.

Death undoubtedly involves major changes for those who pass over. We know little about the details, possibly because we shall have left behind us things earthly, and all will become new. But we will know all that really matters: that what is born of the Spirit is not subject to the dictates of the flesh; that faith, and hope, and the pure love of the Lord Jesus abide forever.

Here on earth our time and space belong to the present universe. They were created with it.[13] On earth we measure our lives by them; after death we are not limited by either of them. It may be that death brings no sudden emergence into the fullness of life and understanding, but we anticipate a new environment and new tutelage. And if time is no longer[14] we have eternity left to learn and to grow.

In the early Christian church there were many who believed that God was still reaching out after those who had never heard the gospel in its fullness or who, having heard, had never understood. Peter wrote,

Christ also hath once suffered for sins, the just for the unjust, that he might bring us to God, being put to death in the flesh, but quickened by the Spirit: by which also he went and preached unto the spirits in prison; which sometimes were disobedient, when once the longsuffering of God waited in the days of Noah, while the ark was a preparing, wherein few, that is, eight souls, were saved by water.[15]

If the gospel is to be preached to those in the "prison house," and if some accept it, both the ministers and those guiding the growth of the newly won will be happy continuing their work as good stewards of the Word.[16]

It is not difficult to imagine the faithful dead working according to the needs of their new situation. Nor should we find anything but comfort in the reflection that those needing their ministry include many who died while children or young people. If "love never faileth" we cannot tell what forms service in the beyond will take, but we can be sure that love and light will be manifested. It was the greatest specialist in the field who said, "Suffer little children to come unto me, and forbid them not, for of such is the kingdom of heaven."[17]

Immortality and eternal life belong together. One of the most significant statements of modern revelation in this connection occurs in the record of the revelation given to Moses and renewed to Joseph Smith in June 1830: "This is my work and my glory, to bring to pass the immortality, and eternal life of man."[18]

The splendor of this pronouncement lies in the association of the two major components of the fullness of eternal life which our Heavenly Father desires for us. Its quality is centered in the loving wisdom of God. Its duration is beyond challenge. It conforms to and adds light to the first biblical statement concerning our creation: "Let us make man in our own image." It is endorsed again and again in the ensuing word that he "hath abolished death, and hath brought life and immortality to light through the gospel."[19]

This is enlightening in two ways: The love of God cannot be satisfied with eternal duration without regard to its quality—its godliness. Nor can infinite love be content with the perfection which Jesus told his disciples to seek[20] if after the age-long struggle to attain such perfection human beings are still to be subject to the caprice of death.

In the final analysis both life and death are clouded in mystery, and there are occasions when no verbal explanations dispel the clouds. But there is no healing in despair or the abandonment of belief. Nor is there promise in constant petitions for the kind of disclosure which we feel would ease or remove our pain. God holds the key of the unknown, and we do well to trust him. Not infrequently the way of trust and unflagging service has been the way of understanding and peace.

There have been times for all of us when we have felt the weight of the unknown into which our loved ones have moved. But men and women of faith have found that they knew all that they needed to know. This was true in the years when to proclaim one's faith was to become a possible candidate for martyrdom. Against this background I have found myself reading with deep feeling the words of the Apostle Peter:

Grace and peace be multiplied unto you through the knowledge of God, and of Jesus our Lord. According as his divine power hath given unto us all things that pertain unto life and godliness, through the knowledge of him that hath called us to glory and virtue. Whereby are given unto us exceeding great and precious promises; that by these ye might be partakers of the divine nature, having escaped the corruption that is in the world through lust.[21]

There were many things neither Peter or other early disciples knew. But they were most sure of what was most important. And they knew this by the testimony of the Spirit of God.

On an Atlantic crossing some years ago I met and came to like the able and widely known Scots minister, John Baillie. Shortly after his death a report of his last sermon was made available. It was published under the title: "When I Awake," and was obviously influenced by his approaching death. I found myself deeply impressed by this paragraph:

Not even the most learned philosopher or theologian knows what it is going to be like. But there is one thing which the simplest

Christian knows—he knows that it is going to be all right. Somewhere, some-when, somehow, we who are worshiping God here shall wake up and see him as he is, and face to face. But where and when we know not....No doubt it will be utterly different from anything we have ever imagined or thought about it. No doubt God himself will be unimaginably different from our present conception of him. But he will be unimaginably different only because he will be unimaginably better. The only thing we do certainly know is that our highest hopes will be more than fulfilled, and our deepest longings more than gratified.[22]

An even greater authority said to the group of disciples he was about to leave:

Let not your heart be troubled; ye believe in God, believe also in me. In my Father's house are many mansions; if it were not so, I would have told you. I go to prepare a place for you....I will...come again, and receive you unto myself; that where I am, ye may be also.[23]

REFERENCES

1. I Corinthians 2:10.
2. Romans 8:35, 38-39.
3. Stephen M. Cohn, *The Philosophy of Religion* (New York: Harper & Row, 1970), p. 294.
4. I Corinthians 15:52-53.
5. Romans 2:7-8.
6. II Timothy 1:9-10.
7. Ephesians 6:13-18.
8. II Corinthians 1:22.
9. Ephesians 1:13-14.
10. Romans 6:23. See also Titus 1:2.
11. Philippians 1:21-23 KJ.
12. I Corinthians 2:9-10.
13. Genesis 1:5, 8.
14. Romans 10:6.
15. I Peter 3:18-20 KJ.
16. Luke 4:18.
17. Matthew 19:14.
18. Doctrine and Covenants 22:23b.

19. II Timothy 1:10.
20. Matthew 5:50.
21. II Peter 1:2-4.
22. "When I Awake," *Christian Devotion*, p. 313.
23. John 14:1-3.

If I take the wings of the morning,
And dwell in the uttermost parts of
the sea,
Even there shall thy hand lead me,
And thy right hand shall hold me.
If I say, Surely the darkness shall
overwhelm me,
And the light about me shall be night;
Even the darkness hideth not from thee,
But the night shineth as the day:
The darkness and the light are both
alike to thee.
Search me, O God, and know my heart:
Try me, and know my thoughts;
And see if there be any way of
wickedness in me,
And lead me in the way everlasting.

—Psalm 139:9-12, 23-24

Chapter 31

The Solemnities of Eternity

In February 1831, when he was two months past his twenty-fifth birthday, Joseph Smith II brought the word of God to the small group of his associates, saying, "Let the solemnities of eternity rest upon your minds."[1]

This was not the first word of counsel which he brought, and was the natural sequence of the inspired word to Oliver Cowdery, Hyrum Smith, Joseph Knight, and others: "A great and marvelous work is about to come forth unto the children of men."[2] It became sufficiently integrated into the language of the saints that it was used in the minutes of the report of the General Assembly of 1835 where the report of the committee on the compilation of the revelations was approved: "The solemnities of eternity rested upon the audience."[3] By this action the Book of Doctrine and Covenants became one of the standard books of the church.

One wonders what was meant by "the solemnities of eternity." We can only approach understanding when we consider the background of similar expressions. When I attempt this my mind goes to the meeting of the First Presidency, Council of Twelve, and Presiding Bishopric, called in response to the divine instruction given in the revelation of 1894. One of the actions of the council was to share in the blessing of Apostle Caffall for his mission to Europe. President Joseph Smith

earnestly invoked the divine blessing upon Brother Caffall...after which Brethren Joseph Smith, W. W. Blair, Alexander H. Smith, and E. L. Kelley laid their hands upon him and set him apart, President Blair being mouth in supplication. The Spirit of the Master fell upon those present and the service was one of joyful solemnity and peace.

The report then concludes:

To God whose hand has led us and whose patience has borne with our infirmities, the generous praise of his church is due. May our renewed consecration under the better conditions his mercy has brought about, bring to him added glory and to his church prosperity and peace.[4]

The solemnities of eternity pertain to the work of the kingdom which is important in the life of the church both here and hereafter. The work of the church militant should be environed and conducted in light of the fullness of the eternal life which is promised to the faithful. This was one of Joseph Smith's deep concerns during the months preceding and immediately following the organization of the church when the boundaries of time were pushed back and he shared the visions of Moses (Doctrine and Covenants 22) and Enoch (Doctrine and Covenants 36). The vision reported in Doctrine and Covenants 76 is also concerned with things eternal, and the account of this vision is of special import in that it is attested by both of the participants:

We, Joseph Smith, Jr., and Sidney Rigdon, being in the Spirit on the sixteenth day of February, in the year of our Lord one thousand eight hundred and thirty two, by the power of the Spirit our eyes were opened, and our understandings were enlightened, so as to see and understand the things of God; even those things which were from the beginning before the world was, which were ordained of the Father, through his only begotten Son.[5]

337

Another vision was shared between Joseph Smith and Oliver Cowdery on April 3, 1836, in the recently dedicated Kirtland Temple. The Lord appeared to them and promises of great blessings were made to them. Later, in a continuing experience, Moses and Elias and Elijah also ministered to them.[6]

These spiritual experiences are reported in the *Church History*. Others by Joseph Smith III can be found in his memoirs (*Joseph Smith III and the Restoration*). I am omitting reference to others for lack of space. The three I am mentioning are readily available. Many others were reported by members and ministers of the church in the pages of the *Saints Herald* and *Zion's Ensign*. I well remember Bishop Roderick May, an overnight guest in my parent's home, offering our evening prayer and including a petition that we should keep our minds and hearts open to such spiritual guidance as the Lord might grant us.

In the closing chapter of *Joseph Smith III and the Restoration*, he tells some of the spiritual experiences associated with his ministry as prophet and president of the church. The recitals are interesting but space only permits reference to a few of them.

Prior to 1873 members of the Twelve were selected on recommendation of special committees selected to search them out. In 1873, however, this procedure was abandoned and thereafter general officers were chosen after their designation by revelation. The 1873 situation was difficult. Two of the Twelve had not been sustained in an earlier conference, and Elder William Marks had died. In the revelation given in answer to earnest prayer W. W. Blair of the Twelve was called to the Presidency, as was elder David H. Smith. And two of the twelve were released from apostolic service and enrolled with the elders. Thus, seven new apostles were called.

Although Joseph had been president of the church for thirteen years, he had approached the conference with considerable diffidence. However, he wrote after he had received the revelation that "the days following its reception I was permitted to enjoy the Spirit to a marked degree." Joseph's comment about the conference was as follows:

In the revelation thus received an acknowledgement of the efficacy of the prayers of the people was definitely stated, and the voice of the Spirit gave clearly what I had to present to them. The matter which had agitated the minds of the ministry was duly considered, and the condition of the church as represented by us in prayer was evidently recognized as requiring the instruction that was given in the message, requiring the Quorums to be more nearly filled.[7]

Joseph's testimony concerning Section 119 also merits consideration. There were but seven members of the Twelve, and one of these (James Caffall) was in Europe. This made it impossible to secure the votes required for binding action. The Twelve brought this to the attention of the church, and was supported by the Seventy in asking for more light. There were differences of opinion concerning the administration of the Sacrament, the use of music in the services of the church, and the attitude of the church toward Sabbath observance. Happy agreement appeared impossible to achieve. But Joseph, greatly relieved by the Spirit which came to him while he was preparing for the gathering and its continuance during the assembly, wrote the following:

The voice of the Spirit came to me in such plain and unmistakable terms that it was no wonder the revelation was promptly and unanimously accepted for the government and guidance of the church. The Spirit bore witness not only to the leading quorums, each in succession accepting it, but to the general membership as well, as is stated in the minutes of the conference.[8]

The mode of revelation given Joseph in 1902 was unusual. The death of President W. W. Blair and the release of President David H. Smith because of ill health made imperative the strengthening of the Presidency. Then, too, the ages of the older members of the Twelve made their work burdensome. There was also some concern that although Alexander H. Smith had been ordained presiding patriarch, that order had not been further strengthened. After the conference was over Joseph wrote,

Direction as to the calling of persons to office and position came as a result of a vision clearly reflecting in their arrangement and gradations in authority as referred to in the revelation. Section 104 . . . The instructions I received by word came as if from One who stood by me, answering my questions and giving direction. . . . I have felt that the most satisfactory method was that, being in the Spirit, I received verbal direction and precise statement as to what was to be given to the church.[9]

Contemplation of the solemnities of eternity is not reserved to the general officers of the church, nor even to the priesthood. It can be cultivated in the sincere and earnest and frequent worship of Almighty God. Jesus certainly practiced such searching of the eternities in his daily prayer life; this culminated in his self-dedicatory prayer in Gethsemane.[10] It is reflected throughout the writings of the apostle John:

God so loved the world, that he gave his only Begotton Son, that whosoever believeth in him should not perish; but have everlasting life. For God sent not his Son into the world to condemn the world; but that the world through him might be saved.[11]

It guided and strengthened Peter:

For we have not followed cunningly devised fables, when we made known unto you the power and coming of our Lord Jesus

340

Christ, but were eye-witnesses of his majesty. For he received from God the Father honor and glory, when there came such a voice to him from the excellent glory, This is my beloved Son, in whom I am well pleased. And this voice which came from heaven we heard, when we were with him in the holy mount.[12]

And Paul wrote to his Son in the gospel, Timothy: "I know whom I have believed, and am persuaded that he is able to keep that which I have committed unto him."[13]

Awareness of the solemnities of eternity has come to many of the saints in the course of their personal or corporate worship. I remember many such incidents—some of them arising in heart-warming conversations rather than in formal meetings. As a young appointee in England I became stenographer for Apostle J. Arthur Gillen. When he became tired he was quite likely to suggest that we go for a walk in a nearby park. When we did so he was apt to bear his testimony in ways which opened up the way of spiritual understanding. The secret here was that as we walked we found ourselves in the spirit of prayer and understanding.

Possibly the best prayer and communion services I ever attended were those conducted by John S. Garver soon after I was transferred to the United States. John was president of the Lamoni Stake at the time, but some years later I was associated with him in charge of an apostolic field. On occasion I talked with him about the techniques of prayer meeting leadership. I learned that John arranged for the church to be unavailable on the Thursday evenings before the monthly communion service. That evening John went to church and there thought of his people individually and as a group, young and old, as they were then and as they were becoming. It did not take long, however, for me to discover that John's life—not just his Thursdays—was behind his preparation.

Later, John and I became members of the First Presidency. One evening I planned to stay in the office to catch up on some routine work, and when John found out about it he insisted on staying with me. He followed me into my office and we fell into conversation—routine forgotten. We talked about the deeper needs of the church, drawing on John's broader experience. We talked, too, about quite a number of the men of the church, both those showing promise and those having difficulties. We stayed together till about ten o'clock. It was a very serious occasion, but I was interested when I looked back to remember that it was a love-occasion without our mentioning this. (John was very close to President Israel Smith. When John's tongue slipped Israel became "Dutch.") John died within a few months, but not before the seeds had been planted for the conference of high priests which was held in 1950.

During the evening when John and I talked together, and the "routine work" awaited a more convenient time, we mentioned our need for the Spirit of light and truth and power but recognized that this was in the hands of God. We sensed our need, and prayed about it then and later. Although the conference was held in the Temple we did not meet to experience the "gifts." We met to praise God. And our Heavenly Father, in his wisdom and mercy, blessed us through the beloved Elbert A. Smith in a way which some of us remember with feelings approaching awe.

"Let the solemnities of eternity rest on your minds." What clearly inspired counsel for the worshippers of any generation! Knowing this, Paul wrote to the saints in Philippi:

"Our conversation is in heaven."

Or, as Moffatt puts it,

"We are a colony of heaven."

The admonition carries its own credentials. And it was reinforced by the example of the Lord Jesus, whose life cannot be understood apart from his repeated renewal in prayer.

There are other vitally important aspects of the life of the Christian, but they are pointed in the right direction by the practice of the presence of Jesus and the presence of eternity in our thought, and our prayers, and our fellowship.

REFERENCES

1. Doctrine and Covenants 43:8b.
2. Doctrine and Covenants 6:1, 10:1, 12:1, 22, 23b, 28:9c.
3. Doctrine and Covenants 108A:3f.
4. Doctrine and Covenants, Appendix E, Section 123:28, 31.
5. Doctrine and Covenants 76:3a, b.
6. *Church History* 2:47.
7. *Joseph Smith III and the Restoration*, edited by Mary Audentia Smith Anderson (Herald Publishing House, 1952), p. 611.
8. Ibid., p. 619.
9. Ibid., p. 625.
10. Matthew 26:39.
11. John 3:16-17.
12. II Peter 1:16-19.
13. II Timothy 1:12.